MANIFESTING JUSTICE

MANIFESTING JUSTICE

WRONGLY CONVICTED WOMEN RECLAIM THEIR RIGHTS

VALENA BEETY

Foreword by KOA BECK

CITADEL PRESS
Kensington Publishing Corp.
www.kensingtonbooks.com

CITADEL PRESS BOOKS are published by

Kensington Publishing Corp.
119 West 40th Street
New York, NY 10018

All Kensington titles, imprints, and distributed lines are available at special quantity discounts for bulk purchases for sales promotions, premiums, fund-raising, educational, or institutional use.

Special book excerpts or customized printings can also be created to fit specific needs. For details, write or phone the office of the Kensington sales manager: Kensington Publishing Corp., 119 West 40th Street, New York, NY 10018, attn: Sales Department; phone 1-800-221-2647.

CITADEL PRESS and the Citadel logo are Reg. U.S. Pat. & TM Off.

ISBN: 978-0-8065-4151-8

First Citadel hardcover printing: June 2022

10 9 8 7 6 5 4 3 2 1

Printed in the United States of America

Library of Congress Catalog Number: 2021953435

Electronic edition:

ISBN: 978-0-8065-4153-2 (e-book)

For LEIGH *and* TAMI,
who trusted me with their story.

For their sister TASHA MERCEDEZ,
*who is still incarcerated for a crime
she did not commit.*

And for my wife, JENN,
*who inspires me with her generous heart
and commitment to making
our world more just.*

CONTENTS

Foreword by Koa Beck   ix

Prologue   1

1. A Journey from Rehab   9
2. Prosecuting the War on Drugs   17
3. A "Long" Drive to Brookhaven   23
4. Reexamining Habeas Post-Conviction Laws to Manifest
   Justice   27
5. Police Investigate and a Case Begins   42
6. Changing Habeas Post-Conviction Law For Racial Justice   50
7. Dr. Michael West and Evidence of Bite Marks   58
8. Faulty Forensics and Future Truths   67
9. Trial and the Prosecution's Case   86
10. Criminalizing Queerness and Encouraging Passing   96
11. Dr. West Takes the Stand   108
12. Women's Bodies as Objects   136
13. The Defense Case for Leigh and Tami   141
14. Verdict and Sentencing   154
15. Punishing Identity   157
16. Women in Rankin Prison, Mississippi   161
17. Wrongly Convicted Women: Criminalizing Sex and
    Pregnancy   175

18. Criminalizing Transgender People   183

19. Undisclosed Evidence   193

20. The Innocence Movement   204

21. Exculpatory Evidence from the FBI   216

22. Imagining Dickie's Mother, Helen Ervin   227

23. A Post-Conviction Hearing   231

24. Prosecutorial Misconduct   249

25. Freedom   255

26. Alternate Paths to Freedom and Restorative Justice   264

27. Tami Vance in Her Own Words   272

Epilogue: The Future Innocence Movement   274

Checklist of Tools for Manifesting Justice   277

Endnotes   283

Playlist, 2012   317

Acknowledgments   319

Discussion Questions   323

Index   325

About the Author   339

FOREWORD
by Koa Beck

Many foundational and existing laws in the United States assume that you are a very specific person. They assume that you had two able-bodied parents who had the money and resources to furnish you with security, ability, protection, and education. They assume you come from a home free of abuse, neglect, and mental illness with community support to help you realize ambitions and goals beyond day-to-day survival. They assume you have a gender presentation that doesn't hinder steady employment, stable housing, or assistance. For huge swaths of the American population, though, this is not the story of their formative life. But when they are put before our legal system for crimes that stem from food insecurity, abuse, transphobia, systemic racism, structural misogyny, and homophobia, this is the metric they are measured against.

Women in the United States have proved to be particularly vulnerable to this egregious standard: women are the fastest growing segment of the incarcerated population and have been for some time now. Across the country, there are more than eight times as many women in local jails and state and federal prisons than there were in 1980. Between 1977 and 2004, the number of women serving sentences of over a year grew almost 800 percent—twice that of the male prison population.

One of the prominent reasons women are subjected to this landscape is because we have erected and perpetuated a legal system that focuses solely on criminal activity, and not the circumstances that have contributed or facilitated it. Behind this data is the real data: many of them are women of color who are imprisoned for nonviolent offenses, such as fraud, drugs, or sex work. Women are more likely to enter prison with a history of mental illness, abuse, and trauma, having come to drug use to cope with victimization.

When reviewing the dramatic uptick of incarcerated women, we are simultaneously being confronted with the ways the United States has criminalized women's responses to gender-based violence, poverty, and addiction. Meanwhile, the broad effort to address women in jails and prisons has been to widen the involvement of the criminal justice system in ways that further criminalize those trying to get by in a system that was fundamentally not made for them, such as arresting women who survive through sex work and dual arrests for women fighting back during domestic violence episodes.

Valena Beety's *Manifesting Justice* speaks to this reality by addressing the holistic parameters of these lives, these crimes, and the critical spaces where they have overlapped. As a former federal prosecutor and innocence litigator, Beety applies tactical analysis and correctives to a process that she has spent her entire professional life both studying and navigating. Her assessment of underutilized legal doctrine illuminates distinct opportunities to understand how criminal law and convictions can be leveraged to account for the lived realities of many, rather than the insistence of how they should have been.

Los Angeles
August 2021

KOA BECK is the author of *White Feminism: From the Suffragettes to Influencers and Who They Leave Behind.*

MANIFESTING JUSTICE

PROLOGUE

The shortest distance between two strangers is the story.
—Patti Digh

We view strangers with suspicion because we cannot predict what they will do. But when we hear their stories, we unearth what is hidden. We find ways to listen, to wait, and to grow intimate. With intimacy we can grow closer until we realize our stories are not so separate, but a part of a tapestry, our lives interwoven.

Though we are strangers, I encourage you to tell your story and to listen to this one.

The prison yard was unusually quiet when Leigh's friend collapsed. With a soft thud, her body crumpled onto the dirt, smearing red dust on her green-and-white-striped pants. These were not her clean pants, the ones kept fresh and bright for rare family visits. These pants were faded and frayed, marked with the stripes showing she had permission to be walking with a friend in the exercise yard of the Central Mississippi Correctional Facility for Women.

Leigh stood next to her comatose friend and yelled for help. She cupped her hands to amplify her voice and strained her eyes to identify approaching guards. Urgently, she called again. As the guards ran closer, she froze, so as to not pose a threat to them.

One guard pushed Leigh aside to try to minister to Leigh's friend. But another turned to her with rebuke.

"Leigh, why didn't you help her?" the guard demanded.

Leigh stared down at the unconscious woman, gripped by a power-ful memory.

Then she turned and met the guard's eyes.

"Because the last time I tried to help someone in trouble, I ended up in prison for a crime I didn't commit."

This is a story about sexual shame. This is also a story about the War on Drugs, and trapping people in prison because of fear, misunder-standing, and hatred. But the root of it is shame.

It is also a story of change and how we can create justice.

Three women meet in a drug rehab institution. One experienced a tragic event in college months earlier. Trying to cope, she throws her personal and sexual vulnerability to the wind. The second woman is newly out of high school and struggling to figure out her sexual iden-tity. The third woman is a lesbian, recently turned thirty, who has lived through homelessness and exile all the while questioning her pur-pose in the world. All three need help. And they find each other. Their relationships buoy them until the outside world shames them for their sexual choices, grasps at lies and stereotypes, and transforms them into victims and criminals.

This is their story.

I am an innocence litigator. For more than a decade, I have repre-sented men and women who were factually innocent—serving time in prison for crimes they did not commit. Someone else had committed the crime, but police, prosecutors, and our courts had made a tragic mistake.

Over the past thirty years, innocence litigators have created a whole new field of law. With the advent of DNA evidence, these attorneys proved in court that their clients were factually innocent. They ex-posed serious failings in our criminal legal system, and they led legisla-tive reforms in many states to prevent wrongful convictions.

In this book I offer a passport to this world, and a new expanded vi-sion of wrongful convictions.

Some of my clients had DNA evidence that could prove they did not commit the crime. The evidence was either in a police storage locker or a courthouse evidence room. I needed the prosecutor's permission to test the evidence. Every single prosecutor refused. I always offered to pay the DNA testing costs, but that wasn't what mattered to the prosecutor.

During those years, judges often told me their hands were tied, that there was no legal pathway to consider my client's plea for relief.

They were wrong; there is a legal pathway. It's called manifest injustice.

Manifest injustice is a legal mechanism to challenge and reverse convictions. It recognizes that convictions tied to racism, police and prosecutor misconduct, over-sentencing, and false evidence are wrongful. Manifest injustice—or miscarriage of justice—empowers a judge to consider the law, facts, and surrounding circumstances in a case and to declare a conviction, or a sentence, unjust.

Judges rarely use it.

In our criminal legal system, what qualifies as legal punishment can be a far cry from what is just. Judges infrequently reverse convictions.

The legal system prioritizes finality and prefers a simple contained narrative. The story is considered over once the person is convicted and labeled as guilty. To reverse that conviction, to free someone from prison, to be able to tell the full and complete story, is to overcome a legal bar that is dauntingly high, even for "perfect" defendants.

Our full stories reveal our motivations, our imperfections, and our humanity. My clients were not perfect, and like so many incarcerated people, they were survivors of crime and violence. My clients suffered in the same way that every incarcerated person suffers in prisons in America: over-arching violence, non-existent health care, token time with family, being caged in remote locations far from relatives with expensive phone bills widening that distance, and only small reprieves except escape through drugs.

Most of my clients did not have the DNA golden ticket to reverse their convictions and free them from prison. According to the prosecutors and judges, they didn't have enough proof to meet the very high standard of "innocence" that the current law demands. While locked in prison and unrepresented by counsel, my client may have filed five different petitions, each of which challenged a different evidentiary problem: the mistaken eyewitness, the police officer lying on the stand, the suppressed statement by a passerby to the crime.

The evidence issues presented across these petitions made it clear that my client had been wrongfully convicted, but courts do not review these errors collectively. Instead, they review the errors raised in each petition in piecemeal fashion. While this makes it much easier for the courts to rule out errors are "harmless," it makes it exponentially more difficult for the incarcerated person to win freedom.

Taken singly, one by one, each error was insufficient to meet the burden on the client—which was now on me as their attorney—to reverse the conviction. Courts often simply refuse to consider the entirety of the errors that were committed, and the result is denial of relief.

The courts' reliance on finality serves a purpose. Finality, enforced through an impossibly high standard to even revisit a conviction, insulates legal actors from reflection and reform. Finality is a shield, deflecting or burying criticisms of prosecutors, defense attorneys, judges, and police.

This dominant story of finality is the reason why the standard for reversing convictions must be manifest injustice. Courts should be obligated to review the picture as a whole to assess whether a trial was fair and just. The wrongs should be added up, rather than individually picked off and discarded as meaningless or as "harmless error."

It is not just the factually innocent who are wrongly in prison. Forensic fraud, "testilying" police officers, prosecutors withholding exculpatory evidence, mistaken eyewitness identification, and false confessions lock away factually innocent people. But these systemic breakdowns also unjustly lock away far more people who are wrongfully convicted and sentenced, even if their factual innocence cannot be conclusively proven or their guilt is not in dispute.

Innocence work often promotes the concept of an "ideal client" with a sympathetic narrative and no prior convictions. The result, intended or not, is a perception that only near-perfect people imprisoned for crimes they did not commit deserve to have the innocence community fight for their freedom. But even with "ideal clients," factual innocence may not be enough. Previously established facts are questioned or labeled fake news, not to mention disputed evidence or facts that simply remain unknown.

In a country that currently incarcerates 2.3 million people, proving factual innocence is also not enough to provide justice. Some innocence work has been co-opted by a denier's narrative, which contends that the vast majority of people who are arrested deserve prison and punishment.

The façade of the "always right" prosecutor should no longer be allowed to demand the conviction and incarceration of millions of people in the United States today.

These convictions can be reversed through manifest injustice. Manifest injustice is a tool that reaches beyond the perfect client who is demonstrably innocent. It can be an independent, fact-based claim for relief.

Through manifest injustice, courts can allow a defendant to withdraw their guilty plea after a conviction. Through manifest injustice, prosecutors can withdraw sentences they had advocated for and free the convicted person in prison, even years later. Through manifest injustice, bail requirements as well as sentencing guidelines can be more flexible. Courts can acknowledge over-incarceration and sentencing errors. Courts can recognize a confluence of errors in a case and their cumulative impact, even if each individual error does not rise to the legal standards created by previous court decisions.

The idea of manifest injustice challenges assumptions of what is natural and what is normal. Judges, lawyers, and civilians should not be accustomed to how our legal system quickly and routinely wrenches away peoples' freedom every day.

Manifest injustice is a correction when the law is too strict and leads to an unjust result. There are other tools that do the same thing—"dismissal in the interest of justice," before a person is convicted, and "coram nobis," after a person has served their sentence.

Before trial, fourteen states and Puerto Rico recognize a judge's authority to dismiss a criminal charge not on legal grounds, but in the interest of justice. Like manifest injustice, "dismissal in the interest of justice" allows a court to dismiss a procedurally proper but unjust charge pre-trial.

At the height of the AIDS health crisis in the 1990s, judges dismissed low-level charges against HIV-positive defendants in the interest of justice. Judges dismissed charges against ACT UP protesters—AIDS Coalition to Unleash Power—who organized "die-ins" and protested the government's failure to support research and find a cure. Courts dismissed charges in the interest of justice to protect protesters and principles of free speech.

Coram nobis petitions can challenge a conviction even after the convicted person has served their sentence. Courts can grant coram nobis petitions "to maintain public confidence in the administration of justice," reversing convictions for de-criminalized behavior, like marijuana possession, or where a "fundamental error" occurred.

In 2014, relatives of George Stinney filed a writ of coram nobis for his conviction to be reversed. The State of South Carolina convicted Stinney of murder in 1944, when Stinney was fourteen years old.

Stinney, a Black boy, was legally and factually innocent, but an all-white jury found him guilty after a one-day trial. The state of South Carolina executed Stinney in 1944, putting a Bible on the electric chair so the boy could fit into the straps.

In 2014, a court vacated Stinney's conviction through coram nobis, recognizing a miscarriage of justice. Coram nobis petitions and manifest injustice claims are being successfully brought today, even when the harm is decades old.

Manifest injustice is a powerful tool that can have a wide-ranging impact and expand innocence work.

Manifest injustice may also be seen as disruptive of traditional innocence work and its cohesive theory of factual innocence. And it is. It is part of a growing movement that asks courts to liberate rather than incarcerate. It is an expansion and not a devaluation of the innocence movement and its global importance. We can celebrate the successes of innocence work, while also consciously discussing an expansion of innocence. We can apply the term "wrongfully convicted" to more people, as our society also begins to recognize criminal injustice more broadly. Manifest injustice is a new direction for growth and change, as a theory and a reality.

The innocence vision is powerful. And when we free wrongful convictions from the technical constraints of factual innocence, we can recognize and remedy miscarriages of justice.

Building awareness is how we turn from the "deserving" narrative of finality to a manifest injustice framework. Galileo said he wasn't the first to discover the stars and planets, he was the first to see them for what they are. Manifest injustice is likewise a story of generational change: the origin of innocence work, the backlash of prosecutors adhering to a status quo, and a current move to reclaim the narrative of what is a wrongful conviction. Police, prosecutors, innocence deniers, and myriad structural system challenges stand as obstacles to freeing and vindicating people harmed by our criminal legal system. Manifest injustice creates a unique avenue to challenge prosecutorial misconduct, police abuse, and broader systemic racism.

The universal adoption of a manifest injustice standard would slow the churning machine of incarceration. Wrongful convictions are blazingly real and encompass a broad swath of people. Incarcerating people of color for decades to punish drug use is real. Women sentenced to a lifetime in prison for their connection to a boyfriend selling drugs is real. Imprisoning poor people for engaging in the same behavior as free, wealthy Americans is real. Convictions resulting from these injustices are wrongful.

The DNA revolution and innocence movement started more than thirty years ago, proving the reality of wrongful convictions in a way that courts and citizens have come to accept. But it is a narrow vision—too narrow to include the vast numbers of less than perfect, less than innocent people whose convictions are obtained through corruption, junk science, racism, and other legally dubious means. For the past twenty years, advocates in criminal justice reform have been arguing to broaden the innocence movement. This book acts as both a mirror and as a path forward from theory to reality. The widespread adoption of the existing tool of manifest injustice can expand innocence work to mitigate longstanding structural inequities rooted in our current system.

This book also provides other ways to manifest justice. When police and prosecutors criminalize transgender people, innocence litigators and activists can speak up about these wrongful arrests, charges, and convictions. When people of color are arrested and charged based on racism, state laws can require the charges be dismissed. When women are over-sentenced for assaulting their rapist or abuser, people can advocate for clemency, for pardons. Many paths exist to manifest justice.

This book is about manifesting justice for people incarcerated too long, for women who took the fall for someone else, for people wrongfully convicted. And this book is about ways we are manifesting justice now.

Let's begin.

CHAPTER 1

A Journey from Rehab

Just past Pine Grove Road in western Alabama, State Route 14 becomes Mississippi State Highway 69 and crosses into Lowndes County, home of the "Black Belt," one of the most fertile plains in the United States. The two-lane road winds north and west through woods, prairie, and farmland for ten miles until easing into Columbus, Mississippi, population 25,000.

In Columbus, Highway 69 becomes "Main Street," the sort of thoroughfare that defines the heart of so many cities and towns across America. At 1011 Main Street is the Pines & Cady Hill Recovery Center, a well-regarded alcohol and drug treatment center that first opened in 1976. It was through these doors in January 2000 that Leigh Stubbs walked to enter the rehab program. She was twenty years old. Sixty days later, she walked out having kicked free of opioids at last. But that was about the last of any freedom for her—she would soon lose a decade of her life to prison.

Leigh's road to Cady Hill began about two hundred miles south, at Pine Grove, an emergency rehab center in Hattiesburg. Leigh knew if she didn't stop using, her mama would kick her out of the house. She also knew her mama loved her. And while Mama Sheila had a big heart, she also had a stern comeuppance for her three daughters, Kristi as the eldest, and especially Leigh and her twin sister, Lorilyn.

Sheila and Pete Stubbs owned and managed Stubbs Mobile Home Park in Collins, Mississippi. After graduating high school there, Leigh had started going to Jones County Junior College. Besides classes, she was working two jobs: manager at the Quickstop on Highway 84, and for the *News Commercial,* the primary newspaper in Collins. Years later, when Leigh needed affidavits in support of her "character," the editor of the *News Commercial* would speak highly of her, offering to re-hire her at any time. He also said her conviction was not who Leigh truly was, and that she had served enough time. Of course, every day Leigh had served was more time than she should have spent in prison—she didn't commit the crime.

But back in 2000, Leigh was trying to figure out her life, her own sexual identity, what made her different from her twin sister. In March of 1999, she broke up with her boyfriend of two and a half years, and by December, she came to her parents and asked for help with a drug problem. She had just marked her twentieth birthday. Leigh's parents sent her to Pine Grove, where Leigh started to pay attention to the causes of her drug use. She did so well that a counselor promised her a job once she had been clean for six months. Leigh got along with the nurses, and they noted how she helped other patients. One of those patients was a twenty-two-year-old woman named Kim Williams.

Kim had begun using drugs when she was fourteen, and her drug use became so severe that she missed too many days in eleventh grade and had to repeat the grade at another school. She had already attended four programs for opioid use disorder between 1999 and 2000. Kim's drug of choice was morphine, which in pill form is Oxycontin.

Her drug use spiraled out of control—if she had ever been in control—following a horrific event in college. Kim's boyfriend Dickie, twenty years her senior, had had multiple operations on his spine and had an ample supply of Oxycontin to manage his pain. And, it turned out, to manage Kim's pain as well. She was arrested three times for shoplifting and convicted once. She was stealing Dickie's morphine and other prescription pain pills. By the time she landed at Pine Grove, Kim wanted to quit acting on impulse, quit stealing, and stop needing drugs so much. Like Leigh, Kim also was figuring out her sexuality. In the past, Kim had hooked up with a couple of different female friends. While it may have been the twenty-first century, this was southern Mississippi. At one party where she kissed her friend, the guys at the party turned hostile, calling them "disgusting bitches."

Kim and Leigh both graduated from the Pine Grove program on January 18, 2000, and they both moved on to long-term rehabilitation at Cady Hill, on Main Street, Columbus.

When Kim arrived at Cady Hill, she was five-foot-two and not on any medications, weighing 118 pounds. By the time she was discharged from Cady Hill two months later on March 5 she weighed 135 pounds and was taking an antidepressant, as were many people at Cady Hill. In her final discharge, Cady Hill listed Kim's response to the rehab program as "poor." Kim was criticized by therapists for not having the "self-will" to address her addiction.

When Leigh drove to Cady Hill in her '94 white Chevy truck, she knew Kim would be there too. She hoped they would be roommates, but instead Leigh's new roommate ended up being Tami Vance, a thirty-one-year-old woman who already had been at Cady Hill for several weeks. Tami was a Scorpio from Dry Prong, Louisiana, and an open lesbian. She had a few drug possession convictions, and she was trying to get clean. After struggling with her sexuality, Tami had accepted herself, learned not to care what anyone else thought of her, to keep on, and to be a kind person. Although both had individual therapy, Tami and Leigh would soon spend time together in group sessions as they made their way through the twelve steps to sobriety. At the time, the program at Cady Hill was all that Mississippi—and most states—had to offer: the Alcoholics Anonymous 12 Step method. The abstinence-only framework meant dealing with withdrawal through talk therapy and sharing circles; journaling when they were dopesick and in physical pain. When Kim came to Cady Hill, she was still suffering from potentially life-threatening delirium tremens. Rehab programs trumpeted the strength of individual willpower, which frequently was a weak match for the severe stranglehold of opioid addiction.

In March of 2000, Tami, Leigh, and Kim finished the sixty-day program at Cady Hill and were pondering whether to stay for a thirty-day extension aimed at developing job skills and transitioning into the workforce. Tami and Leigh got weekend passes and went to see their families to discuss whether to return to Cady Hill. When they left, they saw Kim packing her bags. She was leaving for good—heading for home; her boyfriend would pick her up. She had been planning on leaving Cady Hill to live with Dickie, although recently he had told her he wasn't sure that was a good idea. On Friday, Leigh drove her white Chevy pickup truck south through rural Mississippi, heading to Collins to see her parents. But first, she dropped off Tami in Jackson to visit her mom. When she arrived in Collins, Leigh told her parents she was ready to come home and get back to work. Instead, Mama Sheila encouraged her to give the thirty-day work program at Cady Hill a try.

When Leigh and Tami returned to Cady Hill on Sunday, March 5, 2000, they found the center in disarray. There were new social workers. Suddenly, residents had access to drugs. There were men in the women's section. Cady Hill drug-tested Leigh immediately. Leigh called Mama Sheila.

"Mama, I'm leaving Cady Hill. All hell broke loose this weekend when I was gone."

"What do you mean?"

"Everybody was sleeping with everybody. Mama, they're fixing to put us all on restriction, and I wasn't even there, and I don't think I deserve it. It's not fair." Leigh told her mama that she was coming home. She packed up and got ready to get back on the road the next day.

When Mama Sheila called Cady Hill the next day, the director conceded that the new social workers had gotten out of hand, and then hadn't distributed the assigned medications until late. Although Cady Hill maintained separate male and female facilities, the alarm door separating the sections had been tampered with and was now silent. This wasn't the first time the separation had been breached: on previous visits, Mama Sheila frequently saw a male counselor in the women's facility. (A week after Mama Sheila's call, the man was fired.)

The director deflected and simply told Mama Sheila that Leigh was using drugs again, and that Sheila should focus on her other family members, not Leigh. The mandatory re-entry drug test Leigh took said otherwise. The test came back negative for any controlled substances.

When Tami and Leigh returned to the chaos at Cady Hill, Kim was still there. Her bags, packed since Saturday morning, had not moved. According to the other women at the center, Kim had been sitting on the couch rocking herself to self-soothe on Saturday and Sunday, asking for her antidepression medicine. Why was Kim still here, amidst all that had happened over the weekend at Cady Hill?

Kim's boyfriend, Dickie, never came to pick her up. Perhaps that should have been expected. He hadn't visited her the entire time she was at Cady Hill. Tami, Leigh, and their friend Samantha, who they befriended at Cady Hill, decided to leave. They threw their things into Leigh's truck and made to leave Cady Hill behind them.

"Can I go too?" Kim asked.

And with that, all of them left. But it wasn't the happy celebration of graduating into recovery, it was an angry frustration. The rehab center had let them down, particularly the people who were trying to stay sober.

They weren't the only ones leaving. Another friend, Kathy, decided to leave as well, and after attending an AA meeting at Cady Hill, she got a ride with DB, another Cady Hill resident who had become Samantha's boyfriend after they met during group therapy. All six of them met up in nearby Starkville, the home of Mississippi State University. In a near-empty parking lot, Samantha took her belongings from the back of Leigh's truck and got in the car with DB and with Kathy. They would spend the night with DB's uncle. They had no plans beyond that. And indeed, within twenty-four hours, Samantha returned to Cady Hill.

Tami, Leigh, and Kim headed to a hotel in Columbus for the night. They decided that Leigh would drive Tami to Tami's mother's home on the Louisiana-Mississippi border in Dry Prong, Louisiana. Along the way they would drop Kim off at Dickie's home in Summit, Mississippi. Then, Leigh would head to Collins to Mama Sheila, to see her twin sister, and to get a job.

The next day, March 6, they left for Dickie's house in Summit, a drive of more than five hours. Weeks later, Leigh would tell her mama, "I couldn't leave my friend."

DISCHARGED AND DISPERSED—ON THE ROAD

James and Emmit Ervin, better known as "Dickie" and "Peanut," were brothers living together with their mama in Summit, Mississippi.

Kim knew why Dickie hadn't picked her up from Cady Hill to bring her home. When Kim said she did not want to be around morphine, her drug of choice, Dickie said that would be impossible in his household. As Dickie conceded later, his original plan never included bringing her to his home.

Imagine Dickie's surprise on a Monday night when he found Kim knocking at his mama's door in Summit, nearly four hundred miles from Cady Hill, with two women he had never met: Leigh and Tami. The women talked about taking Kim's seven-person tent so they could camp. After a thirty-minute search, Peanut, Leigh, and Tami found the tent, but no poles—useless. Tami and Leigh went out on the porch to talk, and at that point decided to leave. Kim was in the back bedroom with Dickie, smoking weed and watching *World Championship Wrestling*. There was no reason for Leigh and Tami to stay. They started toward the truck and waited for Kim to retrieve her belongings.

Dickie and Kim were seeing each other for the first time in months. Dickie spent much of his time in the bed. He had an implant in his hip and walked with difficulty. And he had been in a car accident years prior, resulting in spine injuries that required surgery. Dickie received a disability check at the beginning of each month, and he took pills for pain, for sleeping, and for depression. He had a few arrests and convictions for marijuana, but he still used it to ease the pain.

In Dickie's large black medication bag, he had Oxycontin, Ultram, Sonata, Nitroglycerin, and $300 cash. There was something in the bag that belonged to Kim. Dickie had a filled prescription for Xanax for Kim, with a full bottle of Xanax pills.

Kim made a decision. Her time with Dickie was over. She grabbed his full black medication bag and ran out the front door. Kim hopped in Leigh's truck and told them her plans had changed—step on the gas. As they pulled onto on the main road and sped out of town, Kim said she couldn't stay with Dickie. Tami immediately offered that Kim could stay with her and her mama in Dry Prong for a while.

As they drove out of Summit, Kim revealed that she had a bag full of pills and was ready to share.

Days later, Dickie had another unexpected visitor. Kim's uncle, Sheriff's Deputy Truett Simmons from the Walthall County Sheriff's

Department, made the thirty-mile drive to Summit to interview Dickie and Peanut.

After Kim had left, Dickie filed a criminal charge with the Summit police accusing Kim of stealing his drugs. But when Deputy Simmons showed up on Dickie's doorstep, he wasn't asking about the bag of drugs. He was investigating instead whether something had happened to Kim. Dickie later admitted he thought it was odd that Kim's uncle came—in his role as a sheriff from a neighboring county—to interview him at his home. Dickie said, "I didn't—I even asked, isn't it like not supposed to happen that—what do you call it?—a family member investigates a crime? So I was confused. I didn't know exactly what to think."

Deputy Simmons wanted to know about the two women who had been with Kim. Dickie told Kim's uncle that he had never met them before, but that Tami was a "bull dyke." At that point, the wheels started to turn.

In an extensive interview Dickie later gave to Brookhaven, Mississippi, police, he said his first opinion of Tami was "look at this bull dyke and what is she doing with my baby." But then, he said he figured that Tami and Leigh were a couple. "It seemed like it was a, um, like you know how in a male-female relationship the male is dominant, it seemed like this girl Tami was dominant over Leigh."

"During the time that Kim was with you, did Tami ever give you a look or look at . . . you and Kim as though she was jealous or something. Or she didn't like it, or—?" Brookhaven Assistant Police Chief Arlustra Henderson asked.

"You know, it may have been a jealous look," Dickie replied.

"That's what I want to know," Henderson said.

Dickie added, "But it was just one of those things that made you think 'What the shit's wrong with her?'"

By the time the police later interviewed Tami, they specifically asked her about "what she did for sex at Cady Hill."

Dickie also told the police that "Tami and Leigh kept walking back and forth in the hallway and were acting strange or nervous." Dickie's mama would later say that Tami and Leigh were on the porch, whispering in the dark.

Dickie would also tell the police that Kim was truthful and trustworthy, and that he had planned on marrying her, except for her addiction. Despite Kim's prior arrests and charges for shoplifting, and that she previously had taken his morphine, Dickie maintained that he was surprised Kim stole his bag of pills. He told police that he knew she stole from other people, but he didn't think she stole from him.

Dickie believed that Kim talked about his stash of drugs while she was at Cady Hill, and he thought the three women arrived in Summit with a plan to take the drugs and have a party. He was suspicious of Leigh and Tami—they didn't have "the regular Mississippi accent," though he didn't hear Leigh talk much. He thought they sounded like they were from Pierre Part, Louisiana, an area populated by people of Cajun descent, who were crudely referred to as "coon-ass." It was a most derogatory and insulting term for a Cajun.

"They had the accent, it was more coon-ass and you may have a drawl with it," Dickie said. "But some of the words they use are, you know they're coon-asses . . . I know they weren't from like around here."

CHAPTER 2
Prosecuting the War on Drugs

After working as a Rape Victim Advocate, I knew that I wanted to become a prosecutor. I saw how violence impacts survivors. I wanted to end the cycles of violence and stop the perpetrators. I thought prison was the answer, and that I could be a protector.

We all have origin stories. Mine began in the Midwest. I grew up, went to school, and worked in Indiana, Illinois, and Ohio. My dad and grandfather worked for ACDelco, a car parts manufacturer, in Anderson and Kokomo, Indiana. Kokomo, the "City of Firsts," was a pioneering automotive town, and their Delco Radio Division developed the first push button car radio. We were a General Motors family, relying on the company that, in our words, "put every meal on the table." My mom was a high school teacher with the Indianapolis Public Schools system, where she taught home economics and child development. I was a Midwesterner at heart, and in my family history.

When I was twenty-seven years old, I made a big move to Washington, D.C. There, I would finally start my career as a federal prosecutor. I was confident, righteous, and excited, armed with my newly minted law degree and job experience clerking for federal judges. I was proud to be an Assistant U.S. Attorney in the nation's capital, proud to be fighting for others.

But that wasn't necessarily the job. My year as a prosecutor brought me face-to-face with how prosecutions did not always help victims. In fact, victims often resented me.

Of course they did. I quickly learned to have the police arrest victims in order to make sure they showed up in court to testify against the defendant. That was just one of the common and callous tactics adopted in the office. Yet I continued to cloak myself in a shroud of righteousness.

I never thought about being wrong. I didn't think about charging the wrong person as the perpetrator, or about prison as the wrong solution.

I saw prison as the answer through my own experiences growing up. As a kid, I didn't see many men in my family and family circle go to prison. In my neighborhood, I didn't see many harms from far off prisons and over-policing. So I superimposed my own past and my own view on survivors—that they undoubtedly would benefit from incarcerating the person who hurt them.

I remember one incident, when a victim called a prosecutor down the hall from me. The victim was calling from the lobby of our office building, just downstairs. Her boyfriend was with her. He was the charged perpetrator in her domestic violence case. Together, they wanted to talk with the prosecutor about dropping the charges.

At the time, D.C. had a mandatory arrest law that required police to arrest someone if they received a domestic violence call. After the arrest, a local court would frequently impose a no-contact order. As prosecutors, we then brought charges against people who violated these initial no-contact orders, or orders of protection. When a defendant contacted "our" victim, it became a criminal charge.

In this case, there was a civil order of protection in place after the domestic violence arrest. The survivor's boyfriend could not legally be in touch with her—let alone stand next to the victim in the lobby of the prosecutor's building.

The prosecutor called the police, who promptly arrested him. Now he had another charge—violating the order of protection.

We saw police and prisons as the solution to domestic violence and sexual violence.

I ignored survivors' concerns that the charged person was the co-parent of their children. I discounted that the alleged assailant provided a salary and funds for the family. And I diminished that they provided and could provide companionship and support.

I was averse to compassion or sympathy for anyone other than the few people, and few situations, I decided deserved it.

Instead, the common refrain was that if the defendant didn't do this crime, they did something else. He was a bad guy. If she didn't assist with the case, she was a "crack-whore."

A NATIONAL OVERDOSE CRISIS

At the time that Kim, Tami, and Leigh were in rehab, the national overdose crisis was in its beginnings. Notably, Tami, Kim, and Leigh were all white women—in what grew to be an epidemic centered on whiteness, white addiction, and white suffering.

They also lived in rural Mississippi. "Rural" frequently, and inaccurately, read as white. Rural people of color remained overlooked. Mississippi's population is almost 40 percent Black in a state where the largest "city" is 100,000 residents. In rural areas like the Black Belt, the majority of residents are Black. Yet while the whitewashed opioid overdose crisis brought attention to rurality, overdose victims of color were sidelined.

Drug use was stigmatized, but so was rehab. Federal law prohibited doctors from prescribing methadone or buprenorphine to treat opioid use disorder (OUD) at outpatient treatment facilities. Rehabilitation centers like Cady Hill instead relied on abstinence-only treatment models: the Alcoholics Anonymous 12 step method, group therapy, and individual talk therapy. At the time, the prevailing—and anti-scientific—view was that substance use disorder was a moral failing. As such, the cure was individual willpower.

But the definition of addiction is doing whatever it takes to obtain the object of addiction, no matter the consequences. As it turned out, willpower was a weak match for OUD, which is more severe than alcohol use disorder.

In the 2000s, the tide began to turn in favor of enhanced access to evidence-based treatment.

Today, rehab for opioid use disorder includes medication, where patients in recovery receive doses of a prescription opioid agonist, which can break the cycle of addiction. The Cady Hill Recovery Center still provides an intensive residential treatment program but has incorporated medication as well.

Providers can still be hostile to medication treatment, criticizing that it just swaps out one drug for another. Worse yet, there's more stigma in the treatment community for methadone, the medication most frequently used to treat opioid use disorder by people of color, than buprenorphine, the less effective analgesic used by white people.

Significant drug policy changes have occurred since Leigh, Tami, and Kim were in rehab, but what a difference those advances would have made for these women. What if they had all received medicine to overcome their addictions?

If someone used and overdosed, the reality was bleak. People overdosing were hastily dropped off at a hospital or a public park. Worse, sometimes the person overdosing was left to die alone. Anyone using a drug with the overdosing person could be charged with possession of drugs, distribution of drugs, or even worse: drug-induced homicide. Drug-induced homicide is a charge that an individual is responsible for the overdose death because they gave drugs to the person—regardless of whether there was any intent for that person to overdose and die. The intent doesn't matter, just the act. Criminal drug laws were discouraging reporting overdoses, and instead leading to more people dying.

NOT **PROSECUTING THE WAR ON DRUGS**

"Vice"—drugs, alcohol, prostitution—used to be socially demonized but not criminalized. But criminal laws became a vehicle for social ordering and defining who is a criminal. Police created Vice Squads. Prosecutors soon charged and convicted marginalized people for vice offenses.

Prosecutors now have tremendous power over people's lives because of drug laws. Police arrest roughly 1.5 million people every year, largely for drug possession. Prosecutors decide whether to criminally charge someone, what charges to bring, and what penalties to seek. Prosecutors generally have vast, unreviewable authority in this area. The United States spends roughly $47 billion each year on criminal drug prohibition.

Prosecutors turned the tide toward over-charging. A recent national study showed prosecutors are still more likely to over-charge by bringing a felony charge or multiple misdemeanor charges against a first-time offender where no person was injured and no property was damaged. Indeed, a majority of the surveyed prosecutors recommended punishment, even while they acknowledged the incident was a minor crime, or in their words, "no big deal."

Yet prosecutors can choose whether to charge people with drug crimes and ask for prison sentences, or instead choose public health solutions. Prosecutors have the discretion and power to turn the tide back again, voluntarily promoting solutions other than incarceration.

Many prosecutors simply don't understand how their policies and actions harm survivors, people with substance use disorder, and the safety of community members. That can change. Elected prosecutors can invite directly impacted people to speak about their experience with drug use and incarceration. They can provide space for survivors to tell prosecutors about the impact of having family members in prison. Elected prosecutors can bring in medical experts to explain the basics of substance use disorder and treatment. Local harm reduction experts can share the consequences of drug conviction and discuss different types of interventions and support services to deliver better outcomes.

Prosecutors can promote access to medication for treatment of opioid use disorder.

Prosecutors can stop sending people back to prison for a dirty urine drug test. Nearly one in four people are in state prisons for technical violations of parole. Drug testing instead can be a measure of progress during treatment and re-evaluating the person's situation through a health lens.

Elected prosecutors can support proposals to expand public health interventions and services, particularly with funds saved through *not* incarcerating people who use drugs.

While some elected prosecutors are choosing not to prosecute people for drug use and possession, more state legislatures are ending these drug laws. Oregon, through a ballot measure, decriminalized possession of small amounts of drugs, instead assessing a fine and creating Addiction Recovery Centers across the state. Three elected prosecutors publicly supported this ballot measure. Other states are decriminalizing drug possession as well.

Finally, more prosecutors are now re-sentencing people who are in prison for long sentences for drug-related offenses. Some prosecutors are creating freedom instead of taking it away through these "second look" sentencings. They are correcting past harms of over-incarceration for drug use. They can correct for the mistakes that I now know I made as a prosecutor.

Nowadays, the majority of states have Good Samaritan laws in place to encourage people to report overdoses. A Good Samaritan law protects the person who calls 9-1-1 about an overdose or takes a friend to the hospital. Under the Good Samaritan law, that reporting person will not be criminally charged with possession of the drug. It is another form of decriminalization.

But in 2000, when Tami, Leigh, and Kim were released from rehab, Mississippi didn't have a Good Samaritan law. A reporting person who called in an overdose was dangerously risking their freedom.

CHAPTER 3
A "Long" Drive to Brookhaven

On the way to Dickie's house, the women had stopped to buy beer and Wild Turkey bourbon. Now, on the road again, Kim and Tami broke out the Wild Turkey, while Leigh stayed sober and drove. They combined the Wild Turkey with Kim's Xanax and Dickie's Oxycontin. Kim and Tami were ready to get high and put any and all troubles in the rearview mirror.

The women had been prescribed antidepressants while at Cady Hill; it seemed simply part of the protocol. Antidepressants combined with opioids, or alcohol combined with opioids, can lead to respiratory distress. Wild Turkey and Xanax and Oxycontin were a most troublesome combination. Kim and Tami popped the Oxycontin pills and soon passed out. They had driven less than twenty miles.

With two inebriated people in the car and driving after dark, Leigh was heading for Dry Prong, Louisiana, a village of perhaps four hundred people located 150 miles west of Summit. There, Kim would stay with Tami. But, in the dark, and with no GPS, Leigh drove in circles. She didn't know how to read a map, and until that day had never driven past Hattiesburg, which she had passed hours earlier. By 10:00 P.M., having now driven virtually all day, she was exhausted. Leigh finally conceded that she was lost, and stopped in Brookhaven, a town north of Summit. She had driven for two hours but had traveled only twenty miles from Summit.

Brookhaven, long before the town had a name and citizens, was

Choctaw Nation territory. Once, the Choctaw had lived across the Southeastern United States—Georgia, Alabama, and Mississippi. On December 10, 1817, the Mississippi Territory became the state of Mississippi, with 55 percent of the population enslaved, and white plantation owners profiting from cotton. The Choctaw were on land valuable for growing cotton and making money. In 1818, New Yorker Samuel Jayne arrived to make his fortune. He founded Brookhaven, naming it after Brookhaven, Long Island.

In the 1830s, the Choctaw were physically forced off their lands after Congress passed the Indian Removal Act of 1830 to make room for white settlers. Their long march to the Indian Territory promised them, Oklahoma, was part of the displacement of Native Americans across thousands of miles. It became known as the "Trail of Tears."

Brookhaven, not unlike other towns in the South, has an ignominious past. In 1955, in the middle of the day and on the lawn of the county courthouse, white men shot and murdered Lamar Smith, a Black farmer and World War I veteran. Smith had been organizing voter registration for Black citizens, a veteran advocating for civil rights. No one was ever prosecuted for his murder.

At 10:00 P.M., the vacancy light was on at the Brookhaven Comfort Inn. Leaving Tami and Kim passed out in the truck, Leigh parked and went in to reserve a room. She found the night clerk chatty and warned the clerk that she had two passed-out people in the truck. "Don't worry, I'll be dragging in two people, but they're just asleep, they're not dead," she joked.

Leigh made sure to ask about video cameras for her truck, and then requested a ground-floor room so she could keep an eye on the truck herself. She was worried about her personal possessions in the open bed of the truck, and the clothes she had brought from Cady Hill. The front desk clerk assured her that there was hotel surveillance with security cameras in the parking lot, and that the property itself was safe. She told Leigh that the hotel staff would see anyone on the camera.

Leigh parked directly in front of the ground-floor room, in full view of the surveillance camera. She helped Kim and Tami inside and onto the bed. Then she made trip after trip to bring their stuff inside. Exhausted, she collapsed on the bed.

Leigh was awakened in the middle of the night by the sound of

Tami retching into the toilet. Kim remained asleep. Leigh made several trips between the bed and the bathroom, helping Tami, who vomited repeatedly. Leigh retrieved ice from the machine down the hall to cool Tami off and for Tami to chew on so she wouldn't get dehydrated. Finally, all three were asleep again.

Leigh and Tami awoke in late morning. Hungry, they decided to get some breakfast and call their parents, and they nudged Kim to wake her up. Kim didn't move. They decided they'd wake her up after breakfast. Aching to be home at this point, Leigh called Mama Sheila and asked her to grab the local paper so she could start looking at the want ads for work when she got home.

When they returned, Kim was no longer simply sleeping, she was struggling to breathe. She was overdosing.

In the past, Kim routinely used Oxycontin and knew how much she should take to get high. But she had been in rehabilitation for at least two months. Frequently, when people are released from jail or rehab, their tolerance is down because they haven't had access to their drug of choice. This is actually the most dangerous time for someone with substance use disorder. Judges may say that they're sending a person to jail to "dry them out," but the person is most likely to overdose immediately upon release from custody by using their preferred drug at the same dosage they formerly used. Sending people with opioid use disorder to jail can expose them to a most dangerous situation—both in terms of withdrawal and then using again upon release.

Leigh immediately called the front desk on the hotel phone, reaching the same clerk as she had met the night before.

"Call 9-1-1! Our friend is overdosing!"

Tami and Leigh took turns performing CPR on Kim. They could hear the ambulance approaching.

When the paramedics arrived at the Comfort Inn, they found Kim lying on the hotel room floor with Leigh and Tami huddled over her. Again and again the two women pressed on Kim's chest, hoping to get her heart started, trying to resuscitate their friend, waiting to hear a gasp for air. The paramedics took over the CPR and chest compressions, working against time to get Kim breathing on her own. They detected no pulse, no cardiac activity. Clinically, Kim was dead.

But the paramedics had a lifesaving drug with them. In 2000, that drug was only for emergency responders. More than two decades later, it is carried by police officers, social workers, and even some schools in emergency overdose response kits, a critical part of a nationwide response to what has become an opioid overdose crisis. It's available at drugstores. The EMTs gave Kim a shot of naloxone—often known by its brand name of Narcan—a drug that reverses the effect of an overdose.

The Narcan worked: Kim's heart re-started and blood pulsed through her body. Faintly, she was breathing again.

As the EMTs worked, Leigh and Tami explained how, after they were released from rehab in Columbus, they stopped at Summit to visit Kim's boyfriend. There, Kim stole Dickie's medicine bag. Leigh and Tami found the Oxycontin bottle in Kim's purse and turned all the meds over to the paramedics. They also gave the EMTs their home addresses and said they would stay in Brookhaven until they knew Kim was going to recover.

The EMTs strapped Kim to a stretcher and carried her to the waiting ambulance. The ambulance raced through the streets of sleepy Brookhaven, arriving within minutes at nearby King's Daughters Hospital. This was actually Kim's second time in the King's Daughters Hospital emergency room in Brookhaven in the past four months. Her mother didn't live too far away, and Kim had been living with her in December. At the time, neither Leigh nor Tami knew that Kim's family home was so close by. The hospital called her family immediately.

The road trip, once so full of promise, was about to become a twelve-year nightmare.

CHAPTER 4

Reexamining Habeas Post-Conviction Laws to Manifest Justice

I lived in a high-rise apartment one summer, and our windows overlooked another high-rise under construction. The top floor was slightly below our eye level. Every morning I saw neon jackets, hard hats, equipped and confident people walking on narrow wood planks between open metal railings. What looked like orange mosquito netting was draped over the whole thing—twenty-two floors up from the ground. The workers walked without concern, laboring on thin tables, more than two hundred feet above the street. I, an observer, was constantly worried someone would trip, the orange mosquito netting doing nothing but wrapping them in their fall.

Lawyers in the courtroom—be they prosecutors, defense attorneys, or judges—frequently are in much the same position. Just like the builders, working step by step they carry out seemingly mundane tasks every day, ultimately building a population for prisons, a world of condemned people, brick by brick, person by person, paying no heed to the potential costs. They are familiar with the swell of Black and Brown people sitting in the courtroom as well as the mass of guilty pleas. Prosecutors, defense attorneys, and judges interpret what the law is, what the law means, and what it will be. They have tremendous power. Yet the vast majority of these legal players in the courtroom also unthinkingly carry out the routine of their jobs every day.

We are socialized and taught not to see what we see. We ignore any reality that disrupts the standard policy. When we see violent and filthy prison conditions, we are taught to only see them as necessary and immutable. When we see a trans woman arrested, abused, and assaulted by police, we are taught to overlook the injustice and assume this was a necessary police response to a criminal.

Criminal. Prison. Language can transform a person or a place into a flat word, an abstraction, a noun, a world without dimension. Those nouns absolve deeper thinking, absolve examining or even recognizing any attendant shame and discomfort. We maintain the story that our criminal legal system identifies, punishes, and separates "truly dangerous" people from society. Yet the low clearance rate of homicides, arguably the most dangerous of violent offenses, belies that perpetrators are identified. The high rates of people incarcerated gives the false impression that the people being punished are "truly dangerous."

It is time to move from a system replete with manifest injustice to a system that employs tools for manifesting justice.

We can lift up the remedy of manifest injustice—miscarriage of justice—for courts to reverse convictions.

What is a manifest injustice claim? It is that a charge or conviction is unjust. How can a court determine a conviction is unjust? This can be achieved by looking at a confluence of factors—all of the evidence of injustice at trial and in post-conviction, not simply individual factors that can be advanced and therefore picked off one by one. Instead of focusing on limited arguments of factual innocence, we can, through this approach, look at a confluence of factors to determine whether the conviction is unjust. Together, the factors that are dismissed or rejected individually can demonstrate a manifest injustice.

Let's also consider broader change, systemic change. Congressional and state legislative change. We can lift up a Third Reconstruction Era and a Congress to reform our drug policy laws, our sentencing laws, and our federal habeas laws, like the Anti-Terrorism Effective Death Penalty Act (AEDPA). To do all this, let's first examine our history.

CREATING A THIRD RECONSTRUCTION

Black Americans have always faced threats to their freedom. Twice before in the history of the United States, our federal government has taken widespread action against racial injustice through Reconstructions of the law. A Third Reconstruction Era is on the horizon.

The First Reconstruction occurred after the Civil War, when Congress amended the U.S. Constitution to abolish slavery, extend citizenship to Black people, and give the right to vote to Black men.

A backlash across the South, sustained by white mob violence, created legal segregation, legal and extralegal violence against Black men and women, and newly drafted Black Codes to incarcerate and profit from the labor of Black men.

The Second Reconstruction was instigated by the Civil Rights movement of the 1950s and 1960s. The Supreme Court struck down racial segregation laws from transportation to housing to employment to education. The Court ruled in *Brown v. Board of Education* that public schools must racially integrate, setting off a firestorm of pushback and transformation. Congress passed the Voting Rights Act and Civil Rights Act.

A backlash to increasing civil rights was to take away those rights through incarceration.

Now is the time for our Third Reconstruction. The War on Drugs and the 1990s tough-on-crime zeitgeist in Congress reversed steps for racial justice. We can end the War on Drugs. We can create safety without depending solely on the system of incarceration. And we can affirm that justice is not necessarily complete when someone is convicted. In our moment of the Third Reconstruction, we can restore habeas and re-envision the courts' narrative of convictions and finality, of sentencing and punishment.

The writ of habeas corpus—the power to free a person in custody—has always been deeply connected to race in the United States. Expansion of this power to free a convicted person came after pivotal racial turmoil in our country in the 1860s and 1960s. Habeas corpus exists as a remedy for unjust convictions and sentencing.

OUR HISTORY: HABEAS CORPUS AND SLAVERY

Habeas corpus in Latin means "produce the body." The great writ of habeas corpus is a challenge to unlawful detention or imprisonment of a person. As exoneree Rubin "Hurricane" Carter said, "The writ of habeas corpus is not just a piece of paper, not just a quaint Latin phrase. It was the key to my freedom."

Yet before the Civil War, the writ of habeas corpus was used to perpetuate slavery.

Congress passed the Fugitive Slave Act in 1793, the same year that President George Washington laid the cornerstone to the U.S. Capitol building. The Fugitive Slave Act authorized local governments to kidnap and carry off Black people who had escaped slavery. The local government could then "return" these people to their place of enslavement. Slavecatchers frequently abducted free Black people and terrorized Black populations.

Slavecatchers could be charged and convicted for their violence and terrorism. But in 1833, Congress passed the Force Act, allowing federal courts to reverse the convictions of slavecatchers who were imprisoned in Northern states. Federal courts could review those convictions of abuse and violence against Black people, decide if the slavecatchers' actions were in furtherance of a "law of the United States," such as the Fugitive Slave Act, and then free the slavecatchers.

The Compromise of 1850, which is broadly known for admitting California into the United States as a free state, made it even easier for slavecatchers to abduct Black people in the North. Southern white plantation owners were frustrated by the success of the Underground Railroad. These plantation owners enslaved people to work their crops, and they were losing money. The Compromise of 1850 amended the Fugitive Slave Act to force *all citizens* to assist slavecatchers in their pursuit and abduction of Black people who had allegedly run away from slavery.

Those accused of being escaped slaves were arrested and convicted without a jury trial, without the ability to testify, and *without a habeas remedy* to challenge their detention. Judges, always white, received $10 compensation if the accused was determined to be a fugitive, and only $5 if the proof of former enslavement was insufficient. The kidnapping and conscription of free Black people into slavery escalated.

In the 1857 case of *Dred Scott v. Sandford*, Dred Scott, an enslaved man, sued under habeas corpus for his own freedom and that of his family. Dred Scott was born into slavery in Virginia and was property under the law. But he was sold as property to an army surgeon who moved Scott to Illinois, a free state, and then to Wisconsin, also a free territory. The laws were different in those places. In Wisconsin, Dred

Scott married Harriet Robinson, an enslaved woman, in a civil cere-
mony. Scott and Robinson tried multiple times to buy their freedom,
but the army surgeon refused, and took them with him when he moved
to Missouri, a slavery state.

In 1846, Dred Scott and Harriet Robinson sued for their freedom
under a Missouri statute that said any person taken to a free territory
automatically became free and could not be re-enslaved when they returned to a slavery state. They went to trial and won their freedom in
1850.

The army surgeon's wife, Irene Emerson, appealed.

The Missouri Supreme Court reversed the lower court's decision,
re-enslaving Dred Scott and his family. In 1853, the Scotts filed a habeas
petition in federal court seeking their freedom. The federal district
court ruled against them, keeping the Scotts in slavery. The Scotts appealed to the U.S. Supreme Court.

The U.S. Supreme Court issued a now disgraced opinion in *Dred
Scott v. Sandford*, an opinion that would ultimately come to represent
what the Constitution is *not*. The Court ruled that Black people, free
or enslaved, were not "citizens" under the Constitution and were not
entitled to any of its protections. The Court decreed that *no courts*
could consider a habeas petition filed for a Black person, because Black
people had no right to sue in federal court. Justice Roger Taney, who
wrote the opinion, emphasized that the Constitution protected the
rights of property owners to their enslaved workers as their legal property.

Irene Emerson eventually sold Dred Scott, Harriet, and their two
daughters back to Dred Scott's original owner's family in Virginia.
That family freed the Scotts soon after the Supreme Court decision refused to do so.

CIVIL RIGHTS FROM THE CIVIL WAR TO THE PRESENT:
THE FIRST AND SECOND RECONSTRUCTIONS

After the Civil War and the official abolishment of slavery, Congress
transformed the writ of habeas corpus during the First Reconstruction. Southern states were creating Black Codes to continue to control
Black people and restrict their new-found freedom. Indeed, some
southern states included laws for "citizen's arrest" in their Black

Codes. These citizen's arrest laws allowed white civilians to physically and violently detain Black people newly freed from slavery. The Black Codes outlawed conduct performed by a Black person that was otherwise legal for a white person—like being out past state-established curfew or travelling generally. Freedmen were also required to work; if they didn't have proof of employment, they could be charged with the crime of vagrancy. The sometimes decades-long prison sentences for Black men meant the state could lease them out to wealthy plantation owners for their labor, through a new convict-leasing system.

In response to the Black Codes, a bitterly divided U.S. Congress added the Fourteenth Amendment to the Constitution requiring equal treatment of all people, regardless of race. The amendment explicitly overruled *Dred Scott v. Sandford* and declared that all people born or naturalized in the country are citizens of the United States and of the state where they live.

The Fourteenth Amendment prevented states from depriving any person of "life, liberty, or property, without due process of law." States could no longer deny *any* person the "equal protection of the laws."

Congress also passed the Habeas Corpus Act of 1867, expanding habeas relief to "all cases where any person may be restrained of his or her liberty in violation of the Constitution or of any treaty or law of the United States." This meant that federal courts could now reverse convictions of freed slaves convicted under the newly passed Black Codes. These reforms countered racial injustice after the Civil War by expanding the ability of all people to petition to the federal courts for relief.

The Fourteenth Amendment and Habeas Corpus Act of 1867 were a response to the Black Codes and racist criminal persecution of people of color.

The Civil Rights movement, and the attendant Second Reconstruction, were a response to Jim Crow laws in the South that subordinated Black people through state-sanctioned segregation and unequal protection under the laws.

Police brutalized and arrested civil rights protesters who sought to integrate public transportation, public schools, and public restaurants. Here again, habeas expanded as a remedy during the Second Reconstruction. In *Gideon v. Wainwright*, a case brought post-conviction on habeas review, the Supreme Court guaranteed the right to a court-appointed attorney for defendants, including civil rights protesters wrongly arrested and charged. The Court also gave incarcerated people and protesters constitutional grounds to seek habeas relief. Habeas petitions brought in the 1960s resulted in pivotal case decisions by the Supreme Court.

Fast-forward to present day where our carceral state frequently oppresses and estranges poor people of color. The overarching assumption is that a constituent who follows and obeys the law will not be bothered by law enforcement and will not be funneled into the criminal legal system. This assumption ignores who is stopped and frisked without reason, and who is then arrested if they protest a violation of their rights. Many victims of police violence are obeying the law, or are violating only minor ordinances, and do comply with officer demands. Unprotected by law enforcement and often in the margins of government decision-making, poor people of color may see themselves as truly without a state.

The criminal legal system does not just respond to crime, it also surveils and controls poor people of color and people with non-mainstream identities, such as genderqueer and transgender individuals. People at the intersection of these identities face the most hostility and controlling behavior from law enforcement, and the highest rates of incarceration. They are tagged, documented, and controlled by the criminal legal system, even for minor misdemeanors.

The Third Reconstruction can change habeas law, as each prior Reconstruction has, to revive the constitutional, legal, and treaty rights of defendants post-conviction. The purpose of habeas review is to ensure that the government does not violate an individual's constitutional rights. The binds of current statutes, such as AEDPA, should be changed so that federal courts can reverse excessive sentences and unconstitutional convictions.

HABEAS LAW AND THE CURRENT STORY OF FINALITY

People incarcerated in America face a post-conviction court system that prioritizes finality. The system bends, sometimes inordinately, to uphold a conviction. The narrative of finality is tightly woven through government actions opposing habeas post-conviction review. Prosecutors adhere to finality when they oppose petitions to examine newly discovered evidence or to allow DNA testing. Congress argued finality when it limited the jurisdiction of federal courts to review state convictions. Even the Supreme Court lauded the status quo when it voiced concern that actual innocence claims would be "disruptive . . . on the need for finality."

In 1993, the Supreme Court, in *Herrera v. Collins*, ruled that courts don't necessarily have to review evidence of innocence. Although the decision assumes a freestanding claim of innocence, Mr. Herrera didn't meet it. He was executed a few months later. As Justice Blackmun said in his dissent, refusing to allow a convicted person to prove their innocence with new evidence, and then executing them, comes "perilously close to simple murder."

If someone is innocent, even if they have been convicted, it's still murder when the state kills them. Indeed, even if they are guilty, their death certificate will still say "Manner of Death: Homicide."

Our federal statutes, notably AEDPA, mandate that defendants overcome crushing procedural barriers to obtain habeas post-conviction relief. Less than 1 percent of federal habeas petitions are granted. Additionally, the legal system narrows and often denies access to court for people who have taken a guilty plea—the overwhelming majority of defendants. As a condition of pleading guilty, prosecutors require that defendants waive any right to appeal. Defendants may waive their right to know about existing exculpatory evidence that the prosecutor has. Under AEDPA, passed by Congress in 1996, the great hope of post-conviction review by a federal court, the chance to challenge a state court conviction, has shrunk to the size of a pinhole.

The principle of finality also removes moral unease and shame of how we punish people. Finality obliterates the importance of why. Why do we refuse new evidence of innocence? If guilt or innocence makes a judge or prosecutor feel ethical discomfort about how they punish one person, then what about moral unease for how they punish every person? Why do we punish anyone, guilty or innocent, with dangerous and violent incarceration?

Finality removes this moral unease by claiming that conviction and punishment are natural once someone has had a "fair" trial or pled guilty. The concern for the individual, and the process, ends. This dehumanization is apparent throughout court proceedings—the victims, the offenders, the witnesses—none of them are as attentively regarded as the attorneys who are the true players in the courtroom.

The innocence movement exposed how we as a society cannot create draconian exploitative punishment and expect only "deserving" people to suffer.

Yet even as more people are proven innocent, more actors in the criminal legal system—notably prosecutors and police—continue to deny innocence. Innocence deniers seek to control the narrative of who "deserves" to be in prison. Prosecutors re-bring charges against people granted new trials and demand that defendants plead guilty in exchange for a prosecutor's promise of no more time in prison. Courts have ruled that even innocence cases are not about innocence, they're about due process. The current defining question is whether the court and courtroom players followed the rules, not the fairness of the game. The current story is finality.

To change that story, we need to change habeas law in the states and in Congress.

THE ROLE OF HABEAS POST-CONVICTION LAWS AND THE NEED TO REVISE AEDPA

Habeas law, or generally the laws that apply after someone is convicted in the criminal legal system, is a litigant's last resort for freedom. The writ of habeas corpus is ancient, predating the British Magna Carta. The writ requires a court to examine whether a person is being held by the government unlawfully, their body detained.

Historically, habeas review is not about guilt or innocence, it is about liberty and legality. Habeas is such a powerful remedy that the writ of habeas corpus is enshrined in our Constitution: "The privilege of the Writ of Habeas Corpus shall not be suspended, unless when in Cases of Rebellion or Invasion the public Safety may require it." This power to review a conviction is in the hands of federal courts through the U.S. Constitution, and also state courts through every state constitution.

Congress passed the Antiterrorism and Effective Death Penalty Act in 1996 in response to the deadly Oklahoma City bombing by Americans Timothy McVeigh and Terry Nichols. The statute dramatically limits how, when, and why federal courts can revisit a conviction or sentence once it is "final." Under AEDPA, even defendants with evidence of innocence can be ignored in favor of finality.

Defendants can petition both state courts and federal courts to reverse their convictions. But under AEDPA, defendants convicted in state court must first apply to state courts for relief and "exhaust" any state court remedies. When the state court denies their petition, then a defendant can go to federal court. But the federal court must be extremely deferential to the state court's reasons for denial.

Just as Congress can restrict the scope of the writ, Congress can also expand the writ. Congress can reform, or abolish, AEDPA and its limitations on federal courts.

And state courts can define their own standards for reviewing post-conviction petitions.

IDEAS FOR CHANGING FEDERAL AND STATE HABEAS LAWS

Federal habeas law has at least three problems: timing restrictions, deference to state court decisions, and failing to recognize and remedy unjust convictions.

AEDPA is all about throwing out cases on procedural errors, such that federal courts rarely evaluate cases on the merits. AEDPA creates the following key barriers to meaningful relief: defendants must file for relief in federal court within one year of their conviction becoming final; defendants cannot go directly to federal court for relief and instead must first file through the state courts; the federal courts defer to state court decisions instead of viewing a case with fresh eyes; and after rejection, defendants cannot file more than one post-conviction petition without express appellate court permission. The requirement to file within a year is unreasonable for incarcerated people who have no right to counsel and only limited access to documents, investigation, and other means to support their claims. Incarcerated people who do file in that year often see their incomplete petition rejected—and then cannot file again in federal court without court permission. Finally, federal courts are expected to uphold a conviction and defer to state courts—even if they think the decision was wrong.

1. Allow Federal Courts to Review State Decisions De Novo

Many state courts fail miserably when it comes to reviewing post-conviction cases. AEDPA was predicated on the idea that defendants in post-conviction would get a fair shake in state courts. State courts' failure to live up to their end of the bargain has resulted in the effective denial of important federal constitutional rights. Under AEDPA, federal courts defer to the cursory, incomplete, or biased case treatment by state courts. Yet it is the job of the federal courts to step in. Congress should amend AEDPA so federal courts can look at a case "de novo," with fresh eyes and from the beginning.

Shirley Ree Smith, a Black grandmother in California, was wrongly convicted of murder by faulty forensic evidence. In 1996, she had rushed her seven-week-old grandson to the hospital when he stopped breathing. The doctors concluded he had died from Sudden Infant Death Syndrome (SIDS). Yet a local coroner said the cause of death was shaking—even without injuries to the neck, or any of the standard diagnostic signs of shaking. Prosecutors charged Smith with murdering her grandson, and a jury found her guilty.

A decade later, Smith's post-conviction attorneys presented evidence undermining the diagnosis of Shaken Baby Syndrome used against Smith and refuting that the baby had died from shaking. But the California Court of Appeals upheld the conviction, and the California Supreme Court declined to review it. Finally, Smith's case came before the federal appellate court. A panel of judges for the U.S. Court of Appeals for the Ninth Circuit reviewed the medical testimony used against Smith at trial and compared it to what advances in scientific knowledge had shown—that injuries once attributed solely to Shaken Baby Syndrome have other causes that are not the result of intentional shaking. The appeals court reversed her conviction, finding it was a miscarriage of justice.

The state prosecutors appealed the case to the U.S. Supreme Court. They argued that the federal courts must defer to the state court decision. Smith, the prosecution contended, should remain in prison serving a sentence of fifteen years to life.

In an unusual move, the U.S. Supreme Court agreed to review the decision. Justice Ruth Bader Ginsburg said the new scientific information about Shaken Baby Syndrome "casts grave doubt" on the case against Smith, and "it is unlikely that the prosecution's experts would today testify as adamantly as they did in 1997." Unfortunately for Smith, Justice Ginsburg was in the dissent.

The majority of the Supreme Court justices agreed with the prosecutors. The Court found that although there were "understandable doubts" about the conviction, AEDPA required that the federal court uphold the state court's decision to affirm Smith's conviction. Indeed, the Supreme Court held that "judges will sometimes encounter convictions that they believe to be mistaken, but that they must nonetheless uphold." In spite of substantial affirmative evidence of her factual innocence, the Supreme Court, relying on AEDPA, reinstated Shirley Smith's conviction in October 2011.

Shirley Smith was only freed when, in April 2012, California governor Jerry Brown bowed to community pressure and granted her clemency, commuting her prison sentence.

2. Eliminate the One-Year Filing Deadline in AEDPA

Another primary criticism of AEDPA is that the statute simply does not allow time for valid claims to be developed and raised. An incarcerated person without counsel frequently cannot develop a fully supported innocence claim within the time limitation. Defendants, working without lawyers, consequently raise piecemeal claims—one by one—and these successive petitions are often summarily dismissed by federal courts as not being significant enough to overturn convictions.

AEDPA's one-year filing deadline limited access to federal courts for review. And yet, when President Bill Clinton signed AEDPA into law, he issued the following statement: "I have signed this bill because I am confident that the federal courts will interpret these provisions to preserve independent review of federal legal claims and the bedrock constitutional principle of an independent judiciary."

Courts have habeas jurisdiction to hear a claim, and bypass procedural barriers, if it is necessary to avoid manifest injustice. AEDPA created procedural requirements, which callously and frequently deny defendants the opportunity to even have their claim heard because of a procedural problem. But courts, if they choose, can excuse a procedural defect and look at the substance of a claim if doing so is necessary to avoid a manifest injustice.

Traditionally, if a defendant's constitutional rights were not protected, they could have a hearing in court. Furthermore, procedural barriers would fall aside in the face of reviewing a "fundamentally unjust incarceration." A conviction lacks due process if, for example, prosecutors presented false testimony or evidence, whether they did so knowingly or not.

Historically, innocence was incidental to the habeas process. Instead, the focus was on constitutional violations and the right to due process. However, in 2013, the U.S. Supreme Court created a narrow window, an actual innocence timing exception. Incarcerated people claiming actual innocence can still file a petition even if they have exceeded the one-year limit. This is also the "fundamental miscarriage of justice exception," which gives courts equitable discretion to consider habeas petitions to avoid wrongful convictions.

3. State Courts: Confluence of Factors Review

Habeas review can change on the state court level and on the federal level. Although state courts have often failed in their duty to review convictions for manifest injustice, they are an area ripe for change and experimentation.

To avoid a manifest injustice or miscarriage of justice, some state courts have adopted a different review process, looking at a confluence of factors. These states include Massachusetts, Kentucky, Illinois, and Connecticut.

This new approach to post-conviction review means that when a defendant files a habeas petition or coram nobis petition for a new trial, the court looks holistically at trial errors and evidence that expose a wrongful conviction. This collective rather than piecemeal review, in the interest of justice, looks at a flexible confluence of factors, instead of haphazardly at individual errors in isolation.

The court can examine and rule based on the aggregate influence of many errors, from investigation, through trial, and to post-conviction. After reviewing all of the evidence, the court can reverse because of "the substantial risk of a miscarriage of justice."

A miscarriage of justice, or manifest injustice, approach is critically important. The approach accounts for forensic and investigative errors, and a cascade where one error infects the rest of the evidence, leading to other errors. These errors can affect the overarching investigative process, and can affirm confirmation bias—where prosecutors and police only take into account evidence that supports their case.

Miscarriage of justice inquiries outside of habeas law also focus on the violation of substantive rights. They can provide a guidepost for changes in post-conviction law. Federal Rule of Criminal Procedure 52(b) permits the reversal of a conviction on direct appeal if the defendant's "substantial rights" were violated. The Supreme Court and other federal courts have clarified that the purpose of Rule 52(b) is "to afford a means for the prompt redress of miscarriages of justice."

4. Federal Courts: "Evidence as a Whole" Review

As a potential corollary to the confluence of factors approach, some federal courts are looking more closely at the AEDPA requirement to evaluate the "evidence as a whole" in post-conviction. AEDPA added the "evidence as a whole" provision to the controlling statutes in 1996. This provision, and standard, comes from pre-AEDPA Supreme Court decisions, where litigants needed to show either "cause and prejudice" or factual innocence, implicating a "fundamental miscarriage of justice."

Federal courts looking at the "evidence as a whole" can consider evidence from original and successive petitions, reviewing evidence excluded at trial, evidence submitted in prior unsuccessful post-conviction proceedings, as well as the newly discovered evidence. "Simply put, the 'evidence as a whole' is exactly that: all the evidence put before the court at the time of its . . . evaluation." Quoting the Supreme Court in habeas case *Schlup v. Delo*, the "court must consider 'all evidence, old and new, incriminating and exculpatory.'"

Finally, courts have the inherent power to vacate a conviction to prevent a miscarriage of justice. Although AEDPA limited this power in certain circumstances, like successive petitions, this common law power still exists. In *McQuiggin v. Perkins*, the Supreme Court acknowledged the miscarriage of justice exception where AEDPA has remained silent, such as first habeas petitions. It must exist: this authority "is grounded in the equitable discretion of habeas courts to see that federal constitutional errors do not result in the incarceration of innocent persons."

THE TIME IS NOW: A THIRD RECONSTRUCTION AND CHANGING HABEAS LAW

The First and Second Reconstructions of laws occurred because of widespread action against racial injustice: the Civil War and the Civil Rights movement. A Third Reconstruction would acknowledge the racial injustice of our current criminal incarceration system and pass or repeal laws in order to stop the War on Drugs, end excessive sentencing, and reverse mass incarceration. The habeas power to free convicted people expanded after racial turmoil in the 1860s and 1960s. Let's not wait until the 2060s to amend or abolish AEDPA, to free wrongly convicted people—not just the factually innocent—and to widely adopt manifest injustice as a more attainable standard for postconviction relief.

Let's manifest justice now.

CHAPTER 5
Police Investigate and a Case Begins

"Code Blue!"

When Kim arrived at King's Daughters Medical Center in Brookhaven, Mississippi, she was in a coma and in respiratory arrest. She had suffered a massive drug overdose and coupled with too much alcohol and her history of substance use, her life was in danger.

In a written statement to Deputy Truett Simmons of Walthall County Sheriff's Office, Kim's aunt, Janet Simmons, recounted how, while she was in the waiting room, a nurse called out for anyone related to Kim Williams. There was a phone call.

"Hello?"

"Hi, how is Kim doing?" a husky female voice asked.

"Who is this? Did you leave Cady Hill with Kim?"

"Yes."

"Well, you should have stayed there, shouldn't you?"

"Can I come up to the hospital?"

"No."

"I'm not a user. I loved Kim."

Simmons hung up.

A while later, Simmons took another call, this time from a woman whose voice was lighter, younger sounding. This woman identified herself as someone who called the ambulance for Kim, and she was worried about Kim and wanted to stay in touch. Simmons ended this phone call just as abruptly.

FIRST SIGNS OF SEXUAL ASSAULT

Once King's Daughters Medical Center personnel stabilized Kim, they prepared to transfer her by ambulance to the hospital in Jackson, just short of sixty miles to the north. A nurse bathed Kim and removed a tampon from Kim's vagina. That's when emergency room Dr. Joe Moak and the respiratory therapist noticed physical bruises on Kim. Dr. Moak would categorize them as physical abuse—bruises around the nipples, scrapes to her buttocks "as if she had been hit by a board or a belt," as well as swelling and redness in her vaginal area that Dr. Moak described as "like she had been sexually abused in the vagina area and the rectal area."

Kim's family, including Kim's uncle, Walthall County Sheriff's Deputy Truett Simmons, had gathered quickly at the hospital. Dr. Moak informed them of his belief that Kim had been sexually assaulted. Dr. Moak gave Deputy Simmons a report on Kim's condition and considered the authorities notified. Deputy Simmons immediately began investigating.

Later, Dr. Moak called the Brookhaven Police Department. He spoke with Detective Nolan Jones, a man who had a reputation for caring more about making things right than about making people pay. Detective Jones found Tami and Leigh at the hotel and talked to them that same day. When Leigh called Mama Sheila that night, her biggest concern was that Kim's family refused to speak to her. Mama Sheila called Jones.

"Officer Jones, when Leigh tries to talk to the family, they say it's her fault. They hung up the phone on her," Mama Sheila said.

"Not to worry," Jones assured her. "This wasn't Leigh's fault; Kim was coming home from the rehab center one way or another. I'll help explain this to Leigh myself."

DNA DATABASES AND CRIMES OF VIOLENCE

The next day, Detective Jones asked to speak to Leigh and Tami again, this time in person. He revealed that the nursing aid had seen injuries to Kim the night before when she was bathing her. This was the first time that Leigh and Tami had any clue that authorities suspected something more than an overdose had occurred.

However, the nurse who alerted the respiratory therapist and

Dr. Moak did not do so until the bath was complete. If any physical evidence had existed, it had been washed away. Although the hospital could and did then follow the standard protocol to obtain a rape kit, hopes were low. Detective Jones sent what evidence there was to the Mississippi Crime Lab and included Kim's jeans and her panties along with the sexual assault evidence collection kit for testing.

The Mississippi Crime Lab was updating their DNA technology at that time to make their results compatible with a national DNA database being established by the FBI. This was the beginning of what has since become a massive tracking system known today as CODIS—Combined DNA Index System. DNA profiles from evidence in unsolved crimes and from convicted or arrested offenders are uploaded. Those profiles are searchable by law enforcement and prosecutors, state and federal. By 2021, there would be nearly 20 million DNA profiles in CODIS: 14,541,796 convicted offenders, 4,341,864 arrestees, and 1,103,683 profiles from unsolved crimes.

Only police, prosecutors, and lab workers are allowed to access CODIS. As was later demonstrated by the experience of Chris Mumma, a North Carolina innocence litigator, defense attorneys can be expressly prohibited from collecting DNA in the same way a police officer could and would in any case. If defense attorneys do have DNA evidence and obtain a profile, they are not permitted to upload their sample to the CODIS database to see if there's a match. Defense attorneys have to ask prosecutors for permission, and prosecutors frequently say no.

This scenario is all too common in post-conviction innocence litigation. The defense attorney finds untested DNA evidence in the evidence locker—perhaps fingernail scrapings from under the victim's fingernails, or a cigarette at the crime scene, or even a rape kit. They may request permission to submit this evidence for DNA testing and to compare any resulting DNA profiles against their own client who has professed innocence. If the client is excluded, the defense attorney may also request that the unidentified DNA profiles be uploaded to CODIS, to see if the DNA matches anyone in the system and identifies the perpetrator. These requests can be litigated for years in court because prosecutors simply refuse, usually because they fear there will be a match to the true perpetrator, which by its nature will exonerate the person asserting innocence.

Law enforcement, on the other hand, is connected to CODIS and to local, state, and federal lab results.

In 2013, the U.S. Supreme Court reviewed whether police should be able to automatically collect DNA while arresting someone, and upload the sample to this national tracking database. In *Maryland v. King*, the police arrested Alonzo King Jr. for assault, and in the process, they swabbed his cheek to collect his DNA. King had not been charged, let along convicted, and so carried the presumption of innocence. When the police ran King's swab through CODIS, the profile matched to evidence from a 2003 unsolved rape case.

This success in finding the perpetrator of a cold case sexual assault in Maryland led to a Supreme Court decision that diminished the privacy rights of all citizens. The Supreme Court held that for any serious arrest, the police can take DNA, upload it to CODIS, and keep the DNA profile forever. This ruling quickly expanded to all offenses in some states, such as driving under the influence, curfew violation, disorderly conduct in a protest, or domestic violence where the police simply arrest all parties. The collection of DNA in an arrest permanently gives police access to a person's DNA.

CODIS has become part of a massive effort by police to track civilians and gather information, including mining cell phones and collaborating with Google and Facebook. We can each be known and tracked by law enforcement due to the personal information we put into our phones, and if we are arrested at a march or protest, our DNA can likewise be added to a national database to which we have no access—but police and prosecutors do.

And police are having more success with the increasing voluntary sharing of DNA by members of the public—through DNA testing companies like 23andMe and AncestryDNA. When a person shares their own DNA for testing to find out their own genetic history or connections to relatives, that information can be accessed by police.

For decades, the identity of the Golden State Killer remained unknown. The Golden State Killer was a serial rapist and serial murderer responsible for at least a dozen murders and fifty rapes in the 1970s and

1980s in California. He broke into homes and frequently spent hours inside, stealing personal items, going through women's underwear drawers, and assaulting women. If a male partner was in the house, the woman was forced to tie him up and put plates on his back. If the plates fell, the killer declared, he would murder the woman.

Based on victims' descriptions, police knew the perpetrator was a five-foot, nine-inch white man with military or law enforcement training. Yet for decades, even after fifty rapes, police still could not figure out his identity. It wasn't until 2018, nearly forty years after the first attack, that police finally made progress by using a private DNA testing site. It was a high-profile example of how police can force access to private DNA testing sites, while wrongly convicted defendants cannot. Police compared the crime scene DNA to a public genealogy database, and soon were matched with relatives to seventy-two-year-old Joseph James DeAngelo. He was arrested and later pled guilty.

He was a police officer.

The inability of police to solve these rapes and murders unfortunately is not surprising. Research indicates that over the past thirty years, law enforcement has only found and arrested a suspect in 10 percent of major crimes, and prosecutors convicted that suspect *in 2 percent of major crimes.* The vast majority of *reported* crimes of violence go unsolved.

That wasn't the case with Leigh and Tami. In fact, the narrative was written almost immediately just by the facts on paper: Kim overdosed and arrived at the hospital with signs of a possible sexual assault, and she had just been in the company overnight of two lesbians. These two lesbians were right down the street and willing to voluntarily talk to police, plus they had given police their actual home addresses and phone numbers.

This was one sexual assault the county was going to solve and prosecute.

But the rape kit sent to the Mississippi Crime Lab didn't reveal any DNA because Kim's body had been washed before samples were taken. Nonetheless, prosecutor Dunn Lampton, who would achieve accolades later for prosecuting a civil rights era murder and winning a conviction against a white supremacist, was on track to convict Leigh and Tami, who, in his eyes, were violent, vicious lesbians. He considered the lack of DNA evidence a non-issue. He would simply tell the jury that the absence of DNA evidence was a sign of a homosexual assault by women.

DETECTIVE JONES INTERVIEWS LEIGH

On March 9, three days after Kim was admitted to the hospital, Leigh and Tami left the Brookhaven Comfort Inn and drove to Mama Sheila's home in Collins. Leigh took a drug test at Covington County Hospital, her second in a week, and tested clean again. She stayed with her family until the following Tuesday, when Detective Nolan Jones wanted to talk to Leigh and Tami yet again. For the third time, the women voluntarily agreed to speak with Detective Jones. After this third interview, Tami hired an attorney, who would be present for the fourth interview with Detective Jones.

For now, they piled into Leigh's white Chevy pickup truck with Sheila and drove the fifty-five miles to Brookhaven.

They arrived at the police station around 1:00 P.M. Detective Jones greeted them and suggested that Sheila go get something to eat. "This could take a while," he said.

"Thank you, Detective, I'm not hungry," Sheila replied.

"Sheila, no need to worry. I'll be treating Leigh like my own daughter."

"Do we need a lawyer?" Sheila asked.

"This is just routine questioning," Jones replied.

Sheila stayed in the waiting room, separated from Leigh and Tami who were taken to the back of the station. When she heard a man yelling, she didn't realize it was Detective Jones—and that he was yelling at Leigh. Instead, Sheila eventually went out to Leigh's truck and took a nap. When she awoke it was four hours later—5:00 P.M. She was shocked that she had been there for so long.

"Sheila, please, come into my office," Detective Jones told her when she re-entered the police station.

"I know Leigh didn't do this," he said. "But we're going to need her teeth impressions. Leigh has told me she's eager to give them over. In fact, she joked with me that I could have her teeth if I needed them."

"Okay," Sheila said.

"Now what about a polygraph?"

"Why, Detective, that should be no problem," Sheila said.

"You know, Sheila, Kim's family has asked me to find out who did this to Kim. I have to look into this."

"I understand, Detective."

"Did you know that Tami and Leigh were"—he paused—"an item?"

"What?"

"That they're in a relationship?"

"Who told you that?" Sheila asked. "Did they tell you that themselves?"

"It's well known," Jones said. "And I'm sorry, Sheila, but I'm also going to have to keep Leigh's truck here. I can give y'all a ride home."

"What? Do I need paperwork saying you're keeping the truck?"

"No, no. I'll give it to you when you pick the truck back up again. Then I can list what I keep from the truck," Jones said.

"You know, Sheila, Leigh came back clean—she wasn't drinking or using drugs on Monday or Tuesday. But I think Tami is the one who really did this, and that Leigh knows it."

"I hate drug users' code of ethics," Sheila responded.

Two weeks later, when Sheila called about Leigh's truck, the police told her she could come and get it but the police were going to keep the toolbox.

A TOOLBOX THEORY

Detective Jones now had developed a more extravagant theory for Kim's injuries than simple sexual assault. He had watched the Comfort Inn surveillance video and he believed that the video was damning. He saw a body in that truck. In his eyes, the video showed someone going to the back of Leigh's truck, quickly pulling a body out of the toolbox in the back of the truck, and carrying the body at a brisk walk into the hotel room.

Jones called his friend Michael West, a Mississippi dentist, to look at the Comfort Inn surveillance video. He asked Dr. West to take the video home. Dr. West "enhanced" the video on his home computer and zoomed in on still images. Jones, for his part, got Leigh's toolbox, collected hairs from a blue blanket in the toolbox, and sent the hairs to the crime lab. These were to be compared with the rape evidence kit of Kim Williams.

No match. The hairs on the blanket were not Kim's. But Jones nevertheless persisted with his theory. West had stills from the video showing what he believed to be Leigh removing someone, not something, from the toolbox. Dr. West and Jones, now united in their theory, were convinced that the still images showed Kim's body, her legs, her long hair. Jones concluded that Kim hadn't just been assaulted once; she had been assaulted repeatedly, first by being thrown in the toolbox in the back of Leigh's truck. Dr. West believed they had caught Leigh in the act—that the video recording was proof of Leigh removing Kim's limp body from the toolbox.

But Dr. West would end up playing a much bigger role in the case than just reviewing the Comfort Inn surveillance video.

DR. MOAK'S OPINION: ANY SEXUAL
ASSAULT WAS NOT RECENT

By the time Detective Jones spoke to Dr. Joe Moak a second time, Dr. Moak had become more adamant in his opinion. At this point, he said the "sexual assault injuries" that he noticed "indicated that the sexual battery was very forceful and was not a consensual act." He also said "the injuries looked like something a man would do." Dr. Moak dated the injuries "from the coloring" to two to four days before Kim arrived at the hospital. The injuries "were a few days old and were not immediate"—well before Kim arrived in Brookhaven.

The doctor's statement did not fit Nolan Jones's timeline or his theory.

CHAPTER 6

Changing Habeas
Post-Conviction Law
for Racial Justice

My wife's family documents were splayed out before me. First, her mother's birth certificate, from 1956 in rural southern Delaware. The birth certificate classified her parents: Indian. Her mother's parents were Nanticoke, and her father was the Chief of the Nanticoke Nation. To this day, the Nanticoke Nation is still not recognized by the federal government. Yet this government document essentialized her parents down to that one trait. In the 1940 Census documents, her parents were tagged with additional terms: farmer, married, Delaware . . . Negro.

Perplexed, I looked at the birth certificates of great aunts, great uncles: "Legitimate, Colored," "Legitimate, Mulatto," or simply "Mulatto."

This family, who lived in community on the East Coast before white Europeans landed, who had been farmers long before a United States or a Census, were labeled and inserted into a white caste system as non-white. Her family often wasn't recognized as Native American. The group descriptor for non-white was Mulatto or Negro. Looking at the Census pages, listing hundreds of names, the only two identifiers in 1940 were Negro or White.

Within that caste system, people of color were and are de-individualized and face discrimination and punishment in the criminal legal system.

New post-conviction laws and court decisions are acknowledging racism and reversing convictions that are rooted in bias. Post-conviction, we can use these new laws as well as ancient writs to expand innocence and reverse convictions that are miscarriages of justice. Even if federal laws like AEDPA do not change, state laws and courts can manifest justice—and some are doing so already.

COURTS: CONSIDER A "CONFLUENCE OF FACTORS" IN CONVICTIONS—AND INCLUDE RACISM

Frances Choy was seventeen years old when a fire consumed her family home in 2003 in Brockton, Massachusetts. Her parents tragically died in the fire. The high school senior, a survivor, was now an orphan and homeless. But police officers saw Frances in a different light: as a criminal suspect. They arrested Frances. Prosecutors charged her with arson and murder.

In the first trial against Frances Choy, the jury couldn't agree on a verdict. The second trial also ended with a hung jury. Prosecutors tried Frances Choy a third time and in 2011, eight years after the fire, jurors finally returned a guilty verdict.

Sharon Beckman, director of the Boston College Innocence Program, discussed with me how the program fought to reverse Frances's conviction and brought claims of racial injustice.

"It's clear to me that how she was wrongly convicted was a combination of racism, race and gender stereotypes, and a complete dehumanization of her," Sharon told me. "It's clear that an essential ingredient of the wrongful conviction of women is to dehumanize them."

Official misconduct and racism were rampant throughout Frances Choy's trials. Emails between the original prosecutors demonstrated their anti-Asian bias during trial, and to Sharon's point, how they dehumanized Choy. Choy's post-conviction team argued the court should reverse Choy's conviction based on the trial prosecutors' intentional race and gender discrimination.

They also presented fourteen other grounds on which to vacate her conviction, including ones that will be familiar to readers: new evidence of innocence, faulty forensic evidence, and incentivized false testimony.

Massachusetts courts implement a manifest injustice standard: they look at all influencing factors to determine whether a conviction was wrongful and whether justice was done. In this approach to post-conviction review, the court looks holistically at trial errors as well as evidence that exposes a wrongful conviction. They call this a confluence of factors review, and they also examine racial bias in court proceedings.

This expansive review, taken in the interest of justice, adopts a flexible confluence of factors standard instead of reductively reviewing individual errors in isolation. This standard resists the historic "harmless error" approach by courts.

Under "harmless error," courts analyze in isolation each issue raised, and weigh the issue against the otherwise "overwhelming evidence of guilt." As Stephanie Roberts Hartung, professor at Northeastern University School of Law and Trustees Board Member of the New England Innocence Project, shared, "With a confluence of factors approach, the court recognizes ways that each error can itself infect the process—and lead to other errors."

Choy and her lawyers asserted that her fifteen grounds should all be considered, alongside race and gender discrimination, under a confluence of factors to determine whether justice was done.

In September 2020, a judge reversed Frances Choy's convictions using the confluence of factors standard. The current prosecutors agreed that the conviction should be vacated. Soon after, the prosecutor's office decided not to re-prosecute Frances, and dismissed the charges permanently.

Massachusetts is leading the way for state courts to no longer evaluate post-conviction petitions by assessing single errors in isolation, which risks obscuring wrongful convictions. Instead, the Massachusetts courts look at the context and the whole of the evidence. The confluence of factors review is vital to recognizing and reversing manifest injustice.

LEGISLATURES: PROHIBIT DEFENDANTS FROM BEING CHARGED, CONVICTED, OR SENTENCED BASED ON RACE, ETHNICITY, OR NATIONAL ORIGIN

In 2020, California became the first state legislature to counter the legacy of *McCleskey v. Kemp*. The Supreme Court's 1987 *McCleskey* decision protected laws and sentences from being challenged by data showing a racially disparate impact. The California Racial Justice Act, instead, prohibits defendants from being charged, convicted, or sentenced based on race, ethnicity, or national origin.

Whether the evidence of racial bias is brought pre-trial or post-conviction, California judges can respond in a number of ways. Judges can, depending on how far along the case is, dismiss the charges, bring in a new jury, declare a mistrial, or vacate the conviction or sentence. If the defendant can show that they were convicted of a more serious offense than a similarly situated defendant of another race, or given a longer sentence, such a showing can be sufficient to reverse a conviction—at any point in time.

The California Racial Justice Act allows a defendant to file a writ of habeas petition even after they've served their sentence and returned to the community. The Act acknowledges the tremendous hardship of living in the world with a conviction, and particularly a wrongful one.

For defendants with old convictions, the Act allows defendants to file habeas writs for disclosure of "all evidence relevant to a potential violation of that prohibition," as long as the defendant shows good cause to believe the evidence exists.

In the words of the bill's sponsor, California Assembly member Ash Kalra, "It's time to establish a statewide policy that makes it unlawful to discriminate against people of color in the state's criminal justice system."

POLICE: RECOGNIZE ABLEISM AS A CAUSE OF WRONGFUL CONVICTIONS

Our multiple identities can be used against us in the criminal legal system. Our autism flags us as erratic and dangerous to police who respond with violence; our deafness is interpreted as noncompliance and justification to use force to make us comply; our disabilities heighten our own danger from law enforcement particularly when we are already stereotyped as dangerous because of our race. Police extract confessions while ignoring or taking advantage of our mental cognition levels.

Differently abled young Black men are at intense risk of police violence, police coercion, and wrongful conviction. The Centers for Disease Control and Prevention defines disability as "any condition of the body or mind that makes it more difficult for the person with the condition to do certain activities and interact with the world around them." However, in the words of Jay Justice, a disability activist, "My disability does not add to the challenges created by racial injustice. The institutionalized ableism and state-mandated poverty, that is inexorably linked to disability because of the policies enacted by our government, is what adds to the challenges created by racial injustice."

People of color with disabilities have to navigate a criminal legal system that rarely attempts to understand them. Instead, our legal system responds to differing behavior with punishment and criminalization. Police receive little training on how to recognize and interact with people with disabilities, and mistake the inability to raise one's hands, to move quickly, or to understand police orders as noncompliance and defiance. This perception then justifies the use of physical force against a person, to arrest them, and to label them a criminal.

More than 50 percent of people incarcerated in prisons in the United States have a mental disability, and the rate of disability generally is three times higher than outside of prison walls. The disability rate is four times higher in jails than generally recognized in society. Many of these people do not deserve to be in prison and are not aided by incarceration. Hundreds of people with intellectual disabilities have been exonerated of wrongful convictions after falsely confessing to crimes they did not commit. Their desire to please authority figures made them particularly susceptible to police interrogations.

By acknowledging the intersectionality of wrongful convictions, we can free more people who are wrongfully convicted and work to prevent future wrongful convictions.

PROSECUTORS: DROP RACIALLY DISCRIMINATORY CHARGES

If more states and the federal government recognize that charges and convictions based on racial bias are wrongful convictions, the impact can be far-reaching. Take, for example, the charges and convictions of members of the Arizona humanitarian group No More Deaths/No Más Muertes.

No More Deaths is based forty miles from the U.S.-Mexico border and near the Trump border wall. Members leave water in the desert for migrants traveling the dangerous path through the Sonoran Desert from Mexico to the United States. In 2019, federal prosecutors criminally charged members with aiding undocumented migrants. Their criminal act? Leaving water in the desert.

Driving around Tucson at the time, it was easy to identify supporters by the signs in their yards saying "Humanitarian Aid Is Not a Crime." But federal prosecutors made it a crime.

In August 2017, No More Deaths volunteers Natalie Hoffman, Oona Holcomb, Madeline Huse, and Zaachila Orozco-McCormick drove a Dodge truck down a road in a protected wilderness area and left one-gallon bottles of water in milk crates. Prosecutors charged the four members of the Unitarian Universalist church with federal crimes. Those charges included entering a national refuge without a permit and abandonment of property—the water bottles. In a more widely followed case, prosecutors also charged humanitarian Scott Warren of No More Deaths with aiding migrants.

People attempting to cross the Sonoran Desert pass the remains of other migrants who have fled their home countries. There have been more than three thousand documented deaths in the desert since 2001. Organizations like the Texas State San Marcos Project Operation Identification go into the desert to gather the remains of people and try to identify them. They do so, for families to know that their loved ones have died. Humane Borders maintains a map of Arizona migrant deaths, which documents the locations of found remains of migrants crossing the Sonoran Desert. This map helps guide No More Deaths volunteers to locations where they leave water.

Water is lifesaving. According to Scott Warren's attorney, Amy Knight, "[the water placement] is not random, and it's not intentionally flouting barriers, it's based on where it's needed. They're looking at tracks where people go through and have died." Artist Alvaro Enciso has built and installed more than nine hundred crosses to visibly mark deaths in the locations where peoples' remains are found. He calls his ongoing project "Donde Mueren Los Sueños"—"Where Dreams Die." Enciso likewise has left gallon jugs of water near the markers when he installs them.

A humane life-saving act for a stranger should not be criminalized. A humane life-saving act should not be criminalized based on that stranger being non-white or of a particular ethnicity. These prosecutions show a broad and abusive exercise of power by prosecutors, and charges influenced by racism.

Founded in 2004, No More Deaths co-existed peacefully with Border Patrol for years. The women of No More Deaths would regularly and historically go into the desert to leave water for migrants. These volunteers weren't targeted because they were U.S. citizens.

But more recently, the U.S. Fish and Wildlife Services officers began to dump out the water on the arid ground when they found it. When the officers caught women in the act of leaving water, the officers arrested them. Federal prosecutors charged them with federal crimes.

In contrast, similar charged violations, like abandoned property, were waived for the Trump administration to facilitate construction of the border wall in the Sonoran Desert. In defense attorney Amy Knight's words, "They don't really think of [migrants] as people, human beings with lives, families, goals, dreams. They just don't see them that way."

At the No More Deaths bench trial, prosecutors made the macabre claim that increasing the death toll of migrants in the desert would act as a deterrent to migration. Yet they presented no evidence that migrants who found dead bodies and bones were deterred from crossing over into the United States—particularly once they were already in Arizona near the city of Tucson. Prosecutors had no proof that the remains of thirty-seven people in the wilderness refuge in 2017, the year they charged the women, deterred unlawful entry by others.

Nonetheless, the prosecutors' reasoning carried the day. U.S. Magistrate Judge Bernardo Velasco found the women guilty of federal crimes for leaving water in the desert.

A year later, U.S. District Court Judge Rosemary Marquez reviewed the convictions. She questioned whether the defendants' act of leaving water furthered and encouraged illegal smuggling activity: "The Government claims a compelling interest in preventing Defendants from interfering with border enforcement strategy of deterrence by death . . . this gruesome logic is profoundly disturbing . . . it is also speculative and unsupported by evidence."

Judge Marquez wrote that the violations of entering the refuge without a permit and abandoning property "were committed in the course of leaving supplies of food and water in an area of desert wilderness where people frequently die of dehydration and exposure." The water was left with the goal of lessening death and suffering. The Court found the prosecution was too broad and did not accomplish a compelling interest on the part of the government.

Judge Marquez reversed the convictions. After this decision, the federal prosecutors dropped similar charges against four other volunteers for the same actions.

These wrongful convictions offer an example of the potentially abusive exercise of power by prosecutors, a power that intersects with racism. These women defendants provided humanitarian aid to people who were not American—indeed, humanitarian aid to whoever needed it in the desert. Prosecutors transformed their act of leaving water in the desert into a criminal prosecution. These prosecutors used federal criminal law as a prism through which to identify humanitarian acts as criminal because of who they were helping.

These are the cases where our tools come into play. In California, these defendants could have claimed the charges against them, and convictions, should be reversed under the California Racial Justice Act. In Massachusetts, Kentucky, Illinois, and Connecticut, a judge reviewing the convictions on post-conviction could apply the confluence of factors review and consider racism as a factor as well as to determine whether the convictions were manifestly unjust. And here, Judge Marquez reversed the convictions because the prosecution was too broad and did not accomplish a compelling interest for the state.

It is time that prosecutors no longer corner the market on moral outrage. It is time to bring back equity, and recognize that convictions tied to racism, police and prosecutor misconduct, over-sentencing, and false evidence are wrongful.

It is time to reverse these wrongful convictions.

CHAPTER 7

Dr. Michael West and Evidence of Bite Marks

On March 10, Dr. Michael West traveled to the state capital of Jackson, at the request of Detective Jones and Assistant District Attorney Jerry Rushing. Kim was at Baptist Memorial Hospital in Jackson, having been transferred from Brookhaven. The prosecutor and detective asked Dr. West to examine and photograph Kim.

Kim was unconscious and in a coma. Nevertheless, Dr. West took photos and videos of Kim, after her mother gave permission. These were not just any photos—Dr. West recorded and examined Kim naked. He took close-up photos and video footage of Kim's breasts and vulva. He asked the nurses to spread Kim's legs, and then to spread the lips of Kim's vulva, for more photos.

Dr. West photographed what he said was trauma to the vulva, bruising and redness, and "injuries to lateral aspect of the right thigh." He videotaped Kim's naked body with digital video and took photos with a Polaroid 35-millimeter camera.

Michael West was a dentist, and he was also a forensic odontologist, meaning he studied bite marks. No medical personnel at either hospital, including intensive care unit doctors, reported seeing any bite marks on Kim Williams. Dr. West, however, immediately said he found a human bite mark on Kim's thigh.

Dr. West also closely scrutinized Kim's breasts. He found more bite marks. He also claimed he found cigarette burns on Kim's breasts. In the video, Dr. West held up cigarettes, comparing their various sizes to alleged burn marks on Kim's breast. He found a "match" and positioned the cigarette next to Kim's nipple, to "show" the ultimate videotape viewer that the cigarette matched and had caused the alleged injury. He believed someone had snuffed out a cigarette on Kim's breast.

Dr. West went home and drafted his report. When Detective Jones received it, he saw that Dr. West had made a revealing discovery: in his opinion, part of Kim's vulva had been chewed off.

In his expert and pseudo-scientific language, "the injuries to Kim's vagina appear to be masticatory to the left labium majus and avulsion of the right labium majus, due to biting. Hematoma of the glans of clitoris is consistent with severe negative pressure. All of which is consistent with severe oral sex."

In other words, an assailant had chewed Kim's left labia, bitten and torn off her right labia, and then sucked on her clitoris to cause swelling.

The scenario faced by authorities was this: a twenty-three-year-old woman, who spiraled deeper into substance use disorder from a traumatic event the previous year, went into treatment. At some point either at the treatment center or afterward, she had a physically aggressive sexual encounter. There was no evidence to suggest whether it was consensual or not. Kim's memory was damaged by the overdose. An older white male dentist examined her naked body without her consent. She was unconscious while the dentist—a complete stranger—looked over her entire body, rolled part of her body over to see "bite marks" more clearly, thoroughly scrutinized her vulva, and compared cigarettes to her breasts. He did it on videotape so its viewers could later see her naked body for themselves.

That night, Dr. West called the prosecutor, Jerry Rushing, and requested teeth impressions. Within five days, he had the dental models of Leigh, Tami, Dickie, and Peanut.

Within those five days at the hospital in Jackson, nurses discovered an injury that hadn't been observed at King's Daughters—a cut on her head. This injury was discovered only after the hour-long ambulance ride from King's Daughters to Jackson. When Dr. West learned of the head injury, he immediately thought of the toolbox. At his direction,

Detective Jones pried the toolbox latch off the toolbox and handed it to West. Then, with toolbox latch, dental molds, and electric clippers in hand, he returned to the hospital to view and record Kim's body a second time.

Dr. West stepped up to Kim's hospital bed. Her long brown hair was pulled back in a bun. He had the nurse let Kim's hair down, and then West began to clip.

With the permission of Kim's mother, Dr. West shaved part of Kim's head. When the head injury was fully visible, with no more hair covering a large patch of Kim's scalp, Dr. West brought out the toolbox latch.

For Dr. West, it was a match.

He was now convinced that Leigh had put Kim in the toolbox. And he had created the evidence to prove it.

At only one point in his police interview did Dickie Ervin choke up. Kim's boyfriend, on painkillers since his car accident and living with a hip implant, had endured chronic pain for years. Despite hearing about the nature of Kim's injuries, Dickie teared up only when police talked about cutting off Kim's hair. He said Kim loved her hair. Her hair was part of what made her "her."

Dickie told the police how Kim would never wear her hair back in a bun or "any of that shit"—she loved having her hair down. Kim's long dark brown hair hung down, usually to her waist. She hated to cut it, even to trim the ends. And now a dentist had come into her hospital room with electric clippers and shaved it off, close to the skull.

Kim remained in a coma for twelve days. After she awoke, she could not remember what happened the night in question. Thus, the Comfort Inn surveillance footage became important. The footage of the parking lot showed Leigh parking the truck and then removing something from the toolbox in the open bed of the truck. What was it?

Leigh said it was her clothes in a garbage bag. But Dr. West saw something different. Watching the raw footage on his home computer, he saw Leigh lifting Kim's body out of the toolbox.

On March 15, when West matched the toolbox latch to Kim's new head injury, he examined Kim's body anew. This time, he said he matched the toolbox latch to another part of Kim's body—her hip. The strawberry bruise was ample in size. West used that bruise to identify not only a bite mark, but now next to the bite mark he saw a marking from a toolbox latch. In his opinion, "the injuries to Kim's right temple and area inferior to the bite mark on her right thigh are consistent with the trunk toolbox latch." Dr. West had identified yet another instance of assault.

Dr. West wasn't finished. He turned to the four sets of dental molds he had brought with him: those of Dickie Ervin, Peanut Ervin, Tami Vance, and Leigh Stubbs. However, over these five days, the strawberry bruise had faded and with it the alleged bite mark. No matter. On the videorecording he created during his second visit, Dr. West pressed Leigh's dental mold into Kim's naked hip. He then took a photo of the "match"—the visual that he had just created.

As a follow-up, Dr. West decided to perform an analysis by comparing the teeth molds to photos he had taken of the alleged injury five days earlier. Dr. West again found a match: Leigh Stubbs. In his words, Leigh's teeth were consistent with the bite mark. He excluded the others.

The prosecution paid Michael West over $3,000 for his video and bite mark expertise. Later, another bill of nearly $6,000 would be charged directly to Leigh and Tami.

THREATS AGAINST LEIGH

Over the next month, an unknown woman called the Stubbs's home three times. Weeping, she accused Leigh of killing Kim—although Kim had not died. Then a strange man started calling. He said he was close by, and that he was going to get Leigh the same way that she had killed Kim. The man continued to call, playing song lyrics: "You've got nowhere to run to, nowhere to hide." Then his voice came over the phone, "What are you doing? I know . . ."

Initially, Leigh lived at home with her parents, and Tami was at home in Dry Prong with her stepdad and her mama, Sandi. Tami's stepdad worked offshore for ENI Petroleum, and Mama Sandi worked in Pineville, Louisiana, as a dental hygienist.

But after the disturbing phone calls, Leigh and Tami moved together to Columbus, near Cady Hill, where they had met and made mutual friends. They returned to a circle of people who had Cady Hill in common. It was a time when they could simply be around friends who valued sobriety; who had struggled with drug use; who had known people who overdosed. This community knew them and knew Kim— the Kim before her overdose.

The summer months passed with no word from the police or the district attorney's office. Maybe the storm had passed.

CRIMINAL CHARGES IN SEPTEMBER

Kim was discharged from the hospital. While she continued to recover, Lincoln County prosecutors Dunn Lampton and Jerry Rushing went before a grand jury to obtain an indictment against Leigh and Tami. Dr. West was their key witness.

When the grand jury approved and charges were filed on September 20, 2000, Kim was identified as an "un-indicted co-conspirator." Only Leigh and Tami faced criminal charges.

Tami and Leigh were charged with conspiracy to possess morphine and to commit grand larceny, unlawful possession of morphine, and aggravated assault. For the first two, the state alleged Tami and Leigh had conspired with Kim to possess Dickie's Oxycontin pills, stole the pills, and then knowingly had those pills in their possession. The final charge, assault, was an allegation that Tami Vance and Leigh Stubbs caused serious bodily injury to Kim.

Neither the indictment, nor the prosecution's case at trial, ever specifically clarified what that serious bodily injury was. But the state would give the jury multiple possibilities: chewing off Kim's vulva, biting Kim on the hip, burning her nipple with a cigarette, and putting Kim in a toolbox. And their whole case was Dr. Michael West.

The judge initially set bail at $100,000 for Leigh. Leigh's private attorney argued the bail down to $50,000. Leigh's parents paid a percentage fee to Barnhill's Bail Bonding, a bondsman who would post the $50,000 bond—and Leigh was able to go back home until trial.

PRE-TRIAL PROBLEMS

Mama Sheila and Papa Pete Stubbs hired John Ott, a local Brookhaven attorney, to represent Leigh. John Ott arranged for Leigh to take a lie detector test with the district attorney, who said that if she passed, she would not be a suspect.

"Is your first name Vikki?"

"Yes."

"Do you intend to answer truthfully each question that I ask you?"

"Yes."

"Do you know who hurt Kim?"

"No."

"Did you cause any of Kim's bite injuries?"

"No."

"Were you born in Mississippi?"

"Yes."

"Did you put Kim in the back of your truck?"

"No."

"Do your friends call you Leigh?"

"Yes."

"Did you treat Kim's injuries prior to calling nine-one-one?"

"No."

"Have you attempted to withhold any information since you sat down in that chair?"

"No."

Leigh passed.

In January 2001, Ott spoke with Dr. Moak, who timed the injuries as occurring three to four days before Kim arrived at the hospital— meaning before the road trip to Summit and Brookhaven and likely over the weekend at Cady Hill. Ott seemed enthusiastic about the charges against Leigh being dropped.

But then all communication from John Ott stopped.

On May 30, Leigh learned from Tami that they had a trial date set for June 20. Ott was no longer returning Leigh's calls, nor Sheila's calls. On June 4, fifteen days before trial, John Ott called Sheila and told her that Dr. Moak had changed his timeline: now the injuries were only a day old.

At that point, Ott told Sheila that "he couldn't handle the pressure" and he was resigning from the case. Sheila begged him not to—they didn't know any other lawyers and the trial was only two weeks away.

Unmoved, the next day John Ott confirmed that he would not stay on the case and sent Leigh a resignation letter as her lawyer. On Monday June 11, Sheila and Leigh went in person to see John Ott and beg him to stay on as Leigh's attorney. He firmly declined. Instead, Ott handed them Leigh's case file in exchange for her signing and agreeing to the resignation letter.

There was now a week left until the trial date.

Sheila called an attorney in Hattiesburg, Jim Dukes, who met with her and then called the judge presiding over the case, asking for a continuance. Judge Mike Smith, Circuit Court Judge for Lincoln County, was assigned to Tami and Leigh's case. Judge Smith was known to be hard-nosed, and he lived up to his reputation. He refused to grant a continuance—the trial date was set.

Next, Dukes called the prosecutor and told him that it wouldn't be a fair trial on such short notice after a lawyer's resignation. Dukes told the prosecutor that the state would be doing the Stubbs family a grave injustice. Jerry Rushing simply responded that the judge was the only person who could change the date. There would be no request for an extension in time from the prosecution.

With this response, Dukes told Sheila that he couldn't take the case and "no lawyer worth his salt would take a case on such short notice."

The day before trial, Judge Smith agreed to hold a hearing with Ott, Leigh, and Leigh's parents. Leigh still had no attorney. At that hearing, Judge Smith accused the Stubbs family of trying to manipulate the State of Mississippi. He would only give a week extension until June 27.

When John Ott then suggested attorney Bill Barnett, the Stubbses hired him on the spot. Trial would begin June 27. Bill Barnett got to work.

On June 25, District Attorney Dunn Lampton reached out to Barnett with a plea offer for Leigh. The suggested plea was faxed over to

Bill's office in the morning, two days before the trial date. The offer was a recommended sentence of ten years at the Mississippi State Penitentiary if Leigh pled guilty.

Leigh refused.

Before the trial started, Barnett asked for a hearing to challenge Dr. West's bite mark evidence. Barnett was shocked when he looked at the video recording that West had made. The tape from March 10 showed a bruise on the hip; the recording from March 15 showed the bruise but it was much less pronounced. And then the tape stopped. When it restarted, there were indentations. West had imprinted the dental mold of Leigh's teeth directly on the bruise—on Kim, who was in a coma.

Barnett argued that whatever "evidence" that might have existed on Kim's body was altered when Dr. West pressed the dental mold directly into her skin to make an impression.

"What the doctor has done is he has taken the cast of somebody's teeth and he has impressed them into her body," Barnett declared. "A live patient's body. He has impressed those teeth in there and then continued the tape and said, 'Gee, look here. I have a bite mark.'

"He has altered the evidence," Barnett continued. "He's tampered with evidence. He has tampered with her body. That is, I mean that's, that's just uncalled for. There is no way a person should tamper with evidence.

"What's the jury supposed to think after that thing is pressed in there?" he added. "There is a bite mark that wasn't there ten seconds before."

Prosecutor Dunn Lampton was quick to defend Dr. West, his star witness. "As long as he explains what he did. That he put the mold on the skin to compare it to the mark that he saw. That's the way they—"

Barnett cut him off, "There was no mark there. He pressed it in and now there's a mark there. There was no mark there and he pressed it into her skin."

Dunn retorted, "I don't believe that's what the doctor is going to testify to. He is going to say that there was the outline of the bite mark. That he took the mold and put it over what he had determined to be a bite mark to see if it matched."

The judge made his decision. "I'm going to let him testify as to what he did and let the jury decide."

Tami's defense attorney, Ken McNees, then chimed in, "Be dangerous if he did. He's got better sense than to do that."

The judge agreed, "I don't—you know, it's incredulous, from what I know about this man, to suggest that he did that."

And with that, Dr. West was redeemed. His video of the bite mark on Kim's body was going to be shown to the jury. The trial was set to begin that afternoon.

CHAPTER 8
Faulty Forensics and Future Truths

While I worked as a prosecutor in D.C., a close friend of mine, Paul Killebrew, worked at the Innocence Project of New Orleans. Sometimes, when I was dragging my casefiles back from court in a big rolling briefcase, I'd stop, rest on a bench, and call him. He was always out on the road investigating, or meeting with a client in prison, or brainstorming case theories. His work had a life and gave life. My work felt like I was standing in cement that kept pouring and rising, solidifying around me, making me more rigid, cold, and impervious.

Paul told me when the position opened up at the Mississippi Innocence Project. I didn't think I'd take the job—leave D.C. for rural Mississippi—but I wanted to find out about their work for myself. That's how I ended up in Noxubee County, Mississippi, with exoneree Levon Brooks.

History can have a close presence in Mississippi, with the 1960s deaths of three civil rights workers only forty-five miles from Noxubee County, in nearby Philadelphia.

I met Levon that first time in Noxubee County at his mother's funeral. It was hot July but with a forgiving breeze, a day for her to rest. Levon had spent the last few months with his mother in her home in Macon, a rural area where young people would leave on Saturdays and drive to the nearest big town, Columbus, to go to Walmart and socialize. But Levon was in his fifties, and he had spent the last eighteen years in prison for a terrible crime he did not commit. His mother spent those years fighting for his freedom and redemption.

When I asked Levon about his mother's death, he simply said, she was finally able to put her hammer down. She had seen him freed, and they had been reunited in her last days. Levon was an artist, and in prison he drew to lift his spirits and hers, sending drawings home. She always kept fighting for him, and now she could be at peace.

On a whim, Levon's lawyer at the Mississippi Innocence Project invited me to the funeral when I was in Oxford, Mississippi, on my multi-day job interview. The next day I was driving two hours down to Macon with the director of MIP, Tucker Carrington, and his friend, a documentarian. I had only work suits to wear.

But that day at the funeral, it was more than just my ill-suited clothes. I was an interloper. Walking into the small A.M.E. church, among the somber women in white dresses and fans ready to comfort the family, the peaceful, still, and sparse landscape, I was a stranger in the back. The cool wood benches, the memorial, then we rose to bless the departed and depart ourselves.

I didn't go to the burial. I steadied myself for the post-funeral reception and mingling. Me, the awkward white woman. The prosecutor.

But my northern upbringing had misled me. People were welcoming, kind, and generous. Unlike the first question in D.C., they didn't ask what I did. They asked where I was from, due to my accent, and then gave me a pass when I claimed the noncontroversial Midwest. People don't generally have strong opinions about the Midwest.

They asked me to take seconds on food. I made a few people laugh when I—being a vegetarian—ate the fatback in the green beans. Flustered, I exclaimed, "I thought they were potatoes!" I was thankful to appear endearing and inept rather than as my work persona. Family and friends generously broke bread with me. Generosity: something I had been lacking toward victims and defendants in my current job.

After the funeral, I went with the other MIP folks to Levon's home, talking with him, his family, his girlfriend Gloria, and her daughter. When we got in the car to drive back to Oxford, there was a rainbow in the sky. In my journal that night, I wrote,

Today was possibly one of the most moving days of my life . . . going to the funeral, and feeling like everything said had a double meaning—bearing the cross, laying down your burden, that he carried such a burden all those years, and in his letters to his mother he never gave up hope, he kept thinking he would be found innocent. He was so warm.

Two months later, I moved to Mississippi.

FORENSIC EVIDENCE PROBLEM 1: FAULTY TESTIMONY

Levon spent eighteen years in prison for a crime he didn't commit. He didn't have DNA evidence to exonerate him of the crime in rural Noxubee County. But another Black man did.

Three years after Levon's conviction, Kennedy Brewer was convicted of a very similar crime, in the same rural county, and sentenced to death. The DNA in Kennedy's case identified the true perpetrator: Justin Albert Johnson. Johnson, who had been living near both victims when they were abducted, confessed to both crimes. He had been on the police suspect list in Levon's case and Kennedy's case, the only suspect with a history of sexually assaulting women and girls. If police had gotten the right culprit in Levon's case, the second crime never would have happened.

Both Levon Brooks and Kennedy Brewer were convicted based on bite mark testimony by dentist Dr. Michael West and forensic pathologist Dr. Steven Hayne. The alleged bite marks in both cases were actually insect bites, from Johnson hiding both victims in a creek where it took days for their bodies to be found.

West and Hayne were a forensics tag team in Mississippi. They regularly testified together for prosecutors.

West and Hayne are perhaps most known for the Black men sent to die in prison or death row based on their testimony and evidence.

The state of Mississippi wrongfully convicted Levon Brooks based on faulty forensic evidence. That means two things. First, Dr. Hayne and Dr. West testified beyond the scope of the science. Faulty testimony goes further than the foundational validity of the evidence. Second, the scientific evidence itself—bite mark evidence—lacked scientific validity. Bite mark evidence, also known as forensic odontology, has now been widely discredited.

Hayne and West were the go-to testifying experts for prosecutors across Mississippi on a range of cases. In some of these cases the scientific evidence was valid, but their expert testimony went far beyond what the science could show.

When police killed Debbie Loggins, a Black woman, Hayne was asked to defend them. Ms. Loggins was a thirty-three-year-old woman, five-foot-four, who weighed 220 pounds. Carroll County sheriff deputies arrested her in front of her own home, for getting in a fight with her neighbor at 6:00 A.M. Someone had called the police. Two deputy sheriffs handcuffed Debbie's hands behind her back, shackled her ankles, and then linked a third handcuff that connected the other two. Technically this is called a four-point restraints; police refer to it as hog-tying. The sheriffs lifted Debbie Loggins and put her in the back of the patrol car, lying on her face. The sheriffs left Debbie restrained in that position, facedown, while they sat in the front seats and drove to the jail in Grenada, Mississippi.

When they arrived at the jail half an hour later, Debbie was dead. She couldn't breathe. A doctor found she died from asphyxiation. Debbie was not alone; many people have died in police custody while in four-point restraints, in the presence of officers. Including Debbie's own son, who died years later in the Grenada jail, in four-point restraints.

Dr. Hayne performed an autopsy and he testified to a different cause of death: Debbie died from over-exertion. Hayne labeled the death an accident.

When Debbie's family sued the county and the sheriffs under civil rights statute Section 1983, the court decided the police were not responsible. The court held that Debbie's death was "unexpected," and that chaining her in four points didn't pose a risk of serious medical harm in the eyes of the sheriffs.

The police who sat in the front seat of the car while Debbie Loggins died were found not responsible.

In another case, prosecutors in Meridian, Mississippi, charged Linda Griffin with murdering her husband, Frankie. The mortuary had already embalmed Frankie at the funeral home when the police belatedly brought in Dr. Hayne to conduct an autopsy. Hayne found ethylene glycol, a common component of embalming fluid, in Frankie's eye fluid. It is also a component of antifreeze.

At trial, Hayne testified that Frankie had a heart attack. He explained how the autopsy revealed Frankie's severe cardiovascular disease and clogged arteries.

Hayne also testified to the scientific finding of ethylene glycol in Frankie's eye fluid. However, instead of attributing it to the embalming fluid, Hayne testified it was proof of the prosecution's fantastical theory of murder.

PROSECUTOR DAN ANGERO: Now, I want you to assume if you
   would that the decedent consumed a single bowl containing
   cornbread, what I call butter beans, lima beans and chicken
   wings at about 8:15 or 8:30 the night before his death. That
   meal, so to speak—could a meal like that contain a sufficient
   amount of ethylene glycol to poison a man to death?

DR. STEVEN HAYNE: If there's enough fluid with it, Counselor. It
   would take normally approximately 100 milliliters of fluid, so I
   would expect to see some fluid in that. I would not expect it to
   be in the chicken or cornbread unless it was put in there after
   cooking. And the lima beans, there would have to be some fluid
   there to have a volume enough to kill a person.

PROSECUTOR: But it would be possible for the ethylene glycol to be
   placed in the chicken after it was cooked such that it wouldn't
   evaporate, correct?

HAYNE: Yes, sir.

PROSECUTOR: And I believe you said earlier that it has a slightly
   sweet taste; but other than that, no odor or any other indication
   that that's—in other words, if you put it in your mouth, a
   slightly sweet taste; but other than that, you wouldn't really notice that you were ingesting something harmful?

HAYNE: No, sir.

PROSECUTOR: Now, reading your autopsy report, Dr. Hayne, I
   note that you list as the immediate cause of death ethylene glycol toxicity?

HAYNE: Yes, sir.

PROSECUTOR: So had it not been for the ethylene glycol being introduced into his body, it's your professional opinion to be be-

yond a reasonable medical certainty that he would not have died?

HAYNE: That's correct.

The prosecution had charged Linda with murdering her husband by serving his fried chicken and lima beans in a moat of poisonous antifreeze. Never mind that Frankie had a heart attack.

Hayne testified beyond the scope of the science. Defense counsel for Linda Griffin argued the obvious: ethylene glycol is just one component of antifreeze, so Linda would have to drench that fried chicken in antifreeze after the chicken, or beans, or cornbread was cooked. In Hayne's own testimony, Frankie would need to consume at least half a cup of ethylene glycol, so likely double that amount of antifreeze. He would also start showing symptoms of poisoning, instead of nonchalantly jumping in his carpool to head to work for the night shift.

The jury heard Dr. Hayne's testimony and came back with their verdict: Linda was guilty of murder.

The result was so surprising that the judge took an unusual step.

JUDGE LESTER F. WILLIAMSON JR.: It is not appropriate for me to just substitute my judgment for the judgment of the jury; however, I am responsible for a just result in this case. . . . I cannot accept the verdict of the jury. The motion for judgment notwithstanding the verdict is granted, and that will be the ruling of the Court. That's what I feel like I've got to do in this case.

Judges very rarely refuse the jury's verdict. Judge Lester F. Williamson Jr. did so to prevent a wrongful conviction. Few other judges have done likewise, even if they have later called innocence programs to tell them about a case, to alert them to investigate a conviction that "never sat right."

Prosecutors, instead, can play a critical role in stopping wrongful convictions by examining and understanding their own forensic evidence—before using it at trial.

FORENSIC EVIDENCE PROBLEM 2:
FAULTY SCIENTIFIC EVIDENCE

Forensic science was originally created by police. For decades much of the evidence relied on by prosecutors and presented to juries had scant scientific foundation. In its 2009 Report *Strengthening Forensic Science in the United States: A Path Forward*, the National Academy of Sciences (NAS) criticized forensic evidence, particularly hair matching, bloodstain patterns, and bite marks. This forensic evidence was regularly admitted in criminal trials, in part due to a lack of robust pretrial disclosure of evidence by prosecutors.

The NAS Report implored judges to reexamine thoughtless admission of forensic evidence at trial. The report even issued recommendations to ensure that criminal courts only admitted scientifically valid and reliable evidence.

The NAS Report reserved particularly harsh criticism for the forensic odontology sub-discipline of bite mark comparison analysis.

The use of bite mark analysis in North America dates back to the infamous Salem witch trials. A Massachusetts Colony "witch hunter" alleged that a local reverend was recruiting young girls to practice witchcraft. As his only proof, he argued that the reverend's teeth matched purported bite marks on the girls, and the prosecution forced open the reverend's mouth at trial to present his teeth. Reverend Burroughs was convicted and executed. He was hung in front of the people of Salem. He was then posthumously exonerated.

Bite mark analysts purport to match a biter to a bite mark on human skin, by comparing the mark and the suspect's dental mold. Bite mark analysis relies on a belief that each human has unique dentition, and that human skin accurately records those unique dentition features. Neither of these beliefs have been scientifically proven. Instead, the NAS Report found that bite marks on skin change over time, and can be distorted by swelling, healing, and natural changes in the skin. Bite mark analysts also lack a standard for indicating bite marks, and their findings vary wildly.

In sum, the NAS Report damningly concluded that there is no scientific evidence that bite mark comparison analysis can match a bite mark to a biter. Analysts cannot correctly and reliably identify a bite mark as made by a human instead of an animal. Analysts cannot accurately identify a bite mark at all, as shown by their own internal studies.

Instead, bite mark evidence is responsible for dozens of wrongful convictions.

WRONGFUL CONVICTIONS AND
FALSE BITE MARK EVIDENCE

In 1992, a Lowndes County, Mississippi, jury sentenced Kennedy Brewer to death based on false bite mark evidence and testimony. Dr. Michael West told the jury he had discovered nineteen bite marks on the three-year-old victim's body. He testified that Brewer's teeth inflicted many of the bite marks, "to a reasonable degree of medical certainty." According to Dr. West, Kennedy Brewer had bitten the child, repeatedly, using only his top teeth.

The defense called Richard Souviron, a dentist and founding member of the American Board of Forensic Odontology. Souviron challenged the underlying evidence. He believed that none of the wounds on the child's body were even human bite marks, because there were no corresponding lower teeth prints.

At the end of the trial, the jury convicted Brewer of rape and capital murder of a child. The Supreme Court of Mississippi affirmed the conviction on appeal.

But police had found and collected DNA on the victim's body during the pre-trial murder investigation. In a habeas petition filed post-conviction by Vanessa Potkin at the Innocence Project in New York, Brewer successfully asked the trial court to order the State to test the evidence.

The DNA results excluded Kennedy Brewer. His attorneys then petitioned for an evidentiary hearing on the DNA evidence and to challenge the bite marks. The Supreme Court of Mississippi agreed that Brewer was entitled to a hearing "[b]ecause of the compelling nature of the newly discovered DNA evidence." The Court rejected Brewer's challenge to Dr. West's bite mark identification testimony and to the bite mark evidence itself.

With the DNA evidence at hand, Brewer's attorneys identified the true perpetrator. Kennedy Brewer was finally exonerated and released from prison.

The reliability of the bite mark evidence, however, was never revisited in court.

Nearly a year before the Mississippi Supreme Court granted Brewer a new hearing, defense attorney Christopher Plourd instigated a sting against Dr. West. Mr. Plourd's private investigator, James Rix, sent photos of bite marks along with a mold of *Mr. Rix's own teeth* to West. Rix told West that the mold was from the chief suspect in the case. West confidently concluded that the dentition mold—from Mr. Rix—matched the victim's bite mark.

Prosecutors today are more reluctant to use bite mark experts. Yet courts can continue to admit bite mark evidence at trial, along with other unreliable forensic evidence, based almost exclusively on the fact that other courts admitted it in prior cases—precedent. Courts simply rely on sister courts that have adopted the evidence, and also rely on the prosecutors' argument that the evidence has been accepted as valid. This is part of why it is crucial for prosecutors to examine and understand their own forensic evidence. According to the treatise on Modern Scientific Evidence, "rather than the field [of forensic odontology] convincing the courts of the sufficiency of its knowledge and skills, admission by the courts seems to have convinced the forensic odontology community that, despite their doubts, they were indeed able to perform bite mark identifications after all."

ENDING WRONGFUL CONVICTIONS BASED ON FAULTY FORENSIC TESTIMONY OR EVIDENCE

Science, or what is purported to be science, has sent innocent people to prison. They wait behind bars for the future truth to finally be revealed. But even when false evidence or false testimony is revealed, courts won't necessarily free the person they sent to prison.

Cases are frozen at the time of the conviction. Our laws discourage judges from revisiting the evidence and convictions. The premise of science is that hypotheses are tested and re-tested; the premise of our criminal legal system is winners and losers, where finality of a conviction trumps other considerations.

Forensic evidence is likewise trapped in time in the courtroom.

Courts refuse to change the outcome even when the facts change, even when scientific evidence is proven wrong. Science is an evolving story while criminal procedure strains to control or banish alternative narratives once a conviction is final.

We need two solutions: prevent faulty forensic evidence and testimony from entering at trial, and address faulty forensic evidence and testimony discovered in post-conviction.

IDEA #1: FUND PRE-TRIAL FORENSIC EXPERTS TO STOP BAD SCIENCE FROM COMING IN

Prosecutors frequently fail to critically examine their own forensic evidence. Judges are predominantly former prosecutors. They continue the same pattern of accepting evidence, and when they admit the evidence at trial the jury can consider it to be accurate. Forensic testimony can be admitted regardless of its scientific reliability and accuracy. In the vast majority of criminal cases, neither side questions the forensic evidence pre-trial, and defendants often do not have their own forensic experts. Judges admit evidence that they would reject in civil cases.

Aliza Kaplan, one of the original attorneys at the Innocence Project in New York and founder of the Oregon Innocence Project, created the Forensic Justice Project to help defendants before trial. The Forensic Justice Project is a resource for motions for DNA testing and motions for expert witnesses when defendants go to trial. The State Board of Oregon funds their work because, in Aliza's words: "We are part of funding public defense because our defense lawyers don't know about forensic science. They need help on every level before, during, and after. And the state has the crime lab."

Providing access to experts for defendants means less faulty evidence may be admitted at trial or put before a jury. These cases ideally never become wrongful convictions.

IDEA #2: RECOGNIZING FAULTY FORENSIC EVIDENCE POST-CONVICTION: MANIFEST INJUSTICE, JUNK SCIENCE WRITS, AND STATEWIDE REVIEWS

Forensic science is a leading cause of wrongful convictions. In 2009, the publication of the National Academy of Sciences' Report *Strength-*

ening Forensic Science in the United States: A Path Forward prompted scientists and legislators to critique and challenge forensic science disciplines. Even the U.S. Supreme Court recognized that "[s]erious deficiencies have been found in the forensic evidence used in criminal trials." According to the National Registry of Exonerations, over the past thirty years our criminal legal system convicted and incarcerated more than six hundred innocent individuals due in part to faulty forensic evidence.

But for innocence litigators, it is always harder to reverse a conviction than for the prosecutor to convict that person in the first place.

Innocence litigators have to present new evidence and prove to the court that if this newly discovered evidence had been presented at trial, the jury likely would not have convicted the defendant. Courts will generally only reverse convictions that were based on, for example, false bite mark testimony at trial if there's *newly discovered* evidence that bite marks are bogus. Something recent. The court may reject the discrediting evidence as not new, because scientists were arguing against bite marks ever since the discipline was created. The defendant is in a Catch-22 situation: *some* evidence probably existed out in the world at the time of trial to challenge bite marks. That can mean the evidence is not newly discovered and cannot be used to reverse a conviction—*even if it absolutely proves that the defendant was wrongly convicted by false evidence.* The reasoning is that the defendant should have argued that at trial. Finality.

Courts can refuse to hold a post-conviction hearing on whether the evidence at trial was junk science—and the defendant wrongly convicted—even when the more developed science of today conclusively shows that the evidence at trial was bogus. That's a problem.

But we have solutions. First, courts have used a manifest injustice standard to review and reverse convictions. Second, legislatures have created "junk science writs," an avenue for convicted individuals to petition courts to reexamine the science and review the conviction. Third, states have initiated their own state-wide case reviews of convictions in particularly problematic areas of forensic science, like arson, hair microscopy, and bite marks.

COURTS REVERSING CONVICTIONS BASED ON FAULTY FORENSICS USING A MANIFEST INJUSTICE STANDARD

One rogue forensic analyst or expert can cause hundreds of innocent people to go to prison. When found out, courts can respond—by considering claims and reversing convictions under a manifest injustice standard.

For decades, lab analyst Trooper Fred Zain falsified blood sample results. As an analyst in the West Virginia Police Crime Laboratory, Zain regularly testified against defendants when he hadn't even looked at the evidence. He was also regularly promoted through the ranks until he was director of the serology department. Zain had a reputation with prosecutors for being able to "solve" even the most challenging cases.

Glen Woodall's post-conviction habeas petition ultimately exposed Zain's misconduct. Glen's attorney, Lonnie Simmons, fought an uphill battle for DNA testing, convinced that Glen was innocent. Lonnie and Glen won—and the DNA evidence proved them right. Glen was freed from prison, and soon the county prosecutor began a criminal investigation of the crime lab. The highest court in West Virginia appointed a judge and panel of lawyers and scientists to aid the investigation. They discovered a staggering series of fraudulent testimony and falsified evidence by Fred Zain.

Compelled by the widespread forensic fraud, the Supreme Court of Appeals of West Virginia ruled that hundreds of defendants could petition for their convictions to be reversed, or guilty pleas vacated, as a manifest injustice.

JUNK SCIENCE WRIT AND CONVICTION INTEGRITY UNIT SUCCESS STORY: TEXAS AND STEVEN CHANEY

Texas leads the country on forensic science reform. The Texas legislature funds innocence projects and education on forensics with the state bar, and created the Texas Forensic Science Commission. The state also has conducted three statewide conviction reviews.

The first conviction review was on hair analysis testimony, after the FBI publicly acknowledged that its hair examiners had exaggerated and given scientifically invalid testimony against defendants. State crime lab directors were informed by their primary accrediting agency that "we have an *ethical obligation* to take appropriate action if there is potential for, or there has been, a miscarriage of justice due to circumstances that have come to light, incompetent practice or malpractice."

The second statewide conviction review was on fire science or arson evidence. This was after Texas convicted and executed an innocent man, Cameron Todd Willingham, based on arson fire myths. In the political firestorm that followed, the state reviewed all arson convictions.

The third statewide conviction review was on bite mark evidence. The Texas Forensic Science Commission reviewed published scientific literature and research studies and ultimately concluded there is insufficient data to support the use of bite mark comparison in criminal cases. The commission found bite mark evidence unreliable based on, among other things, the inconsistency of how human skin responds and changes. As Lynn Garcia, the commission's general counsel told me, "The first Texas bite mark case involved a guy named Doyle who robbed a house and bit into a piece of cheese. [That case] is from 1954, and that cheese is a better medium than skin for recording an impression, way better."

The Texas Forensic Science Commission's final report called out how often bite mark evidence has been brought and admitted in criminal cases—both inside and outside of Texas—but that "it is now clear [bite mark comparisons] have no place in our criminal justice system because they lack any credible supporting data."

According to Texas Court of Criminal Appeals Judge Barbara Hervey, "With science, [there is] a lot of finger pointing, which is ridiculous because if something goes wrong, it's the system, not necessarily one party or another. And to fix it you really need to work together." In 2018, Judge Hervey wrote the groundbreaking *Chaney* opinion, which questioned the use of bite mark evidence and freed an innocent man.

The *Chaney* decision was the collaborative result of independent work by the Texas Forensic Science Commission, Chaney's post-conviction attorneys, and the Dallas County District Attorney's Conviction Integrity Unit. Patricia Cummings, the Supervisor of the Philadelphia District Attorney's Conviction Integrity Unit (CIU), directed the Dallas CIU at the time; *Chaney* was her first case. She worked on *Chaney* along with Cynthia Garza, who later became the Director of the Dallas CIU.

Cummings and Garza investigated the forensic evidence and Chaney's innocence from within the prosecutor's office, a powerful but sometimes uncomfortable position. Patricia Cummings remembers "early on sitting in the executive team meetings and having to fight like crazy about whether or not bite mark evidence was junk science. Or whether or not various types of evidence that I figured were suppressed were actually *Brady* (exculpatory evidence). That all culminated in one of the head prosecutors kind of smirking and laughing and basically saying, 'Oh, you'll never get to actual innocence in this case. Never. No way, no how.'"

Why not? Because Steven Chaney did not have sufficient DNA evidence in his case. Instead, he had false forensic evidence that the state prosecutor had presented and that the jury used to convict.

"Cynthia and I had to just keep, keep, keep pushing because we believed that we could find what we needed to validate what we both felt, which was he'd been wrongfully convicted, not only based on the junk science and bite marks. But we were concerned that if we didn't have DNA, we would never get to actual innocence."

Cummings and Garza talked with the state experts who then revisited their findings. Those same experts refused to talk with innocence organizations. "We just did all kinds of really cool, interesting, necessary stuff—in the end necessary. Had we not done all of that? I'm not so sure we would have had the result that we had."

A faulty forensics challenge is powerful when it comes from the prosecutor's office. While Chaney's attorneys filed a post-conviction petition on his behalf, Cummings and Garza submitted a report to the Texas Court of Criminal Appeals in support of Chaney's petition.

In December 2018, the Texas Court of Criminal Appeals granted the post-conviction petition, holding that "Chaney has proven that he is actually innocent."

For the Conviction Integrity Unit prosecutors, reversing a wrongful conviction was a mix of emotions. Cynthia Garza says,

It's joy and sadness at the same time. Sadness for the victim, the victim's family, sadness that the system did not work in this case.

Sadness that the person was wrongfully in prison. Sadness that they lost people while they were incarcerated. Sadness about all these things and joy because you get to see them getting released. These feelings can be conflicting because when an exoneration occurs, while everybody is celebrating the release of the wrongfully convicted person, the victim or victim's family may be sitting at home by themselves, and it's sad because they may never get the justice they deserved from day one if the true perpetrator cannot be prosecuted or found, for whatever reason. In Mr. Chaney's case, I cried when I read the [Chaney] opinion. I was so happy for Mr. Chaney and his wife and happy that justice was ultimately served for him. The flipside of that is the sadness I felt in calling the victim's family to let them know the opinion came down and notify them of everything, which included that the true perpetrators who brutally murdered their family members have yet to be brought to justice.

When Steven Chaney was released from prison, he met with the prosecutor who had convicted him. They prayed together. According to Lynn Garcia, "Mr. Chaney forgave him for making a number of assumptions around the bite mark comparison and arguing that [Chaney] should be convicted on that, which was a very key part to his closing argument. The fact that humans are capable of forgiveness and that level of love to me is not of our own making. There's something bigger than us that allows that to happen."

STATE LEGISLATURES CREATE JUNK SCIENCE WRITS OF HABEAS CORPUS

Mr. Chaney's freedom was, in part, thanks to a habeas writ created by the Texas legislature in 2013: a "junk science" writ of habeas corpus. The Texas legislature became the first in the country to enact a changed science or "junk science" writ. Now other state legislatures are creating these writs that allow a convicted person to petition the court and argue that scientific evidence discredits the evidence presented at trial. These writs empower state courts to genuinely and substantively re-evaluate scientific evidence.

The Texas junk science writ does not require proven actual innocence in order to reverse a conviction. However, other state junk science writs do. For example, in 2018 the Wyoming legislature passed the Post-Conviction Determination of Factual Innocence Act. Good news: convicted people can petition the court about faulty forensic evidence, the timing doesn't matter. Bad news: as a recent Wyoming Court opinion put it, "[t]he scope of the Factual Innocence Act is plainly limited to claims of factual innocence."

Remember the concern of all the attorneys in Steve Chaney's case: will we be able to *prove* actual innocence? Are proven lies told to the jury *enough*? These writs should provide relief for people without a standard that they "prove" actual innocence. Our Constitution and due process rights do not support a conviction based on false evidence or lies.

I believe the standard should be whether the court finds a manifest injustice, or a miscarriage of justice, rather than actual innocence.

Under a manifest injustice standard, the court would evaluate whether the resulting conviction was unjust, not whether the evidence conclusively proved innocence. The court could apply a "confluence of factors" review to look holistically at all the errors in the case—like the Massachusetts court did in Frances Choy's wrongful conviction for arson. This confluence of factors review, taken in the interest of justice, doesn't look at the scientific evidence or faulty testimony in isolation. In isolation, proof of false testimony could be dismissed as harmless error. Instead, the court looks at the evidence in conjunction with other errors to see whether justice was done.

In California, the legislature created a broad junk science writ. The California legislature arrived at this broad language because of another bite mark case—that of William Richards.

Prosecutors tried William Richards four times for the death of his wife. In the fourth trial, the prosecutors' forensic odontologist expert testified to finding a human bite mark on Richards's wife that matched Richards. He told the jury that this "unusual dentition occurred in only 2 percent or less of the general population." The jury finally convicted Richards.

Years later, the forensic odontologist recanted his trial testimony in a sworn declaration, stating that his "testimony regarding the statistical frequency of [Richards's] dentition was not based on scientific data."

Furthermore, he no longer believed the lesion on the victim's hand was a bite mark.

Richards presented this newly discovered evidence in court, but the Court of Appeals and ultimately the California Supreme Court ruled that the new testimony of the expert witness from trial was not "new evidence." The Court ruled that the changed testimony "failed to undermine the prosecution's entire case and point unerringly to his innocence."

The *California Lawyer* derided the Richards decision as the worst opinion of the year. The California legislature responded to the opinion by enacting the Bill Richards Bill, which amended the state habeas statute to consider faulty forensic evidence without requiring actual innocence. In 2016, under the new statute, Mr. Richards's conviction was finally reversed. His case proves the danger of imposing an "actual innocence" standard in cases of forensic fraud, and alternatives for courts to implement justice.

IDEA #3: CRIME LABS RELEASE SCIENTIFIC FINDINGS DIRECTLY TO PROSECUTORS AND DEFENSE ATTORNEYS

The behavior of Drs. Hayne and West are a far cry from the typical crime lab. Crime labs don't conduct autopsies or analyze bite mark evidence, or generally delve into arson cases. However, crime labs can have insufficient quality checks. More troubling is that institutionally, crime labs only provide prosecutors with access to their findings in a case.

Here are just a few examples of how police crime labs work exclusively for prosecutors. Defense attorneys cannot ask the lab to test different items, only a prosecutor can. Defense attorneys cannot request a DNA profile be run through databases for a match, only a prosecutor can. Defense attorneys cannot request a familial search through DNA to exculpate their client, only prosecutors can. And defense attorneys cannot request access to public DNA databases, but law enforcement can.

Defense attorneys can only access scientific findings that the prosecutor chooses to turn over to them. The lack of transparency—of police crime labs only disclosing their findings to prosecutors, and then prosecutors deciding what they will disclose to the defense—leads people to take unfair and unjust guilty pleas without full knowledge of the actual forensic findings.

When only prosecutors have access to a scientific file, and they are also the only ones to decide what information to reveal, defendants can be at risk. Tunnel vision describes a natural tendency for humans to focus on a desired conclusion, and then interpret all evidence in a way that supports the conclusion. Through tunnel vision, prosecutors and police may zero in on a suspect and then filter out any evidence that is inconsistent with their theory of the case. Confirmation bias, where we as humans seek information that confirms our beliefs, can play a similar role with prosecutors. These natural biases can mean prosecutors fail to disclose crucial scientific information to defendants.

If prosecutors are taken out as the middleman and the lab directly provides scientific evidence to both prosecutors and defense attorneys, at least one problem around these biases can be solved.

Many crime labs now have online portals where analysts upload their scientific findings and prosecutors access them through the portal. Now, crime labs should give access to their scientific findings to defense attorneys as well. The Houston Forensic Science Center may be the only crime lab in the country that makes their portal accessible to both prosecutors and defense attorneys.

The Houston Forensic Science Center created a password-protected portal on its website that allowed lawyers connected with a case to have direct access to complete laboratory reports, including underlying documentation. The website saved Center employees time otherwise spent providing these documents while also ensuring transparency and accuracy. According to former board members Professor Sandra Guerra Thompson and Professor Nicole Bremner Cásarez, although the Center pursued transparency in order to strengthen public trust, "commitment to transparency has resulted in an added benefit: the creation of a more efficient criminal justice system that saves time and money for all participants."

Indeed, prosecutors may not even know they have exculpatory and material evidence. Prosecutors are required under *Brady v. Maryland* to disclose this evidence before trial, but they may not become aware of the evidence until right before trial, or indeed, after a defendant has pled guilty. Nationally, state court criminal trials only occur in 6 percent of cases; the number is 3 percent for federal criminal trials. Instead, this scientific information can be shared early and systematically, avoiding any failures to disclose pre-trial or pre-plea.

Forensic evidence is critical to cases but can result in convictions based on false information, before figuring out factual innocence. As Jacksonville, Florida's, Prosecutorial Conviction Integrity Review Unit director Shelley Thibodeau says, "It's in the forefront of my mind—was this case based on a bite mark, what about hair analysis? I'm always thinking, is there a concern with the forensics or a way to forensically move the case forward?"

CHAPTER 9

Trial and the Prosecution's Case

PREPARING THE JURY

Prosecutor Dunn Lampton was priming the jurors for a salacious, horrific trial. He started in voir dire, the time when attorneys and the judge can ask questions of potential jurors who should be selected. The judge first asked the following questions that would automatically disqualify a juror:

> "Is everybody able to read and write?"
>
> "Has anybody ever been convicted of a felony or an infamous crime?"
>
> "Within the past five years, have any of you been convicted of the unlawful sale of intoxicating liquors?"
>
> "Are any of you common gamblers?"
>
> "Are any of you habitual drunkards?"

Now that the jurors were "qualified," the attorneys began asking their questions. Lampton started by sharing that his twin brother Dudley lived in Brookhaven, and his sister-in-law worked at the hospital—the same hospital where Kim was admitted and treated. Lampton then said, "I prosecute someone in a family and a lot of times other people in the family will get upset with me. Is there anything that I've ever done that would cause you not to be able to sit on this trial and not to be able to at least listen to what I have to say?"

No one responded.

"There will be physical evidence in this case. There will be some graphic photographs in this case and the jury will have to look at all of it to decide what the facts are. What happened."

Lampton continued. "I'll be honest with you, some of the photographs and some of the video will be pretty graphic. This was also, I believe the evidence will show, a sexual assault. And there will be some graphic pictures of the victim."

Eventually, a jury was selected and after opening statements, the testimony and evidence presentation began.

KIM'S MOTHER TESTIFIES

Kim's mother, Judy Mills, was the first witness to testify. One could only wonder what was going through her mind as she walked through the well of the court, past Leigh and Tami and their lawyers, past the inquiring eyes of the jurors.

It is easy to imagine how emotion would tear at a mother when a doctor says that her daughter's body had been savaged, animalistically ripped apart, by the two women sitting quietly at the defense table.

Likely, she understood Leigh and Tami to be addicts—just as her daughter was. After all, they had all lived at Cady Hill.

Judy had been the matriarch. Her ex-husband had never been able to care for Kimberly in the same way. Judy had done everything she could, including transferring Kimberly to a private Christian high school, Park Lane Academy, so she could still graduate after missing so many school days. She sent her beautiful daughter off to college at the University of Southern Mississippi, a very respectable university in Hattiesburg.

While Judy worked on obtaining a nursing degree, her ex-husband finally succumbed to cancer. And Judy's mother was diagnosed with Alzheimer's disease. Judy hadn't known about Kimberly's personal tragedy that same semester. When Kimberly took time off from school, it made sense to Judy, all the loss swirling around her. But she didn't know about Kimberly's personal loss.

And then, after going for treatment at Cady Hill, Kimberly some-how wound up gravely injured in the hospital, fighting for her life. Judy had gotten the call from her sister informing her that Kimberly had been taken to the hospital, in Brookhaven of all places, and they didn't expect her to live through the night. She was in a coma.

Brookhaven?

The last Judy knew, Kim was in Columbus at Cady Hill.

At the hospital, Judy had her first glimpse of her daughter in months. She could only sit helplessly as the myriad tubes and IVs kept Kimberly alive. Before long, Kimberly was packed into an ambulance for the hour drive to Baptist Hospital in Jackson.

It was not supposed to come to this. Judy had put her daughter in program after program, promising the court in Alabama that Kimberly would go to rehab in response to a shoplifting charge. She tried and tried again to prevent Kimberly from spiraling into a life of pain and addiction.

Although Kimberly, comatose and in a pharmaceutical haze, had no memory of that horrible videotape, Judy would never forget. She re-membered as day by day, the days and weeks blurring together, she had pushed Kimberly to come back to life, to read, to practice writing. And slowly, Kimberly had begun to recover. Judy's own recovery, if there could be one, would begin in the courtroom, on the witness stand. Judy had shuffled Kimberly into the car that morning; dread threaten-ing to suffocate them both. But this was to be a day not of dread, but a day to avenge the cruelties inflicted upon her daughter.

There was likely no doubt in Judy's mind about who could be sick enough to even think to do such a thing, let alone get pleasure—sexual gratification—from it. Those two lesbians, the women who now sat just feet away while Judy, sitting in the witness chair, began to focus on the questions from the district attorney. Leigh and Tami, she be-lieved—no, *knew*—had inflicted the cruelties upon Kimberly.

"And were you aware that anything was wrong or abnormal until you were informed that she was in the hospital?" District Attorney Dunn Lampton asked.

"No, I wasn't."

When she had arrived at Brookhaven, Judy said she had been informed by physicians that Kimberly was the victim of "a sexual assault, and drugs, and a vicious attack on her body."

Judy remained by Kimberly's bedside while her brother-in-law, Walthall County Sheriff's Deputy Truett Simmons, went to talk to Kimberly's boyfriend, Dickie, to try to find out what happened.

She was there when Dr. West asked Judy's permission to examine Kimberly for injuries. Judy had signed the release to allow Dr. West to photograph Kimberly's body. She had watched as he videotaped her, naked and unconscious.

Judy had watched as the electric clippers buzzed and her daughter's long brown locks fluttered to the floor of the hospital room. The once shiny vibrant hair lay lifeless, dead oily coils. Her naked daughter was rolled this way and that. Although the nurses were mindful of the life-giving cords so as to maintain the flow of oxygen and nutrients that kept Kimberly alive, the coldness of the procedure was unsettling. Her daughter's legs had been spread apart for the doctor to conduct his examination. And then, the doctor had confirmed the savagery that had been inflicted.

"Did you later see for yourself what you had been told had occurred here in Brookhaven?" Lampton asked.

"Yes," Judy replied. "I was at Baptist."

"I saw her breasts. They were triple the normal size. Her nipples were red and looked gouged or burned," Judy said. "She had, in her genital area, everything that was outside was inside. It was gouge marks, bite marks or like a wild animal had attacked her. On her hip it was a huge red area. And on her head was three places that looked like she had been hit extremely hard."

Judy had practiced for this day, working with Lampton to ensure that she could follow his instructions to remain calm, to sound professional, like a nurse.

"She was comatose for nearly two weeks."

She paused, then resumed narrating the video for the jury.

"As you can see, part of her labia there was chewed or bitten off. These are gouge or bite marks in the area. This is when she was in a coma. Her eyes are swollen. She was on a breathing machine, in a coma.

"The clitoral area there was—trying to—all of this is not old. This part was gnawed off or chewed off or bitten off or something. This clitoral area had so much force to it that it was trying to die."

Leigh's defense attorney stood up. "Your honor," Barnett said. "I'm going to object to them making medical conclusions about the injuries rather than just pointing the injuries out."

"You'll have an opportunity to cross-examine her," Judge Smith responded dismissively.

Judy Mills kept on.

"It's like chewing marks. You see all of this is very unnatural to the natural look of the vaginal area of a woman. The whole area was severely traumatized and being this red shows that it was not old."

With that, Judy timed the injuries.

Judy recalled when she first found Leigh and Tami's address in Columbus and their listed phone number. Judy remembered the desperate anonymous calls she made in May to Leigh's home, sobbing with anger, crying into the phone about how Leigh murdered her daughter. She remembered the phone call from the prosecutor, saying she and her family should no longer call Leigh Stubbs. Leigh had used caller ID to figure out that the calls were being made from the landline in Judy's home. Mama Sheila had told the police, and then the district attorney's office.

She remembered calling them after that, identifying herself this time, asking after them, making her voice and demeanor as sweet as sorghum. She bore it for an hour, trying to get whatever information she could from them, and also trying to absolve herself without mentioning the calls.

"Mrs. Mills, did you ever have an opportunity to talk with Leigh and Tami?" Lampton asked.

"No. I've had no desire to talk with them."

This was not the answer Lampton wanted, so he tried again.

"Let me ask if you ever made an attempt to find out from them what had happened to your daughter?"

Backtracking, Judy said, "I would like to say when I said I never had a chance to talk with them, I did call them at one time earlier before I knew all the situation and ask them if they knew—could help me find out anything about how Kimberly got hurt. They didn't know how she got hurt."

"Did they mention any injuries to her head?"

"Oh, no," Judy declared. "They didn't mention anything like that. It was easier to blame it on the drugs since Kimberly had had a drug problem."

The defense cross-examination was brief and likely perceived by Judy as dripping with his fawned sympathy.

"Mrs. Mills, I know it's difficult for you," Barnett said. "So I'll try to make it brief. When your daughter was admitted to the hospital, do you know what the initial diagnosis was?"

"I think, at first, they said it was a drug overdose," Judy replied.

"All right," Barnett said.

But apparently, it wasn't all right. Not with Judy.

"May I say, the reason they said that is because these two drug addicts were always the ones that told them that," Judy declared. "So they took their word."

As she stepped down from the stand and walked past the attorneys, past the women on trial, Judy kept her head high and her shoulders back. Whatever emotions roiled inside her—likely smoldering rage that anyone would so terribly harm her daughter—would remain concealed. For now.

DETECTIVE NOLAN JONES TAKES THE WITNESS STAND

Detective Jones, who had worked at the Brookhaven Police Department for a total of twenty-seven years, took the witness stand next.

In his youth, Detective Jones had been a prizefighter, fighting informal bareknuckle drag-outs for cash. He wasn't a big man, but he fought until one opponent blinded him in his eye. Then he became a police officer, and ultimately a detective.

Jones was questioned by Lampton. "I want to hand you what appears to be a photograph. If you can, just tell the jury what that photograph represents."

Jones knew the photo; he had taken it.

"It's the vaginal area that's all swelled."

"And whose vaginal area is that?"

"It's Kim Williams."

"And does that picture fairly and accurately show her body at the time you took that photograph?"

"Yes it does."

"I want to hand you another photograph and ask if you're able to identify that for us, please."

"This is Kim Williams's nipple area, that's all swollen and red, swelled," Jones testified.

"I want to show you another photograph and ask if you're able to identify that for us," Lampton said.

"These look like passion marks overlaid and some bruising on the right hip of Kim Williams."

"And was that seen by you on the eighth when you went to the hospital?"

"Yes, it was."

Jones told the jury his theory: "the girls" had put Kim Williams in a toolbox in the back of Leigh's truck. He said he saw it on the Comfort Inn surveillance tapes.

Leigh knew about the surveillance cameras. She had gone so far as to confirm their existence before deciding to stay at the Comfort Inn for the night. She wanted to make sure nothing in her truck was stolen.

Now that same recording system was being used against her, filtered through the eyes of Detective Jones. Jones was convinced that no assault occurred at Cady Hill. He didn't bother driving over to Columbus; he was convinced any assault occurred in Brookhaven.

"At what point in your investigation did Tami and Leigh go from being Good Samaritans to being a suspect?" Leigh's attorney asked.

"When I viewed the video," Jones testified. "I spent all weekend looking at those tapes. I saw what I believe where, I believe, Leigh Stubbs stepped up in the back of the truck, raised the toolbox and picked a person up out of that toolbox and stepped off the truck and went in Room 109."

WITNESSES FROM CADY HILL

The prosecution called two witnesses who were friends with Leigh, Tami, and Kim at Cady Hill. While residents at Cady Hill, Samantha

"Sam" Brown and Kathy Jones began dating men on the Pine side of treatment. Although treatment for men and women was supposed to be separate, and men and women were only supposed to interact at group talk sessions, Kathy and Sam had both found boyfriends.

Kathy and Sam, however, were called not to talk about the open cross-over and romance between the men and women, but the relationship between Leigh and Tami.

"Was there any particular relationship between Tami Vance and Leigh Stubbs? Was there anything unusual about them and their relationship?" Lampton asked Sam.

Sam responded, "I knew that something was going on between them that night that we left, Sunday. They showed affection toward each other that evening, when they returned from their outing. They left for that weekend and they came back and that's when I knew that they were together. I thought they were."

"And when you say you thought they were together, you mean in a relationship, a sexual relationship?"

"Possibly."

"And how were they acting toward each other?"

"Affectionately," Sam said. "I did see—well, I see them peck each other on the lips and exited the room and went out to have a cigarette."

"Did that make you feel uncomfortable?"

"Yes."

Kathy Jones testified that Leigh and Tami's friendship progressed to an intimate relationship.

Leigh's attorney tried to soften the blow. "Now one other thing you said that concerns me and I want to clear the air on this thing. Is it a problem for you for two girls to carry on a relationship?"

"No, sir," Kathy responded.

KIM'S BOYFRIEND, DICKIE ERVIN, ON THE WITNESS STAND

Kim's old boyfriend, Dickie, briefly took the stand.

"How old are you?"

"Forty-four—forty-five."

"Where do you live?"

"That's a trick question," Dickie replied.

Seemingly off to a rocky start, the prosecution truly dispensed with further preliminary questions.

"I don't know how to ask the question any other way than this. Were you aware of whether any part of Kim's vagina or labia was missing?" the prosecutor asked.

Dickie responded, "Well, I would have been. If it had been missing, I would have known about it."

"Was her—when you knew her, her genital was absolutely normal?"

"Yes, sir, completely," Dickie said.

DR. MOAK'S TESTIMONY

Dr. Moak, the emergency room doctor who first treated Kim, testified for the prosecution. He opined that Kim's body temperature was low when she came into the hospital and she was suffering from multi-organ failure.

"Would that be consistent with ice being placed on someone for several hours?" the prosecutor asked.

Detective Jones had testified that Leigh had made multiple trips to the vending area to get ice. He thought it was suspicious. Their theory was beginning to become clear.

"Yes. Doing something like icing a body down, putting ice around you and chilling the body would be consistent with this type of temperature."

Dr. Moak continued. "The injuries that this young lady had, that I observed were, first, a—her breast, around the nipples, had a lot of swelling and almost like little—I'd like to describe them like teeth marks or scratch marks."

He then stated, "Across her buttocks were red marks that in my notes I described, because of a lack of a better way to describe it, like someone had hit her with a belt or a wooden slat or wooden stick or some kind of object like—there were marks across her buttocks." He conceded that though a rape kit was taken because of a belief that Kim was subjected to sexual abuse, hospital personnel did not examine her anal area or anus.

Leigh's attorney questioned the presumption of assault. "Isn't it true that this definitely could have been rough and consensual sex?"

"Yes, it could have been," Dr. Moak responded.

"You're simply not in a position to tell, just from the examination of a patient, whether it could be consensual or non-consensual?"

"When we use the word consensual . . . it's where two people have sexual relationships because they want to and they have a normal sexual relationship. This pattern of injury that I saw was not that. But if it was a situation where it was a rough—what I want to call an abnormal sexual encounter, it's possible that it could be that."

CHAPTER 10
Criminalizing Queerness and Encouraging Passing

Queer people can be two things in the courtroom: a hate crime victim or a sexual offender. Otherwise, our identity is erased because queerness still equates to criminal deviance.

We as queer people have been put in prison, lost jobs, been denied places to live. Even if our identities are no longer illegal, our sexual orientation and gender identity are still stigmatized and made a curiosity. Strangers will ask me and my wife how we have sex.

Anna Vasquez is a board member of the National Innocence Network and an exonerated lesbian, a member of the San Antonio Four. The San Antonio Four are Latina lesbians, wrongfully convicted of fantasized sexual crimes against children.

Less than 5 percent of women sexually abuse children, and that abuse is usually an adult with a teenager. Prosecutors charged the San Antonio Four with sexual molestation of two young girls, and the state's pediatrician expert testified that the alleged acts were "satanic related." The women had recently come out as gay to their families before the allegations.

When Anna went to trial in the early 1990s, she told me, "The way they looked at gay people, I even got shit from my attorney. 'You're going to have to put on a dress and you're going to have to curl your hair.'" Anna described herself to me as appearing like a lesbian, while some of the other women were "just a pretty girl, whatnot, you're going to be quicker to help her rather than me."

So Anna changed her appearance. "Of course I did, because I'm looking up to this man—who was a complete idiot. I felt I was so fake. That's not me." Anna was so frustrated by the entire experience and being judged. "You should at least know the person before you hate them," she told me.

As an adult, the younger girl, Stephanie, recanted her trial testimony and said she had been pressured and threatened by her abusive father—who had made romantic overtures to one of the defendants and was rejected. The San Antonio Four's wrongful convictions were finally reversed fifteen years later.

At the national Innocence Network conference each year, I rarely saw openly queer exonerees. Anna and I talked about this lack of visibility, and she felt isolated by the scarcity of gay and visible exonerees. There are very few openly LGBTQIA+ people on the National Registry of Exonerations. Are they ignored, passing, or forced to pass by their attorneys?

The question of passing, particularly in a courtroom, is complex. In Mississippi, I wore pastel-colored skirt suits and floral dresses, heels, and makeup to protect my clients from transferred bias. Defendants are encouraged to pass and conform in any number of ways beyond sexual orientation—wearing glasses, wearing a suit, short hair for men and long hair for women, appearing empathetic and most of all not appearing angry.

But passing can harm the self. Innocence attorney and lesbian Karen Thompson insightfully told me, "There are specific questions about butch women in the system that are conflated or ignored. That is really hard for most women to survive when they're not seen in their specificity."

PATHOLOGIZING QUEER PEOPLE

The specter of criminality moves ceaselessly through the lives of LGBT people in the United States. It is the enduring product of persistent melding of homosexuality and gender nonconformity with concepts of *danger, degeneracy, disorder, deception, disease, contagion, sexual predation, depravity, subversion, encroachment, treachery,* and *violence* . . .

—*Queer (In)Justice: The Criminalization of LGBT People in the United States*

Psychiatrists historically labeled LGBTQ+ people as mentally ill. They also labeled enslaved Black people who ran away from slavery as having a mental disorder, "drapetomania." Freedom and self-preservation—relabeled for someone else's ends and control.

Queer people are outside of heterosexual norms, and the false labels abound: dangerous, depraved, violent. Scholars discuss these labels, or "queer criminal archetypes," which directly influence policing and punishing people who are queer or not acceptably gendered.

The strong fictional bond between lesbianism and female psychopathy long predated Tami and Leigh's trial.

Around World War II, criminologists labeled lesbians as "menacing social types" by focusing on incarcerated lesbians. Race influenced these portrayals, with criminologists identifying white incarcerated lesbians as victims or as only "temporary" lesbians. But by the 1960s criminologists labeled all incarcerated lesbians as "sexual aggressors," particularly white working-class lesbians.

Lesbians have been over-represented on death row. In 1993, case studies found that women sentenced to death were frequently characterized as "manly" and "man-hating." They went to trial and were punished both for breaking the law and for defying gender roles and femininity. Even if they were not confirmed lesbians, the media had described these women as possibly lesbian or portrayed them as masculine.

The media rarely discussed how most of the women on death row were survivors of abuse.

Instead, the narratives justified male violence against women by alleging the survivor was a lesbian.

These divisions between lesbian/non-lesbian become confounding, given the number of incarcerated women who have same-sex relationships while in prison. Yet if they admit to it outside of the prison context, their sexual behavior may be used against them as a reason for these women *to be* in prison. LGBTQ+ identities are criminalized, medicalized, and pathologized, despite decades of research now proving that LGBTQ+ people are not intrinsically predatory, pathological, or deviant.

Prosecutors and the media can also portray women who are not queer as sexually deviant and crossing heteronormative boundaries—

leading to wrongful convictions. Exoneree Amanda Knox, even after the true perpetrator Rudy Guede was convicted, was forced to trial by prosecutors alleging a fantasized "sex game gone wrong" involving the homicide victim, Meredith Kercher. Years later, media still publicly asked Knox whether she was "into deviant sex"—as though proving that would also prove guilt of a murder.

Judges, juries, prosecutors, and defense attorneys interpret appearance and criminalize queer identity along these queer archetype storylines of danger, depravity, and violence. These stories may prevail regardless of whether the individual committed a crime or any harm. These stories overlap and intersect with race, poverty, and immigrant status.

The carceral state relies on creating binaries: innocent or guilty, law-abiding or deviant, good or bad. Laws codify norms of acceptable conduct alongside existing prejudices in order to control behavior. Then the criminal legal system ostracizes and punishes people for violating these laws.

But convictions can only maintain their legitimacy if we accept the criminal system's own story that laws, and punishment, are impartial.

They are not.

A HISTORY OF CRIMINALIZING QUEERNESS

In the 1950s, all states criminalized sodomy in some form. Prosecutors and police erratically punished people who appeared queer and had queer sex. Although the laws applied to straight people, gay men were almost exclusively prosecuted for violations. In the 1960s, punishment for sodomy ranged from prison sentences of two to ten years.

Laws against cross-dressing or "disguising" oneself date back to 1845. These laws, known as sumptuary laws, decreed what people could wear and were enforced until the 1980s. People were criminals if they wore less than three articles of clothing that matched their gender at birth.

The proliferation of sumptuary laws in the late 1800s followed the disruption of many hierarchies in society—the abolition of slavery, women demanding financial and social equality, and the expansion of the right to vote beyond white men with wealth. As LGBTQ+ subcultures emerged in large cities, legislatures passed sumptuary laws to reinforce control over gender and sexuality. Police targeted queer people and queer sexualities. Butch lesbians had to prove their three articles of femme clothing to avoid arrest by prying and frequently physically violent police. In New York, individuals couldn't be "disguised" in public, and courts punished "cross-dressing" because "the desire of concealment of a change of sex by the transsexual is outweighed by the public interest for protection against fraud."

The laws and prohibitions signaled that everyone must conform—what to wear and how to act—not just queer people.

In California, a state government that feared growing gay populations responded with fierce punishment and police violence. Los Angeles enacted one of the first sumptuary laws in 1889. Then in 1915, the state of California compounded this law and criminalized oral sex as a felony. Police would arrest people for "masquerading" in another person's clothes for unlawful purposes.

In the *Making Gay History* podcast, Evander Smith and Herbert Donaldson describe a 1965 police raid on a queer New Year's Day Mardi Gras Ball in San Francisco. They were both attorneys who organized the ball and protested its shutdown by the police. They were then arrested and their names were printed in the paper. Evander lost his job.

HERBERT: And then some of the people were just terrified, especially the schoolteachers. I remember a couple of women who were schoolteachers. And they had to be . . . they wanted to be sneaked out the back way so they . . . because [the police] were taking pictures of everybody as they left.

. . .

HERBERT: But didn't they arrest those two guys who were standing on chairs to look at something, remember?

EVANDER: Yeah, I'd forgotten all about that. I don't remember what happened to them.

HERBERT: Well, we represented them and they were convicted.

ERIC MARCUS (interviewer): What were they convicted for?

HERBERT: Lewd conduct.

ERIC: Two guys at the dance?

HERBERT: Yes, uh, huh, because the police, they had to show that all of this police . . .

EVANDER: . . . had been legitimate.

HERBERT: Yeah, so they charged these guys with fondling each other. They hadn't been fondling each other. And Evander represented one and I represented the other. When the jury came in Judge Lazarus said, he said, you know, "I never expected that." He didn't think they were going to be convicted. And then he said, "They've suffered enough. I'll fine them $25."

EVANDER: But you see the tragic life there? Because those poor guys . . .

HERBERT: . . . they didn't do anything!

EVANDER: They have to put down that I was arrested at a lewd dance performing a lewd act with another man.

DONALDSON: At that time 647a was registerable. Remember, under . . . ?

HERBERT: Yes, indeed, there are many people . . .

ERIC: So they couldn't be hired by the Federal government. You could not get a job.

HERBERT and EVANDER: Oh, no. No, no.

EVANDER: Absolutely not. And if they had had a credential . . .

HERBERT: . . . it would have been taken away. They'd have proceeded to take it away.

"Lewd conduct" laws are still on the books and used against trans people and queer people of color. The individual officer decides what counts as "lewd" and who to arrest.

FIGHTING TO CHANGE THE NARRATIVE

In 1950s America, newly created gay and lesbian groups began fighting to change the social story about them. Groups like the Mattachine Society and the Daughters of Bilitis quietly, and then vocally, argued that being queer was not criminal and was not a mental illness. By the 1960s, famed author Lorraine Hansberry was even publishing in the Daughters of Bilitis magazine *The Ladder*, and in *One Magazine*, albeit under a pseudonym.

In 1961, Illinois became the first state to legalize consensual sodomy. This marked a wave of decriminalization, particularly when states adopted the Model Penal Code, which did not criminalize consensual adult sodomy.

As governments decriminalized homosexuality, fewer psychiatrists labeled the behavior as a mental illness. Gay and lesbian activists used the empirical research by Alfred Kinsey and Evelyn Hooker to openly advocate that the psychiatric profession drop its diagnosis of homosexuality as a mental disease. In 1973, homosexuality was dropped from the *Diagnostic and Statistical Manual of Mental Disorders* (the DSM).

The protests at Compton's Cafeteria riot in San Francisco in 1966, and the Stonewall Riot in New York City in 1969, spurred on the decriminalization of sodomy and sumptuary laws, and increased the visibility of queer people. In the 1960s and 1970s, gay and Black activists together fought against targeted policing and being punished for their identities.

Yet some states still criminalized sodomy, and the U.S. Supreme Court upheld those laws. Twenty-five years after Illinois first decriminalized sodomy, the Supreme Court upheld Georgia's anti-sodomy law in *Bowers v. Hardwick* in 1986.

The Supreme Court supported the law by citing social disapproval of gay people. In a concurring opinion, Chief Justice Burger wrote:

> Decisions of individuals relating to homosexual conduct have been subject to state intervention throughout the history of Western civilization. Condemnation of those practices is firmly rooted in Judeo Christian moral and ethical standards . . . Blackstone described "the infamous crime against nature" as an offense of "deeper malignity" than rape, a heinous act "the very mention of which is a disgrace to human nature," and "a crime not fit to be named . . ." To hold that the act of homosexual sodomy is somehow protected as a fundamental right would be to cast aside millennia of moral teaching.

The 1986 decision came in the midst of the AIDS health crisis. Queer people were spat on, struck, and even killed for asserting they were gay. Gay men in particular were dying of AIDS, along with intravenous drug users, another marginalized group. The Food and Drug Administration budget for AIDS research, and for a cure, was piddling. President Reagan refused to utter the word AIDS and address the health crisis.

Simultaneously, gay men and women were being wrongfully convicted during a national hysteria over "satanic ritualistic abuse" by day care providers. The problem didn't exist, but the fear clicked with the criminal archetype of queer people as sexual predators. The first satanic ritual abuse conviction was against Bernard Baran in 1985, a male teacher who was a day care provider and had recently come out as gay. Straight people were also swept up as defendants to these accusations.

But in 1987, queer people united and spoke out against the bias and stereotypes. That year, queer activists organized ACT UP, AIDS Coalition to Unleash Power, to forcefully dispel myths about LGBTQ+ people and AIDS. Organizers led "die-ins" and reclaimed the Nazi-era pink triangle symbol of homosexuality, loudly proclaiming "silence = death."

ACT UP made gay deaths from AIDS visible, and they pushed for conversations with the Food and Drug Administration. Like a generation before with psychiatrists, LGBTQ+ activists used data to change health care. This time, they used research to offer viable proposals for HIV positive people to voluntarily test experimental drugs. Their two-prong strategy of angry activism and reform proposals led the government to fund AIDS research, allow HIV positive patients access to new treatments, and encouraged a new generation to come out as gay.

Some judges dismissed protest charges against ACT UP organizers and dismissed criminal charges against gay people on manifest injustice principles—dismissing "in the interest of justice."

By 1996, scientists found a treatment for AIDS.

By 2003, forty states had decriminalized sodomy.

Mississippi was one of the ten that didn't.

That year, 2003, the U.S. Supreme Court decision *Lawrence v. Texas* finally legalized private sexual conduct between consenting adults. The Court found that anti-sodomy laws were unconstitutional because they violated an individual's right to privacy.

Lawrence v. Texas was not a unanimous decision. Justice Scalia's stinging dissent reads like a summary of stereotypes against queer people: "The Court has taken sides in the culture war, departing from its role of assuring, as neutral observer, that the democratic rules of engagement are observed. Many Americans do not want persons who openly engage in homosexual conduct as partners in their business, as scoutmasters for their children, as teachers in their children's schools, or as boarders in their home. They view this as protecting themselves and their families from a lifestyle that they believe to be immoral and destructive."

But private sexual conduct between consenting adults was now legal, and a competing narrative was being told.

The Mississippi statute criminalizing consensual oral and anal sex, Mississippi Code § 97-29-59, is still on the books even though *Lawrence v. Texas* makes these laws unconstitutional. A number of states still have laws against consensual sodomy. On the books, Idaho criminalizes the "infamous crime against nature," Florida forbids "unnatural acts," and Texas outlaws "homosexual conduct."

While these laws can't be enforced, they can give police cover to arrest gay people. When a sheriff in Baton Rouge, Louisiana, enforced "sting" operations to entrap and arrest gay men under the state antisodomy statute, he told the press, "This is a law that is currently on the Louisiana books, and the sheriff is charged with enforcing the laws passed by our Louisiana Legislature . . . Whether the law is valid is something for the courts to determine, but the sheriff will enforce the laws that are enacted."

But the prosecutor publicly dropped the charges. Stories, narratives, can change. And people in power can make different decisions.

CRIMINALIZATION OF QUEERNESS AT THE TIME OF LEIGH AND TAMI'S TRIAL

Mississippi Code § 97-29-59: Every person who shall be convicted of the detestable and abominable crime against nature committed with mankind or with a beast, shall be punished by imprisonment in the penitentiary for a term of not more than ten years.

If you turned on the radio in 2000, you'd hear Rush Limbaugh and Dr. Laura Schlessinger decrying homosexuality, calling gay people "deviants." Dr. Laura would claim that "a huge portion of the male homosexual populace is predatory on young boys," and warn her listeners of a "militant gay conspiracy." A *Newsweek* poll for March 20, 2000, found that "57% of the general public was opposed to same-sex marriage; 50% said gays should not adopt; 36% said gays should not teach elementary school." Legislatures proposed and passed Defense Of Marriage Acts (DOMA) to prevent same-sex marriage.

This was the cultural background to Leigh and Tami's trial in June 2001.

People who killed queer victims could claim the "Gay Panic" or "Trans Panic" defense—that the victim was making sexual overtures and the assailant responded violently in a panic. This excuse, if accepted, reduced the assailant's responsibility in court—they, after all, couldn't help their revulsion. Yet if a trans or queer person were suspected of harming a straight person, there was no such defense. Trans people could expect to be found guilty, even if they were acting in self-defense.

Janet Mock produced and directed the television series *Pose,* focusing on trans women and queer people of color in the 1990s New York City ballroom scene. Many episodes showcase the reality of being criminalized for being queer.

In one episode, trans woman and house mother Elektra, working as a dominatrix, discovers one of her clients dead from an overdose. She agonizes with her friends who are trans women about whether to go to the police. Their overwhelming concern is that Elektra will be wrongfully suspected, charged, and ultimately convicted for killing him. Instead, they lime the corpse and place the body in a trunk in her closet.

According to Janet Mock, this story is based on Dorian Corey, a trans woman in New York City. Dorian Corey founded vogueing house Corey, won over fifty grand prizes in vogueing balls, and was profiled in the cult classic documentary *Paris Is Burning.* When Dorian died of AIDS, her friends found her abusive ex-lover wrapped in pleather in a trunk in her closet. He had been dead for fifteen years.

Neither guilty nor innocent queer people could expect justice from police, prosecutors, or proceedings in a courtroom.

PASSING AS STRAIGHT

All of this history brings us back to passing.

Tami, with her rocking mullet and cargo pants, fit some stereotypes about lesbians. Investigator Nolan along with Kim's boyfriend both called Tami a bull dyke.

Leigh received more of the men's sympathy because of her appearance—a younger, more harmless, more typically femme co-conspirator. Maybe they even thought she was naïve, only in a lesbian relationship because of Tami's coercion or manipulation. And Kim, she passed—or was forced to pass—as straight, so that all the homophobic hostility was trained on the defendants.

Passing as straight may provide safety for the individual. But passing also jeopardizes the community by diminishing queer visibility.

Fewer people of color can pass as another race. Frantz Fanon described his own hypervisible Blackness in the colonial racism of France:

> My body was given back to me sprawled out, distorted, recolored, clad in mourning in that white winter day.

Fanon describes wanting to disappear into a crowd sometimes and be "a man among other men"—to be a neutral, generic, citizen.

At Leigh and Tami's trial, a straight white male gaze trained on Kim and made it normal to watch her fragmented naked body. The same gaze differentiated and judged the queer defendants as visibly different. "And so it is not I who make a meaning for myself, but it is the meaning that was already there, pre-existing, waiting for me," as Frantz Fanon eloquently described.

The police were more reluctant to prosecute Leigh than Tami—even though under their own "evidence," Leigh's teeth allegedly matched the bite mark.

I imagine an alternate universe, where West decided to match Tami's teeth mold to his imagined bite mark. Maybe prosecutors would not have charged Leigh, armed with her more femme appearance, her youth, her long blond hair, and Mama Sheila's involvement.

Tami could not escape her appearance, could not disappear into the crowd. The stereotypes of deviant, bull dyke, criminal, pinned to Tami, subjecting her to criticism, hostility, and hate—even though Tami was such a kind, giving, and harm*less* person.

And then, maybe Leigh would have been the one coerced into testifying against Tami. Coerced into passing. Coerced into training the attention and blame onto her dear friend, in order to save herself.

These are the decisions our criminal legal system forces people to make.

CHAPTER 11

Dr. West Takes the Stand

The next day and a half of the trial was consumed by the testimony of one person: Dr. Michael West. Dr. West was the prosecution's expert for videos of the parking lot to videos of Kim's body. The videos Dr. West took of Kim were now labeled as medical, or "hospital footage."

Dr. West graduated from dental school, then served as a forensic dental officer in the Air Force for three years. When he left the Air Force, he spent fifteen years as the coroner for Forrest County, Mississippi, ordering and attending autopsies.

Dr. West regularly testified for prosecutors across Mississippi. He had testified about bite marks, wound pattern analysis, and bloodstain pattern analysis—forensic disciplines that came under fire as unreliable by the National Academy of Sciences in 2009. Dr. West also frequently lectured to police training academies in Mississippi and Georgia, and at the Mississippi Prosecutors College.

On the stand, Dr. West rattled off the cases where he had been accepted as a bite mark expert—including Kennedy Brewer's case.

"My final one was *Banks v. State*, which I like to refer to as the bologna case," Dr. West declared. "They weren't too pleased with me there. We had received a bologna sandwich that was evidence in a homicide. Someone had taken two or three bites out of a bologna sandwich and they brought it to me and asked me 'Could this woman have bitten it or could this man have bitten it?' And we excluded the woman as possibly making the bite mark. The man was consistent with the bite mark. Eighteen months later, the defense wanted to see the sandwich. And the sandwich had turned into a ball of fungus and I threw it away and they said I shouldn't have thrown it away. I'm always getting into some kind of controversy."

In a number of these cases, even after DNA evidence didn't match the suspect, Dr. West held firm that the suspect bit the victim, "indeed and without a doubt."

Judge Smith accepted Dr. West as an expert in the field of forensic odontology and bite mark identification.

DR. WEST'S TOOLBOX THEORY

Qualified as an expert, Dr. West began outlining his theory of the toolbox. He said he could see Kim's limp body on the hotel surveillance video and in particular, he saw Kim's head with her two-foot-long dark hair. He said he saw Leigh carrying Kim from the pickup truck into the hotel.

"Of course, this startles me," Dr. West testified. "And I told Nolan [Detective Jones], I said, 'Gosh, I would like to see that toolbox in that truck.' He says, 'I have it out back.' And so we went out, outside there at the police station, and we examine this toolbox."

Jurors listened intently. Dr. West was, if nothing else, an excellent storyteller.

The latches on the toolbox, in his opinion, matched the injuries to Kim's hip and head.

"Gosh, we got a video of her coming out of this toolbox," Dr. West declared. "We got closed head injuries. And I've got patterns that not only make the shape of those latches. Those two latches are thirty-seven inches apart. And if you look at Kimberly, from the head injuries to the thigh injury is thirty-seven inches. I'll go back and examine her again, but this time I'm going to take some electric clippers and shave the hair around these head injuries."

And, he said, that's just what he did.

VIDEO OF KIM SHOWN TO THE JURY

Prosecutor Lampton then began airing the "hospital footage" video, exposing the jury to still frames of Kim's vulva. Dr. West explained, "We're trying to show the asymmetry of the labia majora."

The video moved on to show live footage of Kim's naked body taken on March 10. On the video, nurses rolled Kim, unconscious and connected to a breathing machine and IVs, to show the front and backside of her body.

Dr. West narrated as the video rolled. Focusing on Kim's nipples, he said, "A close-up—I don't know if that's an abrasion, a bite where a nipple had been bitten off, or a burn."

He was seen on the video comparing different cigarettes alongside Kim's breast. "Cigarettes come in different gauges, different diameters. Camel makes them wide. Most cigarettes are double A regulars. But you have Virginia Slims and these cigarettes called Capri that are very, very, skinny, little, tiny cigarettes." Dr. West told the jury there was a cigarette burn on Kim's breast.

Leigh's attorney objected, but Judge Smith allowed Dr. West to continue.

The video focused on Kim's hip. Dr. West made clear that the red mark was not only a bite mark—it was also an injury from the latch on the toolbox. "Only this area, right here, the circular, two semicircular areas, do I consider to be a human bite mark," he said. "The rest is a different type of injury."

On an overhead projector, Dr. West displayed transparencies of the raspberry on Kim's hip. He told the jury that the raspberry was from the toolbox lid being slammed down on Kim.

There appeared to be a problem, however. The size of the latch didn't match the size of the injury.

But Dr. West was ready with an answer. He explained that the latch didn't hit Kim straight on. Instead, he said, the latch did a "drag and skid" across her hip. "Think of that injury on the side of your thigh as this thing comes down and drags across you, hard," Dr. West said.

The implication was clear—as if someone had slammed the lid on Kim and trapped her in the toolbox.

Then Dr. West made a surprising request.

"Is Kimberly available, Dunn?"

"Yes, sir, she is," the prosecutor replied.

And at that moment, Kim rose from her seat and began walking toward the front of the courtroom.

Dr. West called out as she approached.

"Kim, how you doing, honey?" he said. "I may be an expert in a lot of things, hairstyles ain't one of them." He was referring to Kim's partially shaved head on the video.

He positioned her standing in front of the jury.

Pointing to Kim's head, he began. "If we go to where this injury on her head, the side of her temple, has occurred, you'll notice that my ruler goes right back—you can sit, honey—to the area on her thigh that we photographed at the hospital. So not only do I have the size and relationship of the latch, I also have the actual distance of the latch."

And then, Dr. West presented his final conclusion to the jury.

"It's my opinion that someone tried to put Kimberly in this toolbox, with her head at this side and her feet here. Somewhere during that, the toolbox is slammed down pinching, creating the injuries on her thigh at this end and creating the injuries at the side of the temple at this end. At least three over here, and three to five over here. In other words, she got more blows to the thigh than she did to the head. The head probably went on into the toolbox, but we have this action as she's being placed in."

"Any other questions? Anything else you want to show with Kimberly?" prosecutor Lampton asked.

"No," Dr. West said. "I think that should be all."

Kim quietly returned to her seat in the courtroom.

The video footage jumped forward to the hip injury with a bite imprint on it.

Dr. West explained the sudden change to the jury. "Now what I've done here, these are some of my early tests where I've taken the stone models of my different suspects and literally placed them onto the skin to give it a little bit of indentation. For me to study and go back and look."

Dr. West displayed a photograph of the hip injury on the overhead projector. It looked like a fuzzy red mark without defined markings.

"A lot of the fine detail in this bite mark is missing, just for no other reason than its age, three days," Dr. West said. Remarkably, he said he was able to determine *when* the bite mark was made. While Detective Jones called the raspberry a "passion mark" or a hickie, Dr. West called the red area a bite mark.

Then he launched into his explanation of how he was able to determine who, in his opinion, bit Kim. First, he took the dental impression of Leigh's teeth and laid it over the photograph of Kim's hip.

"That dot, that dot, and that dot should represent three teeth," he said, pointing to a blown-up image on the overhead projector. "When I place the stone model onto that area, when I line the portion up for tooth number 7, then the cusp of tooth number 5 and the cusp of tooth number 7 falls right across here and here. And then there is tooth number 8 and 9. They match up in the right position, right orientation, and right angle. But because this injury is at least three days old and I cannot find any fine detail, I must stop short of saying these teeth and only these teeth are the ones on the planet that could make that mark."

Again, he timed and dated the injuries. He sounded official, professional, and above all, convincing.

In that narrow time window, Dr. West said, police told him that only four people had access to Kimberly—Leigh, Tami, Dickie, and Peanut. The latter three couldn't have done it, Dr. West said. "This one could have. And it's more than just a possibility to me, I would see it as a probability."

Leigh was the biter. Not Tami, Dickie, or Peanut.

Leigh.

The video footage zoomed in on Kim's vagina. "The vaginal area," Dr. West narrated. "Notice the swelling. I'm asking the nurses to spread the labia. And notice we have a labia on the left side, but we're missing the labia on the right."

"It's very asymmetrical. This area of the labia appears to have been chewed or masticated. This could be teeth marks, but I can't say with any reasonable assurance. I'm just documenting them here," he said. "Here we see some chew marks on the inside of the labia. We see a gross distortion, swelling, in the clitoris. These injuries are—lead me to think that the left labia had been chewed on, the clitoral region had negative pressure or a sucking of great intensity applied to it."

He continued, "And then, of course, here I am, I am missing the right labia, labia majora. And I can't say, with any certainty, was the, you know, lip missing earlier and just the edge of it chewed or was it bitten off or was it avulsed, bitten and pulled off. I can't say."

Prosecutor Lampton interjected, "If you assume that they were symmetrical prior to these injuries—"

"Then I would—I would be more inclined to say it was avulsed, bitten off," Dr. West testified. "I have chew marks, masticatory evidence on this labia, suction, severe sucking on the clitoral and, like I say, I'm missing the right labia. If it was present, then it is certainly consistent with it being bitten off."

By his own assessment, Dr. West identified the injuries on Kim's body as sexual in nature, the result of oral sex: sucking and biting.

After all the scientific terminology and medical language, Dr. West said the injuries to Kim's vulva boiled down to "severe oral sex."

But, he added, "Who bit her vaginal lip off, I don't know."

THE COMFORT INN SURVEILLANCE VIDEO

The jury was next shown transparencies of still frames captured from the Comfort Inn surveillance video. Dr. West warned them: "It is not easy to see. It is difficult and you have to look at it and study it to know what is going on." Then he focused on Leigh's white Chevy truck parked in the Comfort Inn lot. The frame was time-stamped at 10:47 P.M. on March 6, 2000.

"This silver or light streak is the toolbox lid in that truck, with the lid open," Dr. West said. "This is with the lid down." Using the overhead projector, he switched between two transparency stills from the surveillance footage to show the toolbox lid up and down.

"This is very pixilated. You know, you can have a hard time trying to see that. Now we're going to show you some of the video in its original form and then with it blown up and with some computer enhancement."

Dr. West continued, "Let me tell you about enhancement versus alteration. Today it's amazing—ten years ago, I would have to send photographs off to the FBI. Would cost us $20,000 to get them back and enhanced. Now you can sit at home, with your own computer, with

$1,000 software and do enhancements that used to be only NASA could do. And that's what we've done in this case."

As the prosecutor inserted the videocassette surveillance video in the VCR to play for the jury, Dr. West noted, "It was recorded on a very poor imaging system. This system is not designed to take high-definition pictures and blow them up. This is a very commercial grade system."

The surveillance video showed four camera views combined as a grid on the screen. There was no sound. As the jury watched, the truck, with Leigh behind the wheel, entered one camera's view, pulling into the Comfort Inn parking lot. The jurors saw Leigh get out of the truck and walk up to the front desk—she was seen in the top right quadrant. Leigh met with the night attendant. This was when she asked about the security camera itself, but there was no way this video could communicate the true significance of that moment.

As the video continued, Leigh was seen leaving the front desk with the room keys and walking out to her truck. In the lower left quadrant, she could be seen driving the truck around to the back parking lot. There, she parked in front of the ground floor hotel room she had been assigned. The video did not provide a view into the truck itself. Her actions with her friends was not visible. Dr. West, however, didn't need to be able to see inside the truck to know the situation.

"It's mine and Detective Jones's contention, Kim is in that toolbox right now," Dr. West declared.

At that moment, however, there was a wrinkle in the video, a malfunction, where for that space and time, the video was unviewable. When the video returned, Dr. West turned his attention to the toolbox in the back of the pickup truck. The toolbox was closed.

Dr. West said that he could see a tall "girl" and a short "girl." He said he believed they were two different "girls" because of their clothing—one wore a knee-length T-shirt, the other wore black pants. Dr. West identified them as Tami and Leigh.

Dr. West told the jury that he had "enhanced" a section of the video in five different ways and pieced them together to show Leigh going to the truck, climbing into the back of the truck, opening the toolbox, taking Kim out, and carrying her into the hotel room. He said the actions spanned sixteen to twenty seconds.

He began his narration of the first of the five segments, saying "There's the toolbox—here she is coming around the front, going around there. The toolbox lid is up. There's the head there. Hair hanging down. Toolbox lid goes down. She walks over, steps off, goes into the room. Out comes the other girl, there, turns up the tailgate. Comes around checks that door. Walks around checks that one."

Moving to the second segment, Dr. West said, "Steps up into the toolbox. There is what appears to be a head with hair. Closes it. Turns around. Steps off. Goes into the hotel room. The girl comes out, raises the tailgate. Walks around in front of the truck. Checks the door."

The third segment: "Up in the back, the hair flipping. Closes the lid. Stepping. You see the legs. Walks in."

In the next version, which has been amplified to increase brightness, Dr. West said, "The most important part is the hair, to me. You've got to imagine her scooping her up and holding that head, with the hair, to that side. Then of course, walking around the truck again. Hair flip.

"Then, there is her legs as she's cradling her, carrying her in," Dr. West continued. "And if you'll notice, the one that steps up in the truck, when she turns around, you can see what appears to be black pants. But when the other girl walks in front of the car—the truck—the T-shirt covers the pants."

Dr. West showed another version.

"This is the one I like the best," he told the jury. "All of her actions, right in there. Coming out. Scooping up the head, the hair. Standing up. Closing the lid. Turning around. Stepping off the truck."

Now, another version.

"She comes out. Goes up into the truck. Looks like a limp body, to me, that she's removing . . . And that black splotch right there, I believe, is Kim's head with her hair hanging down. And now, back to the door. Another girl comes out, closes the tailgate. Walks around the front of the car—the truck. Checks the doors and then goes back into the room."

And another version.

"She comes out and steps up into the truck. Gets the body. The head swings. The hair is hanging. Turns around, walks back off the truck."

Ultimately, the jury saw the same sixteen to twenty seconds a total of twenty-five times.

In less than half a minute, according to Dr. West, Leigh picked up another woman whose height and weight were the same as Leigh's and carried her from a toolbox off the back of the truck and into the hotel room.

In that time, Dr. West changed the entire trajectory of Leigh's life.

But the prosecution wasn't finished. Dr. West and Lampton had a surprise for the jury.

They had recorded their own recreation of the events in the Comfort Inn parking lot using a different truck, but in the same location, with the same toolbox, recorded by the same surveillance camera. The jury watched as Dr. West's dental assistant, Tracy, stood by the toolbox. A volunteer named Margaret was in the toolbox with her long hair hanging over the side.

"That is Margaret's hair hanging down," Dr. West explained. "And I believe that that is Kimberly's hair hanging down."

This concluded a long day of testimony. The judge instructed the jurors not to read the article about the trial in the local *Daily Leader* and sent them home.

TESTIMONY ABOUT HOMOSEXUAL ASSAULTS

The following morning, Dr. West began testifying about his expertise: bite marks.

"Dr. West, is there any question in your mind that the injury on the hip that you've discussed was, in fact, a bite mark?" Lampton asked.

"In my opinion, the mark on her hip, within reasonable dental certainty, is a human bite mark," Dr. West replied. "I give my strongest opinion of positive."

He explained how markings may not appear to be bite marks except to an expert. "When the teeth drag over the skin, oftentimes it leaves a mark that a lay person would not see as a bite mark," he said. Referring to the photograph of Kim's hip, he told the jury, "I must admit that to a novice, this may not appear to be a bite mark by any means . . ."

"Are bite marks any more or less prevalent in a homosexual assault than a heterosexual rape case?" Lampton asked.

"In male homosexuality, in those cases of violence, there seems to be a much greater propensity of bite marks," Dr. West said. "In female homosexual activity, I haven't had enough experience or read anything in the literature, but it's documented that male homosexual activity is much greater in bite marks."

Apparently, Dr. West was referring to some sort of unverified literature that homosexuals were more likely to bite people. Perhaps this was not surprising, given that his field of forensic odontology was itself unverified. Everything Dr. West said—from matching points on Leigh's teeth model to the splotchy raspberry injury on Kim's hip, to identifying Kim's body being removed from the toolbox in the back of Leigh's truck, to the "propensity" of homosexuals to bite people, was unreliable and unverified. His forensic odontology, his "wound pattern analysis," his video analysis, were speculation dressed up in scientific names and descriptors.

But on the stand, Dr. West was the king of his dominion, the only expert the prosecution needed to call. To reaffirm West's credentials, Lampton asked, "When you lecture in China or to Scotland Yard or to the FBI or to other dentists, are you telling them basically just what you've told this jury, showing them the way you compare bite marks and the techniques that are used?"

"Well, of course, we go into a lot greater detail, but yes, it's the same protocol," Dr. West said.

Lampton continued.

"So, in a rape case or a homosexual rape case, you would expect to find bite marks? It would not be unusual at all to find bite marks on the skin?"

"No, it wouldn't be unusual," Dr. West answered.

"In fact," Lampton asked, "it would almost be expected?"

"Almost."

A GAP IN THE THEORY

Lampton turned to the injuries on Kim's head and hip. "How much force was involved in causing those marks to the body of Kimberly Williams?" he asked Dr. West.

"I would have to say it's considerable for the injuries that we noted on her thigh," West said. "And those are three days old. For them to have that degree of clarity after three days, I would have to rate it at the amount of injury or pressure as being severe."

"And how much bleeding would have occurred with an injury to the head or injury to the hip?" Lampton asked.

"Scalp injuries bleed a lot," Dr. West said. "With the injury that we saw on the side of her head and the medical record talking of hypovolemic shock, that's the one question I can't answer, where did her blood go."

That was one obvious hole in the prosecution's case. No blood had been found in the hotel room or the hotel bathroom. Likewise, no blood had been found in the toolbox or the truck.

Lampton pivoted back to the toolbox, asking Dr. West if he had performed any "experiments" to determine whether a person the height and weight of Kim Williams could fit inside the toolbox.

"Yes. I had my assistant, Tracy, we put her in the box. She's here today."

Tracy, who was five feet tall and was the woman in the mock recreation video, walked to the front of the courtroom and stood before the jury. "There was plenty of room there," Dr. West said.

Wordlessly, Tracy took her seat again.

Even now, Dr. West wasn't yet finished. His expertise, which perhaps seemed boundless, now covered the pharmacological effects of morphine, Oxycontin, and Narcan. By 2021, Narcan, a lifesaving treatment that reverses the overdose effects of an opioid, was so ubiquitous that it could be purchased at a local pharmacy in Brookhaven. Police had come to carry it routinely. But at the time of trial in 2000, Lampton didn't even know how to pronounce the name.

Dr. West explained the role of Narcan to the jury, and then the impact of morphine or opioids, including the slowing of respiration. He shared his own experience of having given morphine to dental patients prior to removing wisdom teeth. On three or four occasions, Dr. West said he had given too much morphine and the patients had stopped breathing. Dr. West said he used Narcan to revive them.

He made light of what was clearly a dangerous situation. "We always tell them, we put you to sleep for free; we charge you for waking you up," Dr. West said.

Lampton asked Dr. West's opinion on the timing of the injuries, including the vaginal injuries, although the timing of injuries is notoriously prone to error.

"The head injuries, the vaginal injuries, and the hip injuries all seem to have occurred approximately within the same time," he replied. He hadn't seen the injuries until Wednesday, but he placed them as occurring on Monday.

Dr. West made no mention of the difficulty of timing an aging bruise, which is what the hip injury was—a large bruise. Instead, he saw in that bruise two things: an injury matched to a toolbox latch, and a bite mark.

"Based on your determination of bite marks, is it possible that Kim self-inflicted those injuries?" Lampton asked.

"No," Dr. West said. "It's not possible to bite yourself on the side of the hip."

"No further questions," Lampton told the judge.

With that, the prosecutor clinched his conviction of Leigh and Tami. It was only a matter of time.

CROSS-EXAMINING DR. WEST

Tami's lawyer, Ken McNees, went first in the cross-examination of Dr. West.

His beginning wasn't promising.

Curiously, he said, "Good morning, Dr. West, I've enjoyed everything you've said."

But then he got to his first point: Dr. West wasn't an expert in interpreting surveillance cameras.

Dr. West retorted that he had interpreted surveillance cameras in five previous cases, although the cases were never specified. How a dentist, even a forensic dentist, had become an expert on surveillance video cameras and had created evidence for the prosecutor was a fact that was verified only by his word that he had done it before.

"I believe that I saw the actions that Detective Jones described to me the first time I saw the video," Dr. West maintained. "I realize it was difficult to see. And I spent quite a bit of time trying to enhance the video so everyone could see it."

The impact on the jury was unavoidable. Dr. West had made five versions of the same segment of time and the segments were aired twenty-five times. And with each viewing, he told the jury members what they were seeing. At that point, the poor quality of the video no longer mattered. Through his narration, Dr. West had been able to imprint in the minds of the jurors precisely what Dr. West said was there.

"Dr. West, how do you get an adult human body out of that toolbox in one to two seconds?" McNees asked.

Dr. West stepped down from the witness chair to demonstrate before the jury. "You bend down and pick it up and go with it. The person who came in and out of that hotel room appeared to be very anxious. It's adrenaline, fight or flight. What a person can do when they're pumped up is totally different than what they can do when they're relaxed."

"I thoroughly agree, from having been a competitive weightlifter," McNees said. "But, Doctor, one second?"

Dr. West insisted: "Bent down and standing up. Look at it on the tape."

McNees went after the bite marks next.

"Isn't it true, Doctor, that there is more than one school of thought—and among equally educated individuals, if that's possible, regarding the credibility of your science in forensics? Akin to either believing in flying saucers or not?"

Dr. West responded, "I haven't seen a flying saucer, but I know what you mean."

McNees then pressed Dr. West on the lack of blood. "What happened to all the blood?" he asked.

"The only way I think that you could get rid of that amount of blood is put someone in an aluminum toolbox and when you finished, hose it out, and when you took them in the hotel room, put them in the bathtub and ice them down. That's how I would do it," Dr. West replied.

In one short speech, Dr. West summed up the state's theory for how Leigh and Tami could have injured Kim without any blood being found.

PROBLEM ONE: NO BLOOD

Leigh's attorney, Bill Barnett, rose to speak. This was the most difficult defense case of his short career. But even with less than two weeks to prepare, he was fighting. The judge had already chastised Barnett for his hard questioning of a witness, and even fined him $100.

Now Barnett squared off with Michael West.

His first questions focused on the blood. Or really, the lack of it. If Kim was violently put in a toolbox and injured, where was the blood? If she was bitten on her body, and her labia chewed off, where was the blood? If there was a dramatic head injury, where was the blood?

"That's the big problem I have," Dr. West conceded. "I don't know where her blood is, where did this girl's blood go? I don't know and I can't tell you. No one has been able to find any physical evidence to say here's the blood."

Barnett hammered this point. No blood in the toolbox. No blood in the carpet of the hotel room. No blood on the sheets, pillows, or bed cover. And no blood in the bathtub or around the drain.

Barnett then asked unshakable Dr. West about another Mississippi case, *State v. Bourn*, in which Dr. West had found bite marks. In that prosecution, Dr. West found "a really good bite mark" on the arm of an eighty-five-year-old rape victim. The police brought in Johnnie Bourn, took his dental mold, and Dr. West compared the Bourn mold to a photograph of the arm injury—the same methodology used to implicate Leigh. Bourn's teeth, Dr. West had opined, were a match. Dr. West had given the identification his highest rating, "reasonable dental certainty."

But when police took a sample of Bourn's blood to compare to the rape kit, testing showed he was excluded—he was not the rapist. After sitting in jail for eighteen months, Bourn was released when the prosecutors dropped the charges.

Nonetheless, Dr. West was adamant that he was correct. "The bite mark said he was there; semen said another guy was there. If there had been Mr. Bourn's fingerprint on a table and someone's DNA in the vagina, I think they would have went ahead and prosecuted it," Dr. West said. "But since it was just his bite mark and someone else's DNA, they opted not to."

To justify his conclusion, Dr. West had developed his own theory:

Bourn bit the woman on the arm and hit her over the head with a candlestick holder, and then the other man raped her.

"Was there ever any evidence of a second assailant?" Barnett asked.

"Yes," Dr. West responded confidently. "There was someone else's DNA in her vagina."

By Dr. West's circular reasoning, Bourn was guilty even if the rest of the evidence exonerated him. "I believe with no reservations in my heart, Mr. Bourn bit that eighty-five-year-old lady," he asserted.

In other cases, Dr. West made the same argument: he identified the bite mark, and he was certain about the bite mark. The rest of the case was a determination for someone else.

But not so in Leigh and Tami's case. Every determination by Dr. West in their case was an essential component of the state's case. He testified to video evidence of Kim in a toolbox, bite mark evidence of an assault to her hip and vagina, wound expert evidence of marks to Kim's breasts, and even testified about the role of Narcan and overdoses. Dr. West's testimony eventually took up nearly 250 transcript pages. But his evidentiary reports to the police were one page each—one page for the video, and one page for the bite marks.

Dr. West bragged that "there's only three men in the country that's seen more bite marks than me, in my opinion." He mocked any parameters that applied to the study of forensic odontology. Instead, he shared with the jury one of his own experiments.

"We got volunteers from the University of Southern Mississippi and I sedated them and had boyfriend, girlfriend, husband, wives, brothers, sisters come in and we would put one of them to sleep and the other would bite the heck out of them."

In this experiment, Dr. West photographed the bites and then checked in weeks and months afterward to see how the bite mark impression changed. This, he explained, was how he developed his technique, "The West Phenomenon," in which he used blue ultraviolet light to examine bite marks. Other bite mark experts awarded him the 1989 Reidar Sognnaes Report Award for his published findings.

Relying on this past research, Dr. West not only found bite marks on Kim's body, but said he was able to match them to Leigh Stubbs.

By this time, Dr. West had quit his membership in the American

Society of Forensic Odontology, and also quit the International Association for Identification. After a complaint was filed against Dr. West because of his behavior and testimony in the prosecution of Larry Maxwell, Dr. West resigned. In 1990, Maxwell had been charged with the stabbing murders of three elderly people near Meridian, Mississippi. Dr. West used his blue light method for the very first time and concluded that he could see an impression made by the exposed rivets in the handle of the murder weapon on Maxwell's palm. Maxwell had spent more than two years in jail awaiting a trial before he was released in 1992 after a judge ruled that the blue light testimony was not admissible.

"It may well be that Dr. West is a pioneer in the field of alternative light imaging for the purpose of detecting trace wound patterns on the human skin, and it may well be that the future will prove that his techniques are sound evidentiary tools that result in the presentation of inherently reliable expert opinions," declared Kemper County Circuit Court Judge Larry Roberts. "But at this time, I am not so convinced."

Bill Barnett came prepared to cross-examine Dr. West. He asked about the complaints against Dr. West and his resignation. When Barnett brought forth a copy of one of the written complaints, the courtroom atmosphere became electric.

Prosecutor Lampton objected vigorously to the complaint being shown to the jury. He told Dr. West, his star witness, not to answer any questions about it. The judge agreed. He ruled the complaint was not admissible and could not be shown to the jury. The judge urged Barnett to "move on to something else."

It seemed that accusations flowed off Dr. West's back like water. As one attorney later declared, Dr. West was a "snake charmer" with jurors who wound up eating out of his hand, lulled by his colloquial demeanor and attitude of sarcastic indifference to any criticism.

"Are there any other organizations that you were a member of in the past and have resigned from or been expelled from?" Barnett asked.

"Yes, the Boy Scouts of America," Dr. West smirked. "They caught me smoking and threw me out. I was ten. I still smoke."

"Dr. West, I'm trying to get to the truth," Barnett shot back.

"Then you should look at the evidence," Dr. West retorted. "The evidence in this case says that Kim was with these two girls, and after twenty-four or thirty-six hours, she's got severe tremendous injuries; the doctors don't think she's going to live; she has bite marks; she has vaginal injuries; she has injuries from a toolbox; she's lost a tremendous amount of blood. But no one knows what happened."

"Now everything you just said there, that whole diatribe, is simply your opinion up to now, isn't it?" Barnett asked.

"God, that's all I have is my opinion," Dr. West responded. "I can't give you someone else's. That's my opinion."

"You don't understand that you can get an expert to come into this courtroom and say just about anything you want him to say," Dr. West added. "There is a growing number of experts that I'm aware of, who I have no other term for them but whore. They will come in and say whatever you want them to say. I am not one of those types."

Evidence from other cases would ultimately prove the irony of his comment.

Barnett attacked the bite mark impression testimony.

But Dr. West pushed back. He noted that in his experience, such as his testimony against Kennedy Brewer, another Mississippi murder case, biters can leave an impression of only their top teeth. "You don't bite someone on the leg like you're biting a ham sandwich," he declared. "This is usually a combative or a sexual orientation phenomenon. So, don't confuse biting food with biting the lip of someone's vagina off. It's two different things."

Barnett doggedly carried on. He presented research by another expert on how the shape of bite marks indicated whether the bite was made by an animal or a human. According to a treatise on bite marks, the U shape, like the one Dr. West said he found on Kim, was indicative of an animal bite.

Dr. West dismissed the treatise as ludicrous and the author as a "novice." When Barnett moved to have the treatise admitted into evidence, Prosecutor Lampton again objected. And the judge again refused to allow the jury to see the treatise.

After not making much progress in assailing Dr. West's past, Barnett turned to the evidence at hand: the homemade video of Kim's naked body in the hospital, looking to point out errors.

The jury, and everyone in the courtroom, again watched Kim's naked body in the hospital.

Barnett pointed out that Dr. West had misidentified a birthmark on Kim as an abrasion or injury. And he pointed to an injury at the armpit that appeared incongruous with Kim being picked up.

At that, Dr. West beckoned to Tracy, his dental assistant, in the audience. He stepped off the witness chair and joined Tracy in front of the jury. Tracy was being paid by the prosecution to be an exhibit—her body was supposed to demonstrate how Kim's body would have fit in the toolbox.

As jurors looked on, Dr. West picked up Tracy, demonstrating how he believed Leigh picked up Kim.

Barnett quickly pointed out that Dr. West's hand wasn't anywhere near Tracy's armpit.

"Mr. Barnett," Dr. West said, "I'm a married man."

PROBLEM TWO: ALLEGING VAGINA BITE MARKS

Dr. West returned to the witness stand. Barnett resumed the video.

He elicited testimony from Dr. West that it didn't matter if he knew whether Kim's labia was asymmetrical before he examined her. As far as he was concerned, someone had either bitten off the labia, or chewed on the "stub."

"Not knowing how normal her vaginal lips looked before the assault, I had to consider several opinions," Dr. West testified. "The first, of course, is the right lip has been bitten off or avulsed, or the right lip had already been missing, and the base, the stub, of the—in other words . . . The labia lip could be bitten off or it could already be missing then the stump could be chewed, gnawed on, and I couldn't tell you was it the stump being chewed or the lip being bitten off."

Barnett asked questions about Kim's vagina, though he could not bring himself to say the word. "As you continue to look at that part there, now I noticed that when you examined that part of her anatomy that y'all really had to press apart in order to show her female organs there, right?" Barnett asked.

"Yes," Dr. West said. "I asked them to spread her legs and then to spread her lips so that we could see hopefully the entire labia majora and the clitoris, plus the vaginal vault."

Everyone in the courtroom saw this as well. Would the jury have been just as or more concerned with a video of a man's penis and scrotum being shown repeatedly?

"Now, if somebody was going to bite that or suck on it, that would really take an effort to separate everything and get in there, right?" Barnett asked.

"You would have to have the legs spread far enough apart to get your head in there," Dr. West replied. He hesitated, then said, "I'm hesitant to discuss oral sex with females. I've done it, but I'm not an expert."

He sighed. At this point, the subject almost seemed too much even for Dr. West.

"I don't know what to tell you," he said. "Could someone bite her lip off, yes. How would you go about it and all, you would have to get your head down on her vaginal lips. And if you had one of the lips in your mouth, you would bite it off, but she would have to have her legs spread, I would assume."

Barnett pressed on.

"It seems difficult for the nurse to get that spread apart just right, isn't it?" he asked.

"I would say so, yes," Dr. West said.

"And this situation here, we were getting kind of intimate with the lady and she's unconscious?" Barnett asked. "Now, if she was conscious, she couldn't help you do that, absent putting her hands there."

Barnett finally got to his point—perhaps it was consensual oral sex, Kim was awake, and she assisted.

And then, he moved on.

PROBLEM THREE: MIS-MATCHED BRUISES

Barnett skipped forward five days to the recording of Kim's hip made by Dr. West. The back and forth between Dr. West and Barnett turned even more surreal.

"There's basically not a lot of meat to sink your teeth into right there?" Barnett asked.

"I don't believe that it's beyond reason that you could get that amount of tissue in your mouth right there," West replied.

Undeterred, Barnett asked again. "Not a lot of flesh there, is there? It's kind of bone and skin right there, huh?"

"I would have to get Kim and pinch that area to see," Dr. West said. "I don't believe that it's beyond reason that you could get that amount of tissue in your mouth right there," he insisted.

"I'm just going to say that compared to the gluteal portion—" Barnett began.

"It's thinner than the gluteus, yes," Dr. West interrupted.

"And there's basically not a lot of meat to sink your teeth into right there?"

"Compared to the gluteus, no, there isn't," Dr. West conceded.

Barnett steered the cross-examination to Dr. West's assertion that the bruise could have been made by the toolbox latch. He noted that there was not a match.

"That's what I'm trying to tell you," Dr. West explained. "If you close it on her and she tries to either push her in or she tries to push herself out, we would get a cross action on it. I'm not saying that she sat there and this lid was just smashed onto her leg. There's a lot of actions going on and if it hits on the curved surface and she pulls away, which I would anticipate, it would leave that mark. It's not a rubber stamp perpendicular, it's more of a tangible."

For the first time, Dr. West was suggesting that Kim fought when she was put in the toolbox.

Barnett pushed back.

"If this box was empty, why would her leg be up this high in a position to even come in contact with this latch?"

Dr. West dodged the question.

"Why would they want to put her in the toolbox in the first place is my question," he replied. "I have no idea what was in or out of it before she went into it. But from looking at the video, I believe they took her body out of this toolbox and took it into the hotel room. How they got her in there, I'm not sure. Are the marks on her leg and her head consistent with these latches, yes. Are the marks from her head to her leg thirty-seven inches, the distance from these latches, yes it is. Can I completely duplicate how she was forced into the box, no, I can't."

Despite that testimony, Dr. West tried anyway. Tracy was summoned before the jury again, this time on her knees.

"Now," Dr. West said, "If your head is over here, turned that away, and if I hit her with that angle, it would force her head down. You know, it may take two people to hold her body . . . Trying to force her in and when her head is there and getting banged, her hip would be here."

And just like that, Dr. West now included both women in the hypothesis.

As for the lack of a match between the bruises and the latches, Dr. West responded, "I'm not saying she's inside the box and being banged. I believe the blows occurred while she was being put in the box."

Barnett replayed the video of Kim's body focusing on how Kim's hip was smooth until Dr. West put the teeth mold directly on Kim's hip to create the bite mark indentation.

"So, on an unconscious, injured woman, in a hospital, you took a dental impression, and where there were no marks, you pressed that thing into her hip?" Barnett asked.

"Yes, sir, but this doesn't hurt," Dr. West said hastily. "You just take the model and press it into your skin and it's not that you're going to hurt, you just take it and press it for a second and then take it off and take a picture. That's all I was doing."

Barnett responded, "I'm not too concerned with it hurting or not because she was unconscious, but I'm just concerned with the ethics of the whole deal. Don't you feel a little—"

Dr. West cut him off. "No. See, you don't understand how you conduct a test. I'm not trying to manufacture evidence. The evidence on the 10th is what we do the analysis on. This was part of my comparison. I was trying to be as accurate as possible by using the actual portion of the victim's body."

Dr. West puffed up.

"I resent you saying what I did was unethical," he snapped. "You should learn a little more of odontology before you come out here and make stupid questions."

Of course, despite examinations by numerous emergency personnel and other caregivers, no bite marks had been discovered on Kim's body, by anyone, until Dr. West found them.

"Why don't you get your own odontologist and do your own expert analysis and show that your client didn't bite the girl, because I believe your client bit her," West said.

On that note, the trial recessed for lunch.

As he did each day at lunch and at the end of the day, the judge warned the jury not to read any newspapers. There was good reason. The *Daily Leader* was covering the salacious trial daily. And Dr. West had given them plenty of material to publish for their readers.

PROBLEM FOUR: ABSOLUTE CERTAINTY

Dr. Michael West's certainty that he had found a bite mark on Kim was an opinion that evolved and improved with time. His certainty was constructed, much like an eyewitness who at first is less than sure, but at trial, points to the defendant and says, "That's the person. That's who did it." With absolute certainty.

Absolute certainty doesn't necessarily exist in that first moment when a witness is confronted with the image of the defendant. The first time they see a lineup of photos, or even a live person lineup, a witness may feel uncertain. But when someone tells them, "Good, you picked the suspect," their perception changes. The witness's confidence goes up.

When the witness meets with the prosecutor to go over their testimony before trial, their confidence and certainty go up again.

And by the time of trial, certainty has become 100 percent. That's why eyewitness misidentifications have been a leading cause of wrongful convictions. That's why innocence projects have pushed to reform protocols, such as requiring police to document the level of certainty—a confidence factor—of a witness at the time of identification. Another reform is requiring sequential lineups in which police hand the photos one at a time to the witness in separate manila folders, so the officer can't see which photo the witness is viewing and which photo is chosen as the perpetrator. The officer is unable to influence the selection, even unintentionally. Identifying a filler person and exonerating a suspect is just as important as finding the culprit in that moment. Otherwise, the investigation is sent down the wrong path, perhaps all the way to trial and wrongful conviction.

Dr. West wasn't 100 percent certain when he first viewed Kim's body. He didn't mention a bite mark on his video. He even conceded at trial, "I wasn't sure when I first saw it that it was a bite mark." It wasn't until he looked at the Polaroid photographs that he took of Kim's body that he decided the bruise on Kim's hip was a bite mark. He then decided he could see "individual teeth characteristics." And he got the dental molds, which resulted in his final conclusion: a match.

On the witness stand, when Barnett pushed Dr. West about this evolution, West shrouded his actions in science. "You need to understand that a bite mark is a diagnosis," Dr. West said. "Erythema, abrasion, laceration is a clinical finding. *As I examined her body, I'm trying to give a clinical finding. The bite mark is a diagnosis.* That came after the study of my Polaroids."

When the trial resumed after lunch, Barnett played the Comfort Inn surveillance video. This time, when Dr. West identified Kim's long hair, flowing all the way to the bed of the truck, Barnett stopped him. "Something black and long that went down to the bed of the truck . . . might not that have been a garbage bag full of clothes that somebody was taking into the motel?" Barnett asked.

"I don't believe so, no. I think it's hair," Dr. West responded. "I think that's a body she's got in her arms, not a plastic bag."

"How is it that you would determine that that was hair rather than a plastic bag filled with clothes?" Barnett asked.

"I took the truck and put it back at the hotel with the toolbox and re-staged it with a girl holding another girl and her head hanging down and it appeared to be identical," Dr. West replied.

Barnett pressed him. "But other than this period, where it appears to me that she has this plastic bag, do you see any part on that tape where she unloaded her truck?"

"No," Dr. West said.

"So, it's possible," Barnett continued, "that what you think is unloading a body is unloading the truck?"

"Yes. It's possible," Dr. West said. "I don't believe it's probable, but it is possible."

"Did it ever come to your attention or were you aware that my client, Leigh, did have her clothes packed in a garbage bag that night?" Barnett asked.

"No, sir, I'm unaware of that," Dr. West said.

"Would that have changed the way you looked at this case if you had known that?"

"I don't believe so," Dr. West answered. "I do not see a garbage bag. I see her toting a body out of there. I don't care if she had her clothes in Samsonite leather alligator bags, she takes a body out of this toolbox. That's what I see."

"Is it your testimony to the jury that someone from the depth of that toolbox, in one second, two seconds, can lift 120 pounds up, close that lid with their elbow, and walk off?" Barnett asked.

The question frustrated Dr. West.

"I think your question is very misleading," he said. "It appears to me she bends over, picks her up, and then straightens up. I don't see anything mysterious about somebody bending over and picking somebody up. Everything I saw on the video is credible in my mind."

Barnett pulled out a piece of paper. "Well, I'm holding here a video timeline that was prepared that says 10:47:47—I assume that's 10 o'clock at night, 47 minutes and 47 seconds, the toolbox lid goes up. At 10:47:49, the toolbox lid goes down. Again at 10:48:48 the toolbox lid goes up and one second later, at 10:48:49, the toolbox lid goes down. Would you agree with that?"

"You're confusing technical terms with lay terms," Dr. West fired back. "A timeline is a portion of the video tape that the machine reads to set the speed. The little numbers flashing down on the bottom are computer generated onto the tape and have nothing to do with the synchronization of the tape. It's just a label, like Eat at Joe's, Eat at Joe's. This little flashing number at the bottom says 10:47:48, I have no idea if that's accurate."

Then something odd happened that ever remained stuck in Mama Sheila's memory. Barnett mentioned a stack of photos that had not yet been shown to the jury.

"Dr. West, I'm not sure if we looked at those pictures yesterday or not. Did we?"

"No."

"Mr. Prosecutor, have you seen those pictures?" Barnett asked.

"I think I furnished them to you," Lampton responded.

"Yes, sir."

"I have no objection to those being introduced, your honor," Lampton added. "Those are the photographs that the FBI blew up off the videotape."

This was the only time the FBI was mentioned in the entire trial. Apparently, the FBI had seen the videotape, and the prosecutor's office had been in touch with them.

In the audience, Mama Sheila was confused. What was that about? she wondered.

But the moment was lost as Barnett quickly moved on. He pivoted to a critical question, completely unrelated to Leigh's case.

"Just to finish up, I wanted to ask you about one more case. The case that you did on Kennedy Brewer, could you tell me about that case?" Barnett said.

"Which one was he?" Dr. West asked.

"The DNA test was run on him recently because he had raped a victim," Barnett said.

"I don't remember or I don't recall that."

"You don't recall that case?" Barnett asked incredulously. "Would it surprise you to know that the lab that tested the DNA in that case after you claimed that it was for sure a bite mark came back and the DNA didn't match *just yesterday*?"

"Recently?" Dr. West responded blankly.

"Yes, sir."

"This is the first I've heard."

"No more questions, Your Honor." Barnett took his seat.

Kennedy Brewer had been convicted and sentenced to die for the murder of his girlfriend's three-year-old daughter. At Brewer's trial, Dr. West concluded that nineteen marks found on the victim's body were "indeed and without a doubt" bite marks inflicted by Brewer. West further asserted that all nineteen marks were made only by

Brewer's top two teeth and that somehow the bottom teeth had made no impression.

After DNA testing excluded Brewer, he was granted a new trial. But Prosecutor Forrest Allgood refiled the charges of rape and capital murder. A defendant in a capital case in Mississippi cannot be released on bond, so Brewer remained in jail for another five years while Allgood said he would bring the case to trial. He never did.

Ultimately, in 2007, a special prosecutor for another district was appointed to the case. He agreed not to seek the death penalty and did not oppose bail. After eight years on death row and six years in jail, Kennedy Brewer was freed pending a retrial. In 2008, the Innocence Project secured Brewer's exoneration when the DNA crime evidence that had excluded Brewer showed the true perpetrator was Justin Albert Johnson.

Johnson confessed. He also confessed to an identical murder he had committed in the same community while Brewer was in prison. Levon Brooks was wrongfully convicted of that murder after Dr. West testified that alleged bite marks on the body were made by Brooks. In 2008, Brooks and Brewer were both exonerated.

But this unraveling of Dr. West's testimony was still far in the future. It did no good for Leigh and Tami in this trial.

KIMBERLY WILLIAMS TESTIFIES

The final witness was Kimberly Williams. She approached the stand using a cane, with a brace on her leg.

"We've heard a lot of testimony in here concerning you going into the hospital from the Comfort Inn, going into the hospital here in Brookhaven. Do you remember any of that?" Lampton asked gently.

"No, sir," Kim responded.

"Do you remember what happened before you went to the Comfort Inn here in Brookhaven?" Lampton asked.

"Yes," Kim said. "I remember I was in a rehab named Cady Hill and I left with two girls, Tami and Leigh, and we drove to James Ervin's house."

That was Dickie.

"Do you remember what happened at his house?" Lampton asked.

"Somebody took his bag of drugs and then we left his house."

"Do you remember anything after that?"

"No, sir."

Lampton continued. "Do you remember if at that time when you left James Ervin's house if you had been injured in any way?"

"No, sir," Kim responded, "I didn't have any injuries."

"Prior to coming to James Ervin's house, were you and Tami and Leigh friends?" Lampton asked.

"I thought we were," Kim said, casting a look at Tami and Leigh at the defense table.

"Had they ever done anything to you that was inappropriate or made you feel bad or embarrassed?"

"No."

"While you were at Cady Hill, had you had sexual intercourse with any person?" Lampton asked.

"No," Kim responded.

"Had you engaged in any type of rough sex with anyone while you were in Cady Hill?"

"No."

"And had you abused or mutilated your own body in any way?"

"No."

Lampton asked about Dickie.

"James Ervin, did he at any time engage in rough sex with you or abuse you in any way?"

"No," Kim replied.

"Your private parts, your genitalia, your vagina, prior to you going to James Ervin's house on the 7th of March, was it normal?" Lampton asked. "Was your genitalia symmetrical?"

"Yes."

"How tall are you?"

"Five-two," Kim said.

"And how much do you weigh?"

"About 110."

"And is that your height and your weight back on March 7 of 2000?"

"That was the height. I'm sure that wasn't the weight. I was much thinner."

"And why were you thinner back in those days?" Lampton asked.

"Because I used drugs," Kim told the jury.

That was wrong. Kim's records, which the prosecutors and defense attorneys had, showed that when Kim was discharged from Cady Hill on March 6, she weighed 135 pounds.

"And before getting to James Ervin's house, had you had any morphine, had you used any morphine?"

"No," Kim answered.

"Your Honor, I would tender the witness," Lampton declared.

"No cross, Your Honor," said Ken McNees, Tami's lawyer.

"Your Honor, I have no questions," Barnett said.

"Your Honor, the State rests," Lampton said. The State concluded its case.

The defense was about to begin.

CHAPTER 12
Women's Bodies as Objects

We consume visual images of women all the time. We are trained to watch women's bodies, and to not take their bodily privacy as seriously as men's. Women's bodies become public; men's bodies are private. "There is something of a power trip in stripping women and keeping men covered and safe."

OBJECTIFYING KIM'S BODY

Everyone in the courtroom was fully clothed and dressed while they examined photos and video of Kim's fragmented naked body. Attorneys and witnesses described and discussed Kim's body parts, alternating between abstract medical terminology and meat.

Kim was disembodied, her self as a whole separated from her limbs. In the bite mark testimony, the white men described biting into her flesh, the fattiness of her thigh compared to her butt. *There's basically not a lot of meat to sink your teeth into right there? I don't believe that it's beyond reason that you could get that amount of tissue in your mouth right there.*

An individual is unique, living, spirited, whole. Body parts are anonymous, interchangeable. Thighs and breasts are menu choices. They are body parts to be physically or visually consumed, titillating.

Making someone into some*thing* enables treating that person as an object. Dr. West described Kim as body parts that he handled and observed. If he had treated Kim the person this way, it would be assault.

In hospital settings, unconscious women are frequently physically touched and their vaginas invaded by hospital residents. Legally. Women admitted to a hospital for any surgery often unknowingly sign consent forms that permit residents to do "practice" pelvic exams on them while they are under anesthesia for surgery. And that is women with enough agency to sign themselves into a hospital and sign away their rights.

Dr. West violated Kim's body, treating her as an object. He showed his audience a video that scans her full body, then he displayed photos that fragment her body into parts. The photos show Kim's vagina or her breasts or her thigh, for the jury and anyone looking to consume. Her fragmented body allowed the prosecution and Dr. West to piece together a story. West used medical terms—"glandular," "hematosis," "labia"—words that objectify, medicalize, and ignore the privacy and wholeness of the woman. West so thoroughly objectified Kim that no one protested against her vagina being shown on an overhead projector in open court.

Straight white cisgender men created the story that Kim was bitten: on her breast, her thigh, her vagina. The men played as experts on Kim's body while she was voiceless—indeed, she wasn't even conscious. The flesh-biting is a sexualized fantasy, created to bring charges against two women who were lesbians. The prosecutors fantasized for the jury that these two women bit another grown woman for sexual arousal. Their evidence of Leigh's and Tami's guilt was that they were lesbians.

For me, Dr. West's photos and videos of Kim while she's naked and unconscious trigger something else as well. The actions mirror those of an assailant who takes photos or videos of an unconscious rape survivor and circulates those images, amplifying and repeating the harm. The photos and videos create their own harm, making the idea of sexual assault and the unconscious body of the survivor titillating. Women survivors of revenge porn report feeling as though other people are staring at their bodies and imagining what was done to them because of the photos. Here, the male prosecutors and dentist made it permissible for jurors—strangers—to look at Kim, to look at her body, and to imagine their story of what happened to her.

Leigh and Tami were reduced to tropes about violent and vicious predatory lesbians, and Kim was reduced to a victim and her fragmented body parts.

But to be clear, nearly everyone in the trial against Leigh and Tami was white and was disembodied, only seen for a stereotype of who they are, a fragment of their whole selves in service of the prosecutor's narrative. The witnesses, the defendants, the victim. Dickie, Kim's boyfriend, was first and foremost presented through his disability. The prosecutors highlighted their ableist story that Dickie couldn't have been sexual with Kim, and used his marijuana smoking to show his "lack of trustworthiness." Then the prosecutors presented Kim as a permanently disabled woman with Substance Use Disorder. They used an ableist framework to incite pity for Kim and stoke the fantasy that two women physically and permanently disabled Kim through sexualized violence. The prosecutors presented Leigh and Tami as lesbians and "addicts."

Everyone in this case is subjected to hypervisibility in a courtroom narrative that amplifies these stereotyped flat cutouts of themselves. Flat and easy to pin down, to make a demonstration using them. Difference is highlighted, and difference is either tolerated with pity or is punished.

THE HISTORICAL CREATION OF GYNECOLOGY AND MEDICINE

In the 1800s, medicine was not a respected discipline. Medical school students and doctors alike would steal corpses from graveyards to practice and learn what was beneath human skin. Live patients frequently died under their care. Before the American Medical Association was established in 1847, many white men practiced as "doctors" without any formal educational training and little to no practical experience. At a time when surgeries were rare, these doctors performed a shocking number of surgeries on bondwomen during the first half of the 1800s. These doctors relied on the bodies of enslaved women and immigrant women to learn and create the field of gynecology.

In her book *Medical Bondage,* Dr. Deirdre Cooper Owens uncovers that gynecology was a trifling emergent field until the United States government banned importing people as slaves in 1808. At that point, white doctors began partnering with plantation owners to exploit and protect the reproductive ability and health of women who were already enslaved. These white male doctors created slave hospitals in the South to perform surgeries on women of child-bearing age and to examine their bodies. The men would then publish their "findings" as fact in medical journals.

The first women's hospital in the United States was a slave hospital on a small farm in Mt. Meigs, Alabama. In 1844 the hospital was fifteen miles from Montgomery, a slave-trading center at the time. The founder became known as the "Father of American Gynecology." The unheralded Black women in bondage, working as nurses or having their own bodies subjected to surgeries and examinations, were the unsung Mothers of American Gynecology.

The doctors published racist tropes as fact. They repeated lies that women of African descent were impervious to pain, even when the doctors had to forcibly restrain the women to perform their painful surgeries. Black women were not given anesthetic even though it was widely available at the time to ease pain. Today, Black women remain frequently unable to receive pain relief even after major surgeries because of the ongoing racist myth that Black people are preternaturally strong and do not feel pain. In the words of comedian Wanda Sykes,

> Because of racism, Black people, we don't even get our hands on opioids. They don't even give them to us. White people get opioids like they Tic Tacs . . . I had a double mastectomy. You know what they sent my Black ass home with? Ibu-[expletive]-pro-fen.

The doctors in the 1800s built their careers on the bodies of women who were enslaved and poor Irish women who had immigrated to the United States. These men medicalized terms for women's bodies and functions and created an "American Gynecological Society." They fantasized racist physical distinctions between Black women and white women with the aim of justifying white supremacy.

They concocted an "impartial" medical gaze that was anything but impartial.

With the establishment of gynecology, only men could be experts on women's bodies. And only poor women were subjected to their experiments. Slave hospitals in the South with surgeries on enslaved women paralleled charity wards in the North and surgeries on Irish immigrant women. Famous gynecologists would perform surgeries on enslaved women and poor Irish immigrant women in front of audiences, again with no anesthesia.

Gynecology in the South fundamentally relied on agreements between white men: "doctors" and plantation owners. Bondwomen were stripped of their privacy because the law categorized them as property. Their private bodies were publicly exposed, both in open surgeries and in writings in medical journals afterward.

The creation of "medical" labels further objectified and dehumanized women, dissecting them into body parts and conditions. These doctors controlled how women's bodies were viewed, moved, and understood. They made their careers while creating and perpetuating untruths.

In Leigh and Tami's case, Dr. West was referenced repeatedly as a doctor, not a dentist. He was positioned as an expert in examining and identifying the condition of a woman's body. West created and perpetuated a fiction of bite marks on Kim's body. From that grew an attendant story that someone partially bit off Kim's vagina and put Kim in a toolbox. To go one step further, Dr. West testified that lesbians are likely to commit these acts.

This white man, 150 years after the horrific creation of gynecology as a field, was controlling the gaze of the jury. West masked intimate and private pictures of Kim's body and genitalia with medical terms. He objectified Kim's body, and separated her body from her humanity and existence. And he claimed to make expert and medical determinations that were in truth fictional.

Women are still objects without agency, examined and theorized by white medicine. The racialized history of medicine connects with the law to the disadvantage of all women—including white lesbians, people with Substance Use Disorder, and survivors of violence.

CHAPTER 13

The Defense Case for Leigh and Tami

MAMA SHEILA STUBBS ON THE WITNESS STAND

The first witness called for the defense was Mama Sheila.

"Your Honor, I call Sheila Stubbs," Bill Barnett announced.

As she settled into the witness stand, Barnett asked, "Mrs. Stubbs, just tell the jury how you're related to Leigh Stubbs."

"She's my daughter," Sheila responded.

"And you love your daughter, right?"

"Yes."

"And even though you do love your daughter, you wouldn't lie about or for her here today?"

"No, sir, no."

"Now, about this incident that occurred the weekend of the 5th, 6th, do you know firsthand about that weekend?"

"She was home."

"When she went back, did you pack her clothes?"

"I had washed and I packed it all in a black garbage bag because she didn't want to take suitcases out there. So, everything she had was packed in black garbage bags and put in a toolbox so it wouldn't get wet."

"Now, would that be a little old garbage bag or one of the big ones or what size?"

"One of those kind like you put leaves in, outside, great big ones. It has the drawstring."

"Right. Did you speak with anyone up at Cady Hill about what was going on up there that weekend that they were gone?"

"Monday morning, I called and talked to David—he was a director. And I told him what Leigh had told me, and he agreed. He said, 'Yes, we did have some problems.'"

Dunn Lampton shot up, "Objection, your honor, anything he would tell would be hearsay."

"Sustained," the judge declared.

Barnett moved on.

"Mrs. Stubbs, do you know of any violent tendencies of your daughter?"

"No."

"Had Leigh ever spoken to you about Kim Williams before?"

"Yes. They were friends. They had met at Pine Grove in Hattiesburg," Mama Sheila said, and she explained how Leigh and Kim had met.

"Leigh came to me and told me that she had a problem," Mama Sheila explained. "Leigh and her boyfriend—she had a boyfriend for two and a half years and they'd talked about getting married and they broke up in March of '99."

That summer, Mama Sheila said, Leigh "just kind of changed. Everything about her changed. When I questioned her, she said that was her . . . last summer to be a teenager and that everything was fine and she was going to go to school in the fall. But that fall, she went into school, she became more and more depressed."

Mama Sheila told the jury that Leigh, who turned twenty on December 13, had been writing poems. "We had found a poem that she had written about how depressed she was and death. And so, I started talking to her, and she said that she needed help. She told me, 'I can't handle this any longer, I just can't handle this. I'm so depressed, I want to commit suicide, I need help.'"

"So, we checked her into Pine Grove," Mama Sheila said. "She was friends with Kim there. And Kim and another girl and Leigh went to Cady Hill together."

"Is that the extent of her friendship with Kim?" Barnett asked.

"Yes," she replied.

Lampton rose to cross-examine.

"Now where is your daughter today? Where is she living today?"

"In Columbus."

"And who is she living with?"

"Tami."

"And are you aware that she and Tami have a lesbian relationship?" Lampton asked.

"I don't know how to answer that because I've never seen any indication," Mama Sheila replied. "And I know when I go up there, they have two bedrooms and Leigh's bedroom has all of her stuff in it. I've never seen any indication."

"Have you ever asked your daughter?" Lampton pressed.

"No," Sheila answered.

"And you don't know if she's in a lesbian relationship with Tami Vance."

"Not firsthand."

"And you don't know what happened down here in Lincoln County, Mississippi, either, do you?"

"Not firsthand."

"No more questions."

Mama Sheila stepped down from the witness stand.

MISSISSIPPI CRIME LAB ANALYSTS TESTIFY

Amy Winters, a forensic scientist at the Mississippi Crime Laboratory in Jackson, settled into the witness chair. In the majority of cases, she was a witness for the prosecution. On the rare occasion, like this one, she was called by the defense.

Winters testified that Kim's jeans and panties, and the rape kit that Detective Jones had sent to the lab, were negative for the presence of semen. There did appear to be saliva on the exterior of the jeans, so Winters had swabbed the jeans to preserve any DNA. However, neither the prosecutor nor the defense had requested that DNA tests be performed.

During cross-examination, co-prosecutor Jerry Rushing asked Winters a series of questions that were not about forensic analysis, but rather were about oral sex. Rushing became exasperated at Winters's responses.

"I hate to ask you this," Rushing said. "But are you familiar with someone committing oral sex on someone else?"

"Familiar in what means?"

"Well, do they commit oral sex on someone when they're actually wearing their pants or are their clothes removed at the time they do that?"

"I don't know that I could actually testify to that, as to how someone would go about performing that, whether it's typically to have clothing removed or not," Winters replied. "I really don't think that I could testify to that."

"Let me ask you this," Rushing said. "If you saw—had a person who was a victim of a crime and that person had severe lacerations or severe tearing of the vaginal wall, the inside of the vaginal wall, also severe sucking motion of the clitoral area, would you consider the person to be wearing clothes at that time while that was performed on them or not wearing clothes?"

Barnett interjected, "Your honor, I believe that's beyond her expertise. She's a forensic scientist at the crime lab, not qualified to make—"

The judge cut him off. "Why don't you let her answer . . . whether she thinks she can answer that or not?"

Winters responded, "Well, I guess it's always possible that more than likely if someone has had oral sex performed on them that they're not going to be wearing clothes at the time, otherwise, the genitalia would not be exposed."

The next witness, Melissa Schoene, was a trace evidence specialist at the Mississippi Crime Laboratory in Jackson. Schoene physically examined Leigh's pickup truck and the toolbox on March 15 for the presence of blood and hair. That's when she collected the hairs from the toolbox and the blanket in the toolbox. She compared those hairs to hairs from Kim, collected as part of the sexual assault evidence collection kit.

Schoene said that based on her microscopic comparison, none belonged to Kim.

THE COUNSELOR AT CADY HILL

Tina Sullivan, Leigh and Tami's drug and alcohol counselor at Cady Hill, was called to testify next.

"If you were to guess, what would you say would be Tami's outstanding characteristic while there?" asked Ken McNees, Tami's attorney.

"That she was a real person," Sullivan responded. "That she was an honest person with me and her treatment while she was there. She was able to recognize her liabilities and work on them. She was one of those that was willing to work on changing her life and making some changes that would benefit her life."

Sullivan said that on the weekend that Leigh and Tami were gone, Tina discovered the breakdown in the alarm security system. The alarm on the upstairs hall door separating the men and the women gendered facilities failed to work. Sullivan testified that patients were kicked out of Cady Hill after they were caught having sex.

DR. GALVEZ, A FORENSIC PATHOLOGY EXPERT

Barnett then called Dr. Rodrigo Galvez, an expert in pathology who would testify to forensic odontology.

Dr. West was a dentist and a county coroner—an elected official who determines how someone died. Dr. Galvez was a medical examiner whose work was also to determine how someone died, but to do so through conducting an autopsy. He did not win his job in an election.

After medical school, Dr. Galvez took additional training to become a board-certified forensic pathologist. Then he went back to school and became a board-certified psychiatrist. He was noncontroversial. He had never been sanctioned, expelled, suspended, or reprimanded by medical organizations.

Dr. Galvez began his testimony by noting that he did not see any vaginal trauma. "It's important not to make mistakes," he told the jury. "And when I read the first report of Dr. West and then I saw the movies, there was a big mistake . . . There was no trauma to the vagina."

It was seemingly an "Aha!" moment.

But what Dr. Galvez had given life was quickly deflated.

"The trauma was to the vulva, V-U-L-V-A," he said.

"So, I proceed to look at the videotapes, and sure enough, the labia majora, and it was torn more so on the right side than on the left side. There were pieces missing," Galvez concluded.

Significantly, he said that there was no evidence of chewing.

Dr. Galvez testified that he did not see the swelling of the clitoris, didn't see signs of sucking or "severe negative pressure." Dr. Galvez added, "What I can tell you, and I am under oath, with absolute degree of certainty, there is nothing that can prove there was chewing."

But then his testimony—and the defense case itself—went off the rails.

"Could be done by hands, by instrument, sometimes sadistic people get pliers, or those nail pullers," Dr. Galvez speculated. "I know that to you, that is very violent. I've seen it. And when they pull it, clamp and mutilate the nipple, not necessarily chewing. Did I answer your question?"

"Yes, sir," Barnett responded. "Why don't we move on to—why don't we move on to the trauma on her hip."

Dr. Galvez began by explaining that since the latch was at the bottom of the toolbox, if it hit Kim on the hip, there wasn't room for the whole rest of her legs to fit in the toolbox. The latch at the top couldn't have caused the head injury because the lid wasn't heavy enough and the hinges prevented it from being slammed down hard. If Dr. West's hypothesis was that Tami and Leigh were trying to get Kim in the toolbox and she was struggling or looking up, there wasn't the momentum to cause a head injury with the latch. Dr. Galvez then opined about the bite mark on the hip. He was skeptical.

Barnett summarized, "So what you're saying is on the hip it would be very hard to get somebody's entire mouth with every tooth in their mouth to make a bite there?"

"Not to leave so many teeth," Dr. Galvez responded. "You can leave so many teeth marks because you can squeeze and literally take a good bite, but there would be another change, there would be superficial cuts or abrasions or tears on the skin that were not there."

But then Galvez returned to the vulva.

"That in the vulva could be a bite, could be," he suggested. "Although, I am telling you can be done by many other ways, too, because a bite like this chews up a piece of tissue."

Dr. Galvez's primary contribution to the defense was that animal bites are u-shaped, like the mark on Kim's hip, while human bites are round or oval. Problematically, fourteen years later when members of the American Board of Forensic Odontology were asked to examine a bite mark and determine first, whether it was human or animal, and second, whether it matched to the human dentition provided, they couldn't even agree on whether it was an animal or human bite mark.

Ultimately, Dr. Galvez testified that he didn't believe the marks on the hip were the result of a bite by either an animal or a human.

Lampton began his cross-examination by noting that they had crossed paths in the past. This was not surprising for a criminal case in a small town in a rural state.

"Dr. Galvez, good to see you again," Lampton said. "You've testified in this court, you've sat in that chair before."

"Mr. Lampton, I am under oath and I have to tell you the truth, I already had the honor and pleasure to work with you," Dr. Galvez said.

"Thank you," Lampton responded.

"And I take you as a dear friend of mine," Dr. Galvez added.

"We've known each other for several years to say the least," Lampton confirmed. "Twenty-five years. Your hair was dark, so was mine," he chuckled.

This verbal hug fest did not bode well.

And things went downhill from there.

Dr. Galvez revealed that this was his first-ever testimony on bite marks. He had testified as a pathologist and as a psychiatrist, but not on the subject of bite marks. He was not a dentist, let alone a forensic odontologist. He said he did not even know any forensic odontologists.

Lampton asked, "Would you say that the bite mark to the vulva— or you said the mark to the vulva where it was excised or cut off, that that could be a bite?"

"That could be a bite, could be done with other instruments, including the hands," Dr. Galvez conceded. "But in the heat of the moment, sometimes they proceed to tear out pieces of tissue with hands."

"Would you expect to find biting, or would biting be consistent with a lesbian rape type situation? In a homosexual rape?" Lampton asked.

"Yes," Dr. Galvez confirmed. "In homosexual crimes, all, they are very sadistic. Most violent times I've seen in my experience are homosexual to homosexual. They do what we call overkill. They do tremendous damage, tremendous damage."

"They are brutal assaults?" Lampton suggested.

"Yes, sir," Dr. Gonzalez declared. "They're more gory. The more repulsive crimes I've ever seen were homosexual to homosexual."

With that testimonial victory in hand, Lampton moved on to explore Kim's low body temperature when paramedics were summoned to the motel. "Would the low temperature, would that be consistent with someone being placed in a bathtub with ice put on them?"

"Being placed in a bathtub with ice, it will do it, yes, sir," Galvez responded.

Dr. Galvez's testimony capped—some would argue it sunk—the defense case. Tami's attorney didn't call a single witness.

CLOSING ARGUMENTS

Leigh and Tami were facing charges of unlawful possession of morphine and grand larceny, conspiracy to do so, and aggravated assault. Assistant District Attorney Jerry Rushing began his closing argument by referring the jury back to the testimony of emergency room Dr. Moak and to the just-completed testimony of Dr. Galvez.

"Dr. Moak has seen women wounded with childbirth and he says this is the worst. And he used the word 'brutal,' a brutal attack," Rushing said. "Remember when Dr. Galvez took the stand yesterday for the defense? And Dr. Galvez told you about homosexuals and they're the worst attacks he'd ever seen? He told you that they were brutal attacks, didn't he? That's the same word that Dr. Moak used."

"Dr. Moak also saw teeth marks around Kim's breasts," Rushing declared. "He told you that in his opinion, those injuries were eighteen to twenty-four hours old. Note this is after four o'clock on Tuesday, probably closer to at least five or six o'clock. So go back eighteen hours from that period of time, or even go back twenty-four hours, from four o'clock on Tuesday to four o'clock on Monday, who is she with, the only people she's with? It's the defendants in this case."

Based on Dr. Moak's original time estimate—from two to three days—Kim was at Cady Hill and at Dickie's house. But Dr. Moak had reduced his estimate to less than twenty-four hours. The change put

Leigh and Tami in the prosecution's crosshairs—the time when only Leigh and Tami were with Kim.

The prosecutor failed to note how the head injuries remained undiscovered until Kim was at the second hospital, in Jackson, following an hour-long ambulance ride during which Kim experienced seizures.

Rushing shifted his focus to Kim. "You saw her before she testified, walking in here and you saw her take the stand and you saw her condition, how she is today . . . She will never be like she was before, on March 5, 2000. That is forever gone."

Rushing concluded by playing a tape recording of the police interrogation of Tami.

"I know I took morphine and Xanax," Tami said.

"You or Leigh take any of the drugs?"

"I did. Leigh didn't." Tami was honest to the end.

Tami's defense attorney, Ken McNees, stood before the jury.

"I'm glad to be here this morning to represent an innocent woman," McNees began.

He acknowledged that Tami suffered from addiction, but maintained that she was innocent of any assault on Kim Williams.

"You have just heard the tape of my client saying that she took morphine," McNees said. "Tami Vance has taken morphine many times in the past. This is not anything new for Tami Vance to take morphine. Many connections in the Columbus area were there for morphine. These people are notorious takers of drugs, abusers of alcohol. This is nothing unusual. They have their own sources, their own supplies."

Surprisingly, McNees began to sound like Tami was not just a user, but a dealer, someone with easy and continued access, rather than someone who had gone to rehab to seek treatment and help. "They came with their own sources," McNees continued. "They bring it into Cady Hill, and other places. They slip it in. This is not an unusual thing to take place. She took morphine. She had morphine."

"But," McNees finally said, "there is no connective link with the morphine that this young lady, the victim, had with Tami Vance. It hasn't been proven."

McNees pointed out that no drugs were found on Tami or in her control. The black morphine bag was in Kim's suitcase in Kim's possession.

McNees argued that Tami had her own morphine. "Not unusual for drug addicts to have their own morphine," he said. "It's not that expensive. You could have a little pocketful slipped through the door at Cady Hill, maybe. I don't know. Do you?"

And where was the conspiracy? McNees wondered. Kim knew where Dickie's drugs were; Kim had taken his drugs before; Kim took them this time. There was no conspiracy.

Finally, McNees pointed out perhaps the most obvious point of all: there was no blood. "There's been no blood to even link the location," he said.

Bill Barnett, Leigh's attorney, attacked the prosecution's timeline. If Leigh and Tami arrived at the hotel with Kim in the toolbox, when did the alleged assault occur? While on the road from Summit to the hotel?

If so, then how did they put all of Kim's clothes back on her without getting any blood on themselves or the clothes? How did they get Kim in the toolbox or the truck without leaving any blood there?

Where's the blood? He implored the jury, noting that there was no blood in the truck, in the toolbox, there was no blood on Kim's clothes, there was no blood in the hotel room, no blood in the sheets. How could a woman's labia be bitten off and there be no blood?

Barnett moved on to another weakness in the prosecution's theory. How challenging would it be for Leigh to singlehandedly pick up a woman who was her weight and size and lift her out of a toolbox within one second?

He noted that Dr. West claimed the tape showed Leigh bringing Kim's body from the truck but did not see her unloading any luggage or personal items. Barnett repeated what Leigh told the police—she was unloading her clothes that were in a big trash bag.

Barnett emphasized how Dr. Moak's timeline for the infliction of injuries changed from two to four days to twelve to forty-eight hours.

This change eliminated the possibility of anything happening at Cady Hill, before Leigh and Tami returned on Sunday afternoon. Detective Jones hadn't bothered to go to Cady Hill to investigate.

Barnett pointed out that these women were all *friends* and that when Leigh and Tami were leaving and Kim asked to come along, Leigh had assented. Then, Leigh had offered to drive Kim to Summit, in addition to dropping Tami off in Louisiana.

"Friends help friends, and that's what was happening that night," Barnett said. "Friends don't treat friends the way the prosecution would have you believe either one of these two girls treated Kim Williams that night."

He reminded the jury that Leigh and Tami had always cooperated with law enforcement. They talked with the police every time they were asked, and they had even voluntarily returned from out of town. Leigh had agreed to leave her truck with the police. They both voluntarily gave their dental molds. Leigh took a lie detector test. And she had no prior record of committing any crimes or even being arrested.

Barnett then unloaded on Dr. West.

"He's a dentist," Barnett said sarcastically. "And he's telling you folks about vaginal injuries? A dentist?"

"I want to talk about one more thing before I move on. And I don't know about y'all, but I know this ain't Kansas City or New York somewhere, but this stuff about homosexuality and all that kind of stuff, you know, I don't think whether somebody is homosexual or not makes any whit of a difference whether they're innocent or guilty of a crime. You know, maybe a hundred years ago there was some preconceived notions about this stuff, but hey, this is 2001," Barnett said.

Despite this statement, Barnett made sure to argue that Leigh was not a confirmed homosexual. "I don't believe that there was anybody that got on that witness stand, pointed at my client, and said, 'She's a homosexual.' I think somebody got up there and said they were roommates; said they had separate rooms in the house. I don't think that makes a person a homosexual."

In his final appeal, Barnett urged the jury: "We can't convict these girls on junk science. That can't happen. It can't happen."

* * *

The prosecution is entitled to the last word to the jury. The defense only speaks once. Because the prosecutor has the burden of proof they get the final argument, a chance to address issues raised by the defense.

In his rebuttal, Lampton first explained why he did not file any charges against Kim. "I just did not have the heart to come in and try to prosecute her at this stage in her life. I needed her to testify as a witness."

Then he zeroed in on the testimony of Dr. Moak and Dr. Galvez.

"Moak had never seen a woman with these kinds of injuries to her private parts. Never. He said it was brutal," Lampton said. "Dr. Galvez says that a homosexual assault, that he has seen homosexual assaults, and in his opinion, a homosexual assault is the most brutal, involves torture. It's the most senseless kind of assault that he sees. He's using both his psychiatric expertise and his pathological expertise to give this jury the information that, if you believe Dr. Moak when he described the brutality of it, then you would look to see that there is evidence that it is a homosexual rape. There was no semen found and there were bite marks."

The bite marks were of critical importance in Lampton's eyes. "The bites are important because it indicates a homosexual assault. It indicates a sexual assault. Bite marks to the breasts, bite marks to the side, bite marks to the vagina preclude the fact that it could be self-inflicted. You heard Dr. West's testimony and his highest level of certainty is that it is, in fact, a bite mark."

As a measure of his confidence, Lampton said the jurors would have Leigh's dental mold in the deliberation room with them, where they could compare the mold to the photograph of Kim's hip themselves. "You can tell for yourself that that is, in fact, a bite mark," Lampton assured the jury.

But what about the blood?

Lampton noted that Leigh was seen on the surveillance video getting ice from the hotel ice machine. His theory: Leigh got the ice to stop any swelling and bleeding. "That's where the blood went. It went down the drain of the bathtub."

Despite the absence of blood, the timeline boxed Tami and Leigh in as perpetrators.

"We know Kim was brutally injured and we know that it happened while she was in their control, while she was with them. Ladies and gentlemen, if she was injured and they were the only people that were there, and that's what they themselves say, then they had to have injured her, without any question at all."

Lampton wrapped up.

"When you look at all the evidence, you'll realize that while it's a circumstantial evidence case, these two women who were living together, were lovers, whether because of the drugs or the alcohol or their lifestyle, they viciously attacked Kimberly Williams for no reason and tried to cover it up," Lampton said.

Lampton told the members of the jury that the evidence was clear, as was their duty—to consider the evidence presented. And once they did, Lampton told the jurors they would "realize without question" that there was a conspiracy; that Leigh and Tami were guilty of possession of morphine; and that, "without question," Kimberly was the survivor of a sexual assault and "these two women are the ones that caused those injuries to her, and they caused them equally together."

CHAPTER 14
Verdict and Sentencing

Judge Mike Smith released the jury to deliberate. The jurors brought the dental molds back with them, along with the photos, and perhaps most importantly, the videos. They were given a TV and VCR to go through the videos again, if they wished.

Within two and a half hours, the jury reached their verdict. They had been released at 11:09 A.M., and at 1:45 P.M. they told the bailiff they had their conclusion.

It was a unanimous verdict.

Tami and Leigh were guilty on all counts.

Each juror was polled individually. And each nodded their head, individually, when called on, affirming their decision.

Unanimous.

Judge Smith dismissed the jury and proceeded directly to sentencing.

He asked if the victim had a statement. Kim's mom, Judy, spoke up.

"I have put Kimberly in the Lord's hands and He has delivered her from her enemies," she said. "She will shine. She will be a bright star. You have chosen to turn your heads away, to live wicked ways and, therefore, you'll destroy yourselves in your own wickedness. I've got nothing else to say except that the judgment, the jurors, made the right decision."

The judge then asked Tami and Leigh if they had anything to say.

Tami spoke first.

"Kim, you are one of my very best friends and I do not know what happened to you. I am sorry for you and your family, I truly am. And I really wish I knew what had happened to you, but Kim, I don't, and I did not do this."

Leigh declined to say anything.

Judge Smith was ready.

"The testimony is unrebutted that these two defendants had a lesbian relationship," he began. "I don't know whether the victim is of that persuasion or not. The defendants' own expert testified that such people of that persuasion do overkill, do tremendous damage, brutal assault, the most brutal crimes he has ever seen."

He paused. "In addition to the worst injury to her vaginal area that Dr. Moak has ever seen, her other injuries are much more severe."

He addressed Leigh and Tami directly. "You were convicted of all counts of all crimes, particularly possession of these drugs," he said. "I don't think this crime would have happened, this assault would have happened, if it hadn't been for these drugs. I think it goes to show the danger of these drugs and the severity of the drug problem in our country. Hydrocodone . . . If you don't think drugs will kill you, just look at the victim."

The judge began ticking off their sentences.

For the charge of conspiracy to possess morphine and commit the crime of grand larceny: "I'm going to sentence each of you to the maximum on Count One, five years," Judge Smith ruled.

For the charge of possession of morphine: "Because of the severity of the injuries that I believe these drugs caused to the victim, to the maximum of twenty-four years on Count Two."

For the charge of aggravated assault: "The maximum of twenty years on Count Three, due to the severity of the injuries."

"Count One is to be served concurrently with Counts Two and Three. But Counts Two and Three are to be served consecutively."

The grim total: forty-four years in prison.

As a further insult, the judge ordered Leigh and Tami to pay half of the total cost of the expenses of the prosecutor's office, the cost of the medical records, the experts' testimony, and securing all the evidence. That meant they had to pay Dr. West for his testimony.

Judge Smith concluded the proceeding simply. "I place the defendants in the custody of the Sheriff of Lincoln County to begin serving their sentence."

With that, the three days of trial were over, and Leigh's and Tami's lives in prison were beginning. Leigh was twenty-one years old, Tami was thirty-two.

CHAPTER 15
Punishing Identity

I'm brushing my hair in the bathroom. I glimpse my wife as she steps out of the shower.

PROSECUTOR: Dr. West, in a homosexual rape case, you would expect to find bite marks, it would not be unusual at all to find bite marks on the skin?
WEST: No, it wouldn't be unusual.
PROSECUTOR: In fact, it would almost be expected?
WEST: Almost.

We're living in West Virginia. She, a courageous and committed soul, moved to rural West Virginia for us to have a home together. Imagine, a queer lesbian couple in one of the largest towns in West Virginia—a small town anywhere else. West Virginia is like Mississippi that way. The most populated places in the state, as few as there are, are about fifty thousand people. Our neighbor Flip, a big Navy fan, always got along great with my wife who is an Army veteran and badass. Flip was a true neighbor who enjoyed helping us with household repairs, like reversing our ceiling fans on tall ladders or installing new porch doors. But what if we didn't have such kind neighbors? What if our neighbors instead thought of us as violent and dangerous, because we loved each other?

PROSECUTOR: Members of the jury, when you look at all the evidence, you'll realize that while it's a circumstantial evidence case, these two women who were living together, were lovers, whether because of the drugs or the alcohol or their lifestyle, viciously attacked Kimberly Williams for no reason and tried to cover it up.

In West Virginia, I used to require that my Criminal Procedure students participate in ride-alongs with local police officers. It was a small town and I knew the law enforcement leaders. But I hadn't yet realized the number of police officers who sexually assault young women nationally. Society fails women when we refuse to address law enforcement rape of women, particularly women of color and trans women. The second highest complaint of violence by police after use of force is sexual assault. The consistent dehumanization of women pervades the criminal legal system, including the harassment and abuse of women who are only tangentially connected.

DEFENSE ATTORNEY: Dr. West, there's basically not a lot of meat to sink your teeth into right there?
WEST: I don't believe that it's beyond reason that you could get that amount of tissue in your mouth right there.

Nothing, thankfully, ever happened to any of my students.

But the officers were candid about their profiling of Black people, and particularly of interracial couples. The students' reflection papers compelled me to reach out and tell the leadership at the police department. Yet the same experiences occurred the following year. I don't know if it's more upsetting to consider it was the same officers committing the same behavior, or that it was different officers than the prior year, committing the same behavior.

PROSECUTOR: Detective Nolan Jones, at what point in your investigation did Tami and Leigh go from being Good Samaritans to being a suspect?
DETECTIVE JONES: When I viewed the video. I saw, what I believe, where Leigh Stubbs stepped up in the back of the truck, raised

the toolbox, and picked a person up out of that toolbox and stepped off the truck and went in Room 109.

Certain identities are criminalized in the United States. Police can be suspicious of anyone who is not white, not a cisgender male, not middle class or wealthy, not a citizen, not able-bodied, or not performing heterosexuality or gender conformity. Police even arrest straight white wealthy men sometimes, but these defendants are far more likely to be able to negotiate or buy themselves out of punishment.

Laws codify existing prejudices and status. Segregation laws, anti-miscegenation laws, Defense of Marriage Acts, the denial of citizenship status for non-white people, the list goes on. How police, prosecutors, and judges implement these laws solidify tangible differences in wealth and social status—which become the social basis to justify the biased laws. Actors in the legal system use the resulting disparities to perpetuate the idea that they punish the "right" people.

At the time of Leigh and Tami's trial in 2001, anyone performing oral sex—sodomy—was committing a crime in Mississippi. Mississippi's sodomy law was broad and covered oral and anal sex, including oral sex between people of the opposite gender. Mississippi first criminalized sodomy in 1802 making "unnatural intercourse" a felony. A 1950s Mississippi Supreme Court decision found a blowjob was "unnatural, detestable, and abominable, and . . . it was within the intention of the Legislature to make it a felony."

But who gets prosecuted and punished is not just about who has violated the law, it's about power. When Dr. West testified about oral sex on women, he conceded, "I've done it, but I'm not an expert." He committed sodomy, and his own sexual behavior was illegal. But Michael West was on the stand, not behind bars.

When I lived in Mississippi I was in a serious relationship with a Black man. He was a smart and talented man with an exceptional family. His mother—a judge; his father—a litigator before the U.S. Supreme Court; his brother—an elected district attorney. All of them were influential, respected, and successful. Yet they were not immune to racism. They experienced discriminating policing, stops, and even wrongful arrests simply because they are Black. And me, as a white woman, further endangered my partner because police profile Black men with white women. In his town, a Confederate Memorial stood in front of the county courthouse. From the front it looked like a male soldier with a flag, and from the side it looked like a sheeted member of the Ku Klux Klan.

When police and prosecutors unjustly enforce laws, we must have other remedies before someone loses their freedom. When judges and juries unjustly convict people, we must recognize manifest injustice, and free them.

CHAPTER 16
Women in Rankin Prison, Mississippi

Interstate 55, down from Memphis, intersects with Batesville on its way south to Jackson, Mississippi. Perhaps surprisingly, Batesville is home to Magnolia Grove Monastery, a mindfulness practice center established by followers of Thich Nhat Hanh. Batesville also has a Chili's. I watched and celebrated the Saints victory over the Colts in the 2010 Super Bowl at that Chili's—my adopted regional home team, since Mississippi doesn't have professional sports teams, versus my birthplace home team for Indiana. At the time, alcohol couldn't be sold on Sundays in my nearby town of Oxford, and the restaurants closed on Sunday and Wednesday evenings when people went to church services and mid-week potluck dinners. Chili's, half an hour away, was open on Sundays, had a TV, and had beer.

I'd also stop at that Chili's late at night on my way back from visiting Rankin prison. Technically named Central Mississippi Correctional Facility, I could make it to Rankin in just under two hours from Batesville, speeding down the interstate with the Mississippi Delta to the west. Rankin prison, nicknamed after the county, is just east of the state capital, Jackson. The last stretch of the drive includes an oak-lined road far older than the tar and asphalt. Then the road curves past Whitfield, the state mental hospital. Whitfield was itself built on a former penal colony, and originally was known as the Mississippi State Insane Asylum. Similar to the farm prisons of the South like Parchman in Mississippi and Angola in Louisiana, Whitfield Hospital was at one time self-sufficient with 3,500 acres and working inhabitants. But people incarcerated at Parchman prison farm had a target date to end their sentence. At Whitfield, people walked in and never walked out. Whitfield today has an official nursing home for residents.

Whitfield also now has a unit for Substance Use Services, though many Mississippians with substance use disorder are farther down around the bend in the road at Rankin prison. Rankin is the only prison for women in the state, meaning no matter where they're from they can't be moved to a prison closer to their family, or to their children. The only option for women is Rankin. Trans women are often placed in male prisons around the state that don't correspond to their gender.

Leigh and Tami moved to Rankin after they were sentenced by Judge Smith. I'd visit them every month or two, updating them on their case, asking about them and their health, and checking if there were any other women we should be representing. Not that the Mississippi Innocence Project had the bandwidth—we were a small nonprofit and clinic out of the University of Mississippi School of Law. But at least we could try.

Sometimes the only way these women got out of prison was thanks to community mobilization, pressure on politicians, and attention from outside of the prison walls. Community fury is powerful, and prosecutors should not have a corner on outrage.

The stories below show how community outrage freed people when the legal system stalled.

Our guide through Rankin is another one of my clients, Tasha Mercedez Shelby. Incarcerated for over twenty years and still in prison today, Tasha has worked jobs inside at the Hair Zone, in the mailroom, as a tutor, and in the chapel. Most of the women she knew in this chapter are cisgender women.

Individuals who are identify or are perceived as gender-nonconforming, such as people who are trans or non-binary, face additional challenges because they are often forced into prisons that don't correspond with their gender. Tasha knew an intersex person who identified as masculine through delivering mail to the women's Maximum Security Unit—the MSU. MSU is solitary confinement. Tasha delivered mail from friends who sent "masculine" toiletries, a form of humanity. People who are gender non-conforming are cruelly housed in solitary confinement when prisons fail to consider other solutions—and even the solitary confinement units are gendered.

Each Christmas, the prison chaplain would send gift bags to the people incarcerated in the prison. The gift bags were gendered: "feminine gifts" or "masculine gifts." Tasha was working in the chapel when she received a note from a trans woman in solitary confinement housed in the male MSU. She wanted a feminine gift bag.

When the chaplain said yes, Tasha put together the bag: barrettes, hair bows, "girly" shampoo, and deodorant. Even in these small ways, the recognition of someone's identity matters. And it is often people on the outside creating both that recognition and change for incarcerated people.

STATE-SANCTIONED SEXUAL ASSAULT

Tasha, Leigh, and Tami were incarcerated with about 1,400 women at Rankin. The majority of incarcerated women are sexual abuse and assault survivors, who enter or leave with trauma-induced disabilities including PTSD, depression, and anxiety. Transgender and gender nonconforming people in prisons suffer physical and sexual harassment and abuse in prison at even higher rates than cisgender women.

Tasha, Leigh, and Tami spent years being strip-searched for every visit with family members or with me, their attorney. Each visit, the women had to remove all of their clothes and be examined and searched by fully clothed guards. The purpose of strip searches is nominally to search for contraband; it is overwhelmingly to denigrate the individual and their body, insult and humiliate them, emphasize their powerlessness, and turn them from a human with a soul into an object, a body. The message is that their body does not matter and that their body does not belong to them.

Tasha, Leigh, and Tami rarely mentioned the searches. They were a mandatory concession in order to see their family, friends, or attorneys.

One horrific example haunts me. A prison in Illinois was conducting a routine "training exercise for cadet guards." The guards brought two hundred incarcerated and handcuffed women into a room with male and female cadets, prison guards, and even civilian observers. The guards forced the incarcerated women to take off all their clothes and stand naked in front of the watching people.

The incarcerated women stood so close together that their bodies touched. They were ordered to remove tampons and sanitary pads, menstrual blood dripping down their legs and onto the floor. The guards, the cadets, the civilians, were all watching, all fully clothed. And under those staring eyes, the guards ordered the women to do what they're required to do before every family member visit, before every attorney visit: "raise their breasts, lift their hair, turn around, bend over, spread their buttocks and vaginas, and cough."

This was a routine training exercise. It's also rape culture. It is state-sanctioned sexual assault.

TASHA MERCEDEZ SHELBY: WRONGFULLY CONVICTED

I first learned about Tasha from Leigh and Tami. They told me about two women whom they believed to be innocent in prison. Tasha was one of them.

Tasha moved to Mississippi when she was a teenager. She attended high school through the tenth grade, when she became pregnant with her son Dakota and left school to work. Time passed, Tasha raised her son, and she started dating Big Bryan. Big Bryan was a few years older and had just gotten his long-haul trucking license. Big Bryan had a son of his own who was the same age as Dakota, two and a half years old. They called him Little Bryan. Little Bryan was big for his age, weighing thirty-three pounds and standing three feet tall.

He was already half the height of Tasha, who is a little person at four feet nine inches tall.

They were soon all living together in their own home, a trailer in Biloxi, close to the long beaches and water of the Gulf. Little Bryan was on a nebulizer for his asthma and had absence seizures, where he would stare off into space. Tasha and Big Bryan worried about him and took him to the pediatrician, who recommended a neurologist. The family made an appointment with the neurologist for mid-June.

Despite the concern about Little Bryan, the blended family was happy. Tasha was pregnant with a little girl. When she gave birth to that little girl in May, they named her Devin. Tasha had a C-section and at the same time she had the surgeon tie her tubes; their family was complete.

Tasha was on bedrest after surgery and the birth of her daughter, and she stayed in the hospital days after giving birth. Tasha's doctor prescribed her pain pills for the C-section, but she couldn't afford them. The doctor advised against any heavy lifting, bending over, or exertion that could rip the stitches in her body. She had a hard enough time picking up her newborn baby. Her relatives would come by and pick up Dakota to give Tasha a break while Big Bryan worked a night shift at 9 Lumber.

It was on one of those evenings when Dakota was with relatives, and Tasha had put the baby and Little Bryan to sleep, when she heard a loud thump from Little Bryan's room. She went into his room to find Little Bryan convulsing on the floor. He had fallen out of his bed and was having a seizure. He couldn't breathe.

Tasha called the hospital where she had just given birth to Devin, and they told her to come in immediately—driving would be faster than an ambulance.

Tasha then called Big Bryan to come home and started performing CPR on Little Bryan. When her fiancé arrived, they all rushed to the hospital—so fast that police pulled them over. Big Bryan yelled at the police that he needed to get to the hospital. He started to drive off, but not before one of the officers jumped in their van and took over for Tasha performing CPR.

In the Emergency Room the doctors tried to revive Little Bryan.

It was too late. Little Bryan was brain dead from the lack of oxygen. His brain was swollen, and he had a trace of bleeding in his brain. They took him off of the oxygen machine the next day.

The hospital called the police to investigate if Little Bryan's death was the result of child abuse. The police interrogated Tasha. She said what she always has said since: she heard a thump, Little Bryan was on the floor having a seizure and not able to breathe, and she started performing CPR. She was never able to revive him.

At the time of Little Bryan's death, doctors did not yet know how damaging short falls can be, or how seizures can interact with a short fall. Instead, in 1997 the theory of "Shaken Baby Syndrome" was more prevalent in legal and medical fields than it is today. That theory held that when a baby—usually less than six months old—presented with three specific symptoms (bleeding around the brain, bleeding in the back of the eyes, and brain swelling), then the child must have been shaken to death.

Little Bryan had brain swelling and a tiny spot of subdural hemorrhaging, but no retinal hemorrhaging. Even though Tasha's story never changed, no one believed that short falls or seizures could account for Little Bryan's symptoms. The autopsy report concluded that Little Bryan's death was the result of homicide. As the only person who had been at home with the child, Tasha was arrested and charged.

It was her first time ever being arrested.

Big Bryan married Tasha shortly after Little Bryan's death. Then Tasha was booked into jail to await her trial.

Tasha waited three years. By that point, relatives had taken both her daughter and her son; Big Bryan did not keep custody of their newborn daughter.

When Tasha went to trial, her defense attorneys agreed with the diagnosis that Little Bryan had been shaken to death—everyone did. But her attorneys argued that Big Bryan was the culprit. Tasha was four feet nine inches in height, and she had given birth via C-section and had her fallopian tubes removed less than two weeks earlier. How could she pick up a thirty-three-pound toddler and shake him forcefully enough to kill him? Tasha told her attorneys about the short fall, she told them about the appointment with the neurologist scheduled for a week after Little Bryan's death, she told them about the seizures and Little Bryan's asthma and nebulizer. None of it mattered.

In the very first sentence of the State's opening statement against Tasha Shelby, the prosecutor told the jury, "On May 30th, 1997, Tasha Shelby shook a two-and-a-half-year-old child, Bryan Thompson, so violently that the child died the next day from those injuries." By the end of the trial, the prosecutor told the jury, "[t]he things in this case, ladies and gentlemen, that are not in dispute . . . Bryan Thompson was violently shaken to death. That is undisputed." At the time of trial, that statement was correct: it was undisputed.

The State's star witness was medical examiner Dr. LeRoy Riddick. Dr. Riddick had performed the autopsy. He testified that Little Bryan was violently shaken to death. He dismissed that the injuries could be caused by a short fall or another non-abuse-related accident.

Tasha's defense witness, similar to Leigh and Tami's defense witness, agreed with the State that the cause of death was Shaken Baby Syndrome.

In 2000, the jury found Tasha guilty of capital murder. She was terrified of going to death row. But then the jury sentenced her to life in prison instead, without any hope of parole.

In 2008, Audrey Edmunds became the first person to be exonerated on the basis of the newly discovered unreliability of Shaken Baby Syndrome.

In 2010, I first met Tasha. All these years later, I am still representing her. Since the time of her trial, advancements in pediatric medicine, traumatic medicine, and biomechanical engineering have undermined the State's essential contentions. The Centers for Disease Control and Prevention now identify falls as the most common cause of traumatic brain injury in children less than four years old.

The advancements in science also led the State's original forensic pathologist, Dr. LeRoy Riddick, to change his opinion on the cause and manner of death.

In 1997, Dr. Riddick concluded that Little Bryan's death was a homicide—in line with the prevailing wisdom of the time. However, upon reexamining his records in 2015, Dr. Riddick believed that he made a mistake with his diagnosis.

Dr. Riddick changed the cause of death on Little Bryan's death certificate from homicide to accident. He then testified for Tasha at a Post-Conviction Relief Hearing, along with three other defense medical experts.

The courts have not yet reversed Tasha's conviction or granted her any relief. She remains at Rankin. And as such, she is our guide through this chapter of wrongfully convicted women in Rankin.

WOMEN ON DEATH ROW

As the only prison for women in the state, Rankin is home to the women on death row in Mississippi. At the time of my regular visits to Rankin, there were only two women on death row. Both were white and both were completely isolated. Lisa Jo Chamberlin was sentenced to death in 2006. Michelle Byrom was on death row until 2014.

Lisa Jo admits to her crime. But Michele Byrom was innocent, and freed thanks to community outrage and journalistic investigations.

Not many women are sentenced to death, but when they are, prosecutors often use gender stereotypes against the women, characterizing them as "abnormal." Poor parenting, rarely used against cisgender men, is frequently claimed against cisgender women defendants.

Michelle Byrom was one of those women.

Michelle's son Eddie Jr. shot and killed his abusive father Eddie Byrom Sr. Michelle was in the hospital when her son killed her husband. Indeed, she was in treatment on multiple prescribed medications at the hospital. Nevertheless, Tishomingo County Sheriff David Smith came to the hospital to interrogate Michelle about the murder. He encouraged Michelle to help out her son, to take ownership. He told Michelle that she must have hired someone, an accomplice, making this a conspiracy to murder. Michelle told the sheriff that she would take responsibility for her husband's death.

After Michelle's statement to the sheriff, the local prosecutors charged her with capital murder. At trial, Eddie Jr. testified against Michelle, stating under oath that his mom had hired his friend Joey Gillis to kill Eddie Sr. The jury found Michelle guilty.

Before sentencing in capital cases, defense attorneys present evidence of why their client should not receive the death penalty. A psychologist had evaluated Michelle and uncovered that Michelle's stepfather had sexually abused her. Michelle ran away from home to escape the sexual violence and worked as a stripper to support herself. Her relationship with Eddie Sr. began when she was only fifteen years old and Eddie Sr. was thirty-one. Eddie Sr. physically and sexually abused Michelle, forcing her to have sex with him and with other men. Michelle tried to leave but her husband threatened her with violence every time. With no resources to support herself and her son, Michelle stayed.

The male prosecutor at trial, Arch Bullard, used this against her. "There's been arguments made that maybe Eddie wasn't the husband or the father that he should've been," he told the jury. "Why didn't she just leave him? Why didn't she divorce him? Why didn't she seek sanctuary somewhere else?"

Michelle did—she would ingest rat poison in order to have a reprieve in the hospital from her home life. Michelle suffered from depression, alcohol dependence, and mental health issues. Her male attorneys did not present this information, or any of Michelle's history. They then waived her constitutional right to a jury sentencing and asked the judge to sentence her instead.

Circuit Judge Thomas Gardner sentenced Michelle to death.

It was only in 2014, when Attorney General Jim Hood requested an execution date of March 27, that Michelle's case actually received any scrutiny. That attention and ultimate outrage came from citizens and the media.

Journalists uncovered four written confessions by Michelle's son—all of which were known by the defense attorneys at the time of trial, and by the judge who sentenced her to death. Eddie Jr. even led the police to the murder weapon.

These white men in the courtroom had committed the true conspiracy—not conspiracy to murder, conspiracy to convict an innocent woman. Eddie Jr., Joey Gillis and Tishomingo Sheriff David Smith; then prosecutor Arch Bullard, Michelle's defense attorneys, and Judge Thomas Gardner all knew about the repeated confessions by Michelle's son. The only people who didn't know about the confessions were the jury. When the defense attorneys tried to admit some of the confessions at trial, Judge Gardner denied their request.

In 2014, weeks before Michelle's scheduled execution, citizens organized a call-in campaign to the governor's office. The *Jackson Free Press* covered Michelle's case and exposed the confessions. It worked.

In a shocking move, the Mississippi Supreme Court denied the attorney general's request for an execution date, and then reversed Michelle's conviction on March 31, 2014. Days after Michelle was initially set to be executed by the State of Mississippi by lethal injection, she was instead leaving prison.

Michelle was free thanks to community advocacy.

But that's not the end of the story.

The prosecutor re-brought the same charges against Michelle. He demanded that Michelle be incarcerated until her new trial, rather than released on bail. The prosecutor couldn't charge the true perpetrator because Eddie Jr. had pled guilty to a lesser offense in exchange for testifying against his mother.

Michelle sat in jail for a year pending the new trial, just as Kenny Brewer had, incarcerated while the prosecutors waited them out.

Michelle's prosecutor was in no rush. But after sixteen years in prison, and fourteen of those years on death row, Michelle wanted to live the rest of her life free. The prosecutor offered her an Alford plea—she could plead guilty to the crime but maintain her innocence, instead saying the state had enough evidence to convict her rather than that she was guilty. In exchange, Michelle would get a sentence of "time-served" and walk free.

Michelle took the Alford plea. The prosecutor and judge agreed to release her from jail.

Michelle didn't know how little of her life would remain. While she was on death row she had developed breast cancer. The cancer bloomed across her body to stage IV, a reality she learned only when she went to a doctor as a free woman. Michelle died of breast cancer after three and a half years of freedom, in 2019.

Her son, Eddie Jr., who killed his father and set up his mother to take the blame, had choice words on her death: "Life's a lot like poker, sometimes you just don't have a winning hand . . . I believe she did the best she could with the hand she was dealt."

He helped deal that hand against her, along with the police and players in the criminal legal system.

Michelle was not the only woman ever wrongfully convicted on Mississippi's death row, set to be executed for a crime she didn't commit. Sabrina Butler, a Black woman from Columbus, Mississippi, was the first woman on Mississippi's death row. At just seventeen, Sabrina was charged with murdering her baby son Walter. In her own powerful book Sabrina writes: "I was a teenager who, less than 24 hours before, had lost my precious baby boy. Ambitious men questioned, demoralized and intimidated me. In that state of mind, I signed the lies they wrote on a piece of paper."

Sabrina lived on death row for thirty-three months, and in prison for five years, until she was exonerated and proven not guilty in 1995 with proof that her son died from natural causes.

The prosecutor who brought the murder charge against teenage Sabrina, Forrest Allgood, also wrongfully convicted at least three Black men with the assistance of Dr. West: Kenny Brewer, Levon Brooks, and Eddie Lee Howard. In 2015 Forrest Allgood's reign as prosecutor in Columbus finally ended when he was defeated by challenger Scott Colom. Scott's father, a widely known and well-respected attorney, was a board member of the Mississippi Innocence Project. Change is possible.

Michelle Byrom and Lisa Jo Chamberlin were isolated from anyone else in the prison. But on occasion, the women on Mississippi's death row could have a reminder that they were human. They could have another person touch them kindly.

Tasha Shelby was the hairdresser at the Hair Zone—a salon in the women's prison. Tasha earned her cosmetology licenses while inside, and women could pay from their canteen to get their hair done up, share gossip, and get some personal attention.

Tasha cut Lisa's and Michelle's hair, an intimate experience for these women on death row. She tended to Lisa's long brown hair, an act of normalcy bringing them together. Even under the constant gaze of guards, it was a reminder of being human, of having an identity. Lisa would be bubbly and talkative the whole time, excited to see Tasha, catching up on her nails and hair. Michelle was subdued and quiet, never causing any trouble.

The guards would set up a barber chair in a little room in the Maximum Security Unit. Tasha had been in the MSU when she initially came to Rankin because she has a life sentence for a crime she did not commit. All women with a life sentence first go to MSU and then work their way to more freedom—within the prison, that is.

MSU is solitary confinement. The United Nations Mandela Rules, named after South African president Nelson Mandela who was imprisoned for twenty-seven years during South Africa's apartheid, define solitary confinement as twenty-two hours a day or more without meaningful human contact. Solitary confinement has existed in the

United States as a "solution" since the founding of our country. Cells are designed to block human interaction with solid metal doors, a combined toilet-and-sink in the cell, and little or no access to windows or natural light. Food can be inserted on a tray through a slot in the metal door. People in solitary can't participate in educational or vocational programs, and generally can't have televisions, radios, and only limited reading material. They exercise in a single person cage; sometimes outside sometimes not. And again, visits with family are limited and frequently no-contact.

The Mandela Rules prohibit prolonged solitary confinement, defined as more than fifteen days, because solitary confinement harms people. Isolating people from anyone else actually changes our brain activity. We as humans suffer mentally and physically from enforced isolation with panic attacks, paranoia, hallucinations, depression, self-harm, and suicide.

When Tasha first came to MSU she cried so hard that one of the sergeants took notice.

"Shelby, what is wrong with you?"

"Sergeant, it's just me in here. And . . . I've never gone this long without a hug."

One of the hardest sergeants then came and sat on the metal cot next to Tasha. She turned to Tasha and hugged her. Tasha cried into her arms.

Tasha never forgot. Each time she'd cut Lisa's and Michelle's hair, she'd ask the guard if she could give them a hug at the end. A simple gesture. A physical kindness that women on Mississippi's death row could otherwise only receive from a chaplain or guards.

ORGANIZING COMMUNITY ACTIVISM TO FREE WOMEN

Through Tasha, I met still other women—women who were freed due to community activism.

Tasha shared a cell with Jamie Scott, a Black woman sentenced along with her sister Gladys to life in prison for stealing $11.

Jamie and Gladys had no prior arrests or convictions when they were arrested by the Scott County Sheriff's Department for armed robbery on December 24, 1993, Christmas Eve. At the time, both sisters were working full time at a nearby chicken-processing plant and at

Hardee's. The sisters started working before graduating from high school in order to support their families. Three teenage boys confessed to a robbery, and implicated Jamie and Gladys in the crime. In exchange for sentences of ten months to two years each, the boys gave statements to the police. They said that Jamie and Gladys were the masterminds of the robbery, even though the sisters hadn't even been present. Gladys was nineteen years old and Jamie was twenty-one.

The teenage boys testified at trial. Howard Patrick testified that the deputy sheriff told him that "if I didn't participate with them, they would send me to Parchman and make me out to be female." Only fourteen years old, Howard was kept in jail until the Scott sisters' trial.

The jury found Gladys and Jamie both guilty of armed robbery and sentenced them to two life sentences—each. Gladys was pregnant at the time and gave birth to her child while incarcerated, shackled to a hospital bed.

Attorney Chokwe Lumumba took on the sisters' case on direct appeal and post-conviction. In post-conviction, he obtained a written statement by the only Patrick boy who didn't testify, Chris. In the signed affidavit, Chris said the Scott sisters had nothing to do with the $11 robbery. Lumumba gathered affidavits from other witnesses that the sheriff's office was coercive.

The courts refused to grant any relief to the Scott sisters.

In 2010, Jamie's kidneys began to fail and she went on dialysis. When the prison moved Jamie to its intensive care unit, family members and supporters began a petition for her to be released from prison. Jamie and Gladys's mom, Evelyn Rasco, began a "Free the Scott Sisters" blog, and talked with nonprofit organizations and the press. Lumumba by that point had become a councilman in Jackson, Mississippi, and he would later become mayor of Jackson. Lumumba filed a request for medical release. The prison denied it.

Then Lumumba filed a petition for pardon with Mississippi governor Haley Barbour, and organized a rally at the state capital for the next day. After sixteen years of incarceration, Governor Barbour granted clemency to Jamie and Gladys. He ordered them released from prison—on the bizarre condition that Gladys had to donate a kidney to Jamie. She did.

Community organizing had freed the two women and helped them regain their lives outside.

Can we do the same for Tasha? We're on social media, in contact with reporters, and I've talked with her family about purchasing a billboard, explaining her case in downtown Jackson, Mississippi—and in Los Angeles. We've drafted letters to the governor and the commissioner for the Mississippi Department of Corrections, asking for her sentence to be commuted. In the meantime, we fight her case in the courts, with claims of innocence and manifest injustice. In our last court hearing, she had friends, family, church members, professors, lawyers, and even state legislators in the audience supporting her. Next time we will have more.

CHAPTER 17

Wrongly Convicted Women: Criminalizing Sex and Pregnancy

Innocence projects represent a shockingly low number of women. There is a softball explanation for this gender-disparate reality: more men are incarcerated than women. Thus, the odds are that more men are wrongfully convicted than women. In addition, many DNA exonerees are men wrongly convicted of sexual assault. They were freed because someone finally tested the rape kit and the sperm: not a match.

But this chapter is for women who are wrongly convicted or whose convictions are manifestly unjust. This chapter is for women who aren't seen as victims, who aren't seen as innocent. I speak here of women routinely arrested, with charges affecting thousands of them.

This chapter is a familiar story of controlling women's bodies through incarceration. Prosecutors and police may vigilantly patrol, arrest, and charge girls and women for crimes involving how they use their own bodies. Girls and women may be legally innocent and yet morally condemned for these crimes, such as sex work and drug use, particularly if they are pregnant. Women are, frequently en masse, wrongly convicted of prostitution, and child endangerment due to legal or illegal drug use during pregnancy.

In this chapter, I'll address prostitution charges against youth and trafficked individuals, child abuse charges for drug use by a pregnant person—regardless of whether they know they are pregnant—and prosecutorial discretion to bring these charges. May innocence advocates also fight for the freedom of these women, and prosecutors educate their offices on legal innocence and the fallout from these prosecutions.

MASS MISDEMEANOR WRONGFUL CONVICTIONS

Recently, innocence work has drawn attention to widespread faulty drug convictions. Not every misdemeanor drug case can be challenged, but police and prosecutor patterns of behavior and mass wrongful convictions can. These cases include faulty police roadside drug tests, where a cashew is misidentified as a crack-rock, or the police testimony of smelling burnt marijuana—while planting drug evidence in the car. Innocent defendants, usually men, took pleas in these misdemeanor or nonviolent felony cases because the stakes were relatively, seemingly, low.

Innocence organizations represent these men in mass misdemeanor cases, zeroing in on police or prosecutor or crime lab malfeasance. This is valuable work. However, innocence organizations do not represent trafficked women who are convicted of prostitution, pregnant women who are taking prescription medication and convicted of child endangerment, and girls and queer youth who cannot legally consent to sex but are arrested and convicted for sex work. These are also mass misdemeanor—or felony—wrongful convictions.

LEGAL INNOCENCE AND SEX WORK

Ninety-one percent of trafficking survivors have been arrested for a sex offense, and 42 percent of them were minors when they were arrested. Children cannot be guilty of prostitution if they are below the age of consent as a matter of law. They cannot legally say yes to sex. But instead of acknowledging their legal innocence, many prosecutors charge, convict, and label children as prostitutes and deviant sexual criminals.

Girls are not seen and treated as girls. They are labeled as knowing adults, with courts objectifying girls by their body parts and apparent physical maturity. Additionally, prostitution is not a race-neutral charge. Black girls are more likely to be trafficking victims, and more likely to be arrested for prostitution, than white girls. They have a higher likelihood of being punished and incarcerated through the juvenile criminal legal system.

Police, prosecutors, and judges misperceive Black girls as less "innocent" and more adult than white girls, even of the same age. Their adultification means that Black girls are labeled in the courtroom as willing participants in sex trades, rather than as victims.

Black girls have been hypersexualized since the time of slavery. Today, they are more likely to be caught up in the sex trade, either by a "boyfriend" or as a means of survival. Traffickers interviewed by the Urban Institute shared that they "believe[d] trafficking Black women would land them less jail time than trafficking white women if caught."

Due to these factors, Amnesty International has called for sex work decriminalization as a racial justice issue. Decriminalization would allow sex workers to go to police if they feared or suffered violence. It would allow more women to leave the trade without the stigma of a criminal conviction.

"Feminine" is historically and continually reinforced as white, straight, and middle-class. Actors in the legal system target and punish women and gender non-conforming people who do not fall into those categories. Police arrest people they perceive as visibly and easily associated with sexual "deviance," be that influenced by race, class, or sexual orientation. They disproportionately profile trans and queer women as sex workers, leading to criminal prosecutions.

Innocence organizations do not challenge these patterns of charging by prosecutors. Yet they are wrongful convictions, and they are charging patterns that can be changed.

The Trafficking Victims Protection Act (TVPA), and many state anti-trafficking laws, define sex trafficking as "a commercial sex act induced by force, fraud, or coercion, or in which the person induced to perform such act has not attained 18 years of age." Police, however, frequently maximize their prostitution arrest numbers, instead of assisting or protecting sex workers and trafficked individuals. Police still arrest the trafficked individual: for prostitution, possessing a weapon or drugs, or truancy if they are a minor.

As white saviors, police and prosecutors may even treat an arrest as a charitable "rescue." This ignores how sex workers' criminal convictions make it even more difficult for them to attain stability to leave the sex trade. Criminal records block employment opportunities, access to affordable and safe housing and public benefits, and even funds or admission to higher education.

In some states, prosecutors cannot criminally charge and prosecute youth for prostitution because of Safe Harbor laws. These laws provide immunity for minors from prostitution prosecutions when they cannot legally consent to sex in any other context. Safe Harbor laws also support sex workers and trafficked people to leave dangerous circumstances.

Thirty-five states have enacted laws that permit the courts to vacate the prostitution-related convictions of underage teenagers. Those teenagers, of course, were nonetheless arrested and prosecuted in the first instance and never represented by innocence organizations. The fact that underage people may be engaging in independent survival sex work shouldn't complicate their innocence under the law.

MYTHS AND REALITIES OF DRUG USE DURING PREGNANCY

During the 1980s crack-cocaine epidemic, news outlets hysterically pushed out stories on "crack babies." The narrative posited that a new generation of children would suffer birth defects and lifelong health problems because their mothers had used cocaine. Crack babies became a symbol for "bad" moms, and a reason to criminalize and punish individuals who used drugs while pregnant. Dubious charities like C.R.A.C.K.—Children Requiring A Caring Kommunity—provided "free" and even compensated sterilization to women of color with a history of illegal drug use.

Time gave us the ability to witness those so-called crack babies grow up. Years later science proved one thing: those children became healthy adults. In fact, the use of crack cocaine during pregnancy is no more harmful for the baby than smoking cigarettes—which is decidedly legal. The alleged problem of "crack babies" was based on junk science.

In our drug overdose crisis, prosecutors are restoring laws from the crack-cocaine epidemic, charging women for using opioids while pregnant. In twenty-three states, prosecutors can bring child abuse charges for parental drug use beginning at the time of conception—long before the mother may know she is pregnant.

CRIMINALIZING DRUG USE TO "HELP" PREGNANT MOTHERS

In 2014, Tennessee legislators created the crime of fetal assault. Sullivan County District Attorney Barry Staubus testified in favor of creating the new crime. Sullivan County was in the throes of a severe opioid overdose epidemic and prosecutor Staubus reasoned that the new crime would "help" women with drug use disorder.

Staubus testified, "I think when we see this statute . . . we are going to be able to bring lots and lots of women into a program we're creating specifically for drug addicted mothers." One legislator described the criminal prosecutions as "offering mothers the help they so desperately need but cannot obtain on their own." Another legislator supported the bill reasoning "drugs tend to take your right mind away . . . [with the] discipline . . . [of the] court system . . . [the mothers can] go back to being the nurturing caring parents that they would want to be."

The statute only stayed on the books for two years but during that time prosecutors brought fetal assault charges almost exclusively against low-income women. Prosecutors relied heavily on information from health care providers who told police about drug use. Once charged, these women experienced jail, bail, fines, and probation with the threat of more punishment. Pregnant women faced the same challenges and punishment that most people face when they are prosecuted, including enormous pressure to plead guilty.

They also faced losing custody of their children.

Despite the justification of "helping" women, the only "care" poor women received from the state were criminal charges, prosecutions, and convictions.

INTERPRETING LAWS TO CONTROL THE
BEHAVIOR OF PREGNANT WOMEN

What range of habits, conditions, actions, or inactions, will our government criminalize if done by a pregnant person? Once prosecutors criminalize the behavior of pregnant women due to the possible impact on a fetus, such line drawing becomes blurry.

In 2011, Mississippians voted down a proposed personhood amendment to the state constitution. Since then, other states have proposed similar amendments. The personhood amendment would codify that life begins at conception. Assumably, the law could criminalize a pregnant person's behavior starting at conception as well. What would be illegal behavior for a pregnant person?

In 2011, 14 percent of women in Mississippi reported smoking cigarettes in the third trimester of pregnancy, which is a known risk factor for a fetus. Smoking and proximity to secondhand smoke is unhealthy for a fetus. Drinking alcohol is a known contributor to fetal alcohol syndrome. Indeed, eating fish and drinking unpasteurized milk can also be problematic. And personhood laws could move beyond reckless endangerment to criminalize failure to act—failing to have adequate prenatal medical care, for example, or failing to submit to bedrest.

As the Maryland Supreme Court stated in a similar case, "criminal liability would depend almost entirely on how aggressive, inventive, and persuasive any particular prosecutor might be." The Court was considering whether a pregnant woman who ingested cocaine could be convicted of creating a substantial risk of harm to another person.

In Alabama, legislators passed a "chemical endangerment" law to criminalize meth labs and punish the exposure of a "child" to an "environment in which controlled substances are produced or distributed." Prosecutors used this law to criminally charge pregnant women who tested positive for drug use. Prosecutors equated the womb with a meth lab. Alabama courts agreed.

This meth lab child endangerment law was never intended to apply to pregnant people who wanted to carry their babies to term while struggling with drug use. Those pregnant defendants are legally innocent.

Alabama has prosecuted hundreds of women for drug use during pregnancy, a mass pattern of behavior that can be challenged by innocence organizations. Many state courts have ruled that the state cannot criminally punish a pregnant person for continuing their pregnancy despite an underlying health problem, such as substance use disorder.

These laws are not really about harm to the fetus. They are about negatively labeling the mother. If a pregnant woman had a prescription for the exact same drug, the law usually created an exception. Having a prescription for the same substance has been the difference between guilt and innocence—and incarceration. The legal line applies regardless of the health of the child at birth.

There is always the exception, however, at the discretion of the prosecutor. Alabama prosecutors brought charges against Kim Blalock, a married stay-at-home mother of six, whose newborn tested positive for opioids because Kim took prescription hydrocodone for her degenerative disc disease. She had taken the prescription for four years. The local prosecutor charged her with prescription fraud, for allegedly not informing her orthopedist that she was pregnant.

PROSECUTING STILLBIRTHS

While I lived in Mississippi, state prosecutors charged a Black teenager from Columbus, Mississippi, Rennie Gibbs, with depraved heart murder. Ms. Gibbs suffered a stillbirth and tested positive for controlled substances. Prosecutors alleged that her drug use recklessly put the fetus in danger and caused the stillbirth.

Sixteen at the time of her stillbirth, Rennie Gibbs faced a mandatory life sentence if convicted. The language of the statute that she was charged under, however, was limited to "injury to a pregnant woman resulting in miscarriage or stillbirth" *by another person*. That law did not apply to pregnant people themselves and, therefore, they were legally innocent of such charges. They may also be factually innocent: almost a quarter of all pregnancies naturally end in miscarriage or stillbirth with no one at fault.

Power lies in the interpretation of these statutes by prosecutors, and who they choose to target and punish.

FALLOUT FROM CRIMINALIZING PREGNANT WOMEN

With the resurgence of "motherblame," the fallout is real. Pregnant people with Substance Use Disorder are again discouraged from seeking prenatal care for fear they'll be criminally charged for drug use and sent to prison. They will be separated from their children, its own punishment for the parent and the children. Hospitals now regularly drug-test women in labor, with or without their consent. A positive test means prosecutors can criminally charge the mother with neglect or child abuse—or even delivery of drugs to a minor.

These drug tests also trigger mandatory reporting laws to Child Protective Services, and the mother can lose custody of her newborn, or her other children for whom she is the primary caretaker.

Yet while courts will mandate ongoing drug testing of mothers, they do not mandate drug testing of fathers in the home.

Neither the incarceration of pregnant people nor the separation of parents from newborns has a positive or healthy impact on either the parent or the child. The American Medical Association and the American Academy of Pediatrics oppose these prosecutions because they undermine the health of pregnant people and of their newborns. According to the American Academy of Pediatrics, "punitive measures taken toward pregnant women, such as criminal prosecution and incarceration, have no proven benefits for infant health."

For too long, women and girls have been wrongly convicted by creative prosecutors who ignore legal innocence. If elected prosecutors educate their offices on drug use disorder and its impact, more women and their children can remain together. If innocence organizations represent mass claims of wrongful prosecution on behalf of juveniles charged with prostitution, girls can become women outside of the juvenile incarceration system. If legislatures pass Safe Harbor laws, trafficked women can receive assistance and options, rather than further punishment and incarceration.

But the question should no longer be "if" but "when." It is past time to advocate for justice for these women and girls.

CHAPTER 18

Criminalizing Transgender People

Despite the growing attention to misdemeanor wrongful convictions by innocence litigators, the innocence movement ignores misdemeanors specific to trans men and women and nonbinary individuals.

Police have long targeted trans women and arrested them because of their gender performance. The Sylvia Rivera Law Project, named after a famed New York transgender activist, documents the many ways police use broadly written laws to criminalize trans people. A few examples are false arrests for someone's driver's license not matching their appearance or gender, using the "wrong" bathroom, or arrest for "intent to prostitute." Police arrest and courts convict trans women in Phoenix, Arizona, based on a law that criminalizes waving at cars, talking to passersby, and asking if someone is a police officer.

When trans people are low income or people of color, they are particularly at risk of police harassment, arrest, incarceration, and violence. The Black Trans Lives Matter movement is fighting for recognition within racial justice activism of violence and discrimination against trans people.

Trans and queer people are also disproportionately targeted, arrested, and charged for low-level offenses such as trespassing, vagrancy, and shoplifting. Prosecutors bring statutory rape charges against queer youth more often than against straight teens.

Statutory rape is a charge where two people have consensual sex but one of them is underage. Prosecutors frequently absolve these charges through "Romeo and Juliet" exceptions where the older partner's sexual conduct is still illegal but age-appropriate.

In some states, these exceptions explicitly apply only to straight youth. Texas' Romeo and Juliet statute, for example, only applies if the actor "was not more than three years older than the victim and of the opposite sex." A straight teen in Texas will go unpunished, while a queer teen above the age of seventeen will face a jail sentence of two to twenty years and sex offender registration. Approximately one-fourth of people on sex offender registries are *under the age of eighteen.*

Furthermore, 20 percent of incarcerated youth are LGBTQ+ and/or gender-nonconforming, and 40 percent of incarcerated girls are queer or gender-nonconforming. Prosecutors and police also target queer girls for statutory rape charges.

These are wrongful convictions not currently within the public scope of innocence work.

When police and prosecutors criminalize queer, trans, and gender-nonconforming people, innocence litigators and activists can speak up about these wrongful arrests, charges, and convictions.

This is how we manifest justice. We call on courts to dismiss charges pre-trial in the interest of justice, and to reverse convictions as manifest injustice, through writs of habeas corpus or coram nobis.

WRONGLY CONVICTED AND INCARCERATED TRANSGENDER INDIVIDUALS

Sharing these stories is important to recognizing wrongful convictions of transgender and nonbinary people. These stories reveal the power of prosecutors to charge, convict, or free people. A prosecutor has discretion to drop charges that are based on a discriminatory arrest. A prosecutor can refer a defendant to alternate restorative justice resolutions. Or, like in the cases below, a prosecutor can seek heightened and excessive charges, punishing the person for their gender identity.

For LGBTQ+ people of color, prosecutorial discretion frequently works against them. Darnell Wilson and CeCe McDonald's cases are just two examples.

DARNELL WILSON

When I was in Mississippi, I learned about Darnell Wilson. Darnell Wilson is a Black transgender person incarcerated in Mississippi, where they are still incarcerated today in a men's prison. They are in prison for stealing perfume and bras from a Kohl's department store. The police tased Darnell, who fled in their mother's car, trying to cross the state line from Mississippi into Memphis, Tennessee. They didn't make it.

With their prosecutorial discretion, the DeSoto County, Mississippi, prosecutors charged Darnell with felony grand larceny. The items found in Darnell Wilson's car did not equal $500, but the police alleged Darnell took more than just those items and threw them away outside. The prosecutors' allegations that the Kohl's perfume and bras totaled over $500 meant they could charge a felony offense.

Darnell refused to plead guilty and took the stand at their trial, appearing as a femme trans woman. They confessed at trial that they went to Kohl's to steal women's items. "The reason that I shoplift is to take care of bills at my mother's house." On cross examination, the prosecutor asked them about the items and a security camera image of them with the items inside the store.

PROSECUTOR: You're holding a lavender or a purple—what color
    bra is that you've got there? . . . So you've got in your hand here
    a purple and beige bra, right?
WILSON: I'm sure it is a bra. It looks like one.
PROSECUTOR: Was that for you?
WILSON: I have one, and I will wear one again.
PROSECUTOR: You wear bras?
WILSON: Yes, I do, of course.
PROSECUTOR: And this is you in Exhibit No. 13, right?
WILSON: Yes, it is.

. . .

PROSECUTOR: You normally get money from male companions?
WILSON: Yes.
PROSECUTOR: For what?

WILSON: For what? Oh, well, let me put it this way, in my past I used to be a prostitute, if you want me to break it down to you. I'm quite sure you're going to get to it so I'm going to lay it on the line for you. Three counts of so-called aggravated robbery— before you bring it up, let me bring it down to you—they weren't aggravated robberies. I, what you call, provide a service. You know what I'm saying? It's like you being married and your wife ain't doing something that you need her to do, and you come to me and you get something that you need. So you pay me; and then if you don't pay me, then that means that you want your money back so you want a refund. And in my line of work, I don't give refunds. So, therefore, your ego gets in the way. So you feel like you've been talked out of your money by what you assume to be a female that turns out to be a male. So then you go and fabricate and trump up a story and say that you were allegedly robbed. It's part of the game. That's life. You take the good with the bad. The good is you gave me your money. The bad is that you went and lied and said that I took it from you.

PROSECUTOR: So you're saying you dress up like a—are you a man or a woman?

WILSON: A female impersonated, transsexual transgender, homosexual, all of that. And excellent at what I do.

PROSECUTOR: So in your line of work which you said was shoplifting or in prostitution you would need bras and panties, right? . . . And as part of that you would also need perfume, right?

WILSON: Of course.

PROSECUTOR: . . . May I ask you a question, Mr. Wilson?

WILSON: You may.

PROSECUTOR: . . . Still doing the prostitution thing?

WILSON: Of course. It pays the bills . . . These bills were going to be paid. The thing about it was, I wasn't putting a pistol on nobody. Taking and robbing—yes, I was boosting, but robbing and boosting are two different things. Taking something forcefully, that's when you're doing something really major. Don't get me wrong, the Bible says no sin is greater than the next, but the Bible says God knows your heart. So I was doing something wrong to do something right.

PROSECUTOR: Because one of the ten commandments is thou shalt not steal, isn't it?

WILSON: Yes, it is. There's a whole lot of ten commandments. Thou shalt not commit adultery, but I'm quite sure men do that, don't they?

PROSECUTOR: Oh, I'm not talking about men. I'm talking about—

WILSON: But you said—if you say ten commandments, there are ten, right?

Most of the prosecutor's questions were irrelevant and legally improper, but the defense attorney failed to object and the judge allowed the character assassination. The jury convicted Darnell Wilson of felony grand larceny and felony fleeing on June 22, 2010. The prosecutor charged Darnell as a habitual offender, under Mississippi's three strikes law. Under this law, the court sentenced them to life in prison without parole for stealing bras and perfume. If Darnell had been convicted in Tennessee, even if for a felony, they would not have received the life sentence that they did in Mississippi.

Where is the community activism for freeing Darnell? Where is the habeas petition for this manifest injustice? And even more broadly, where is the momentum to eliminate three strike laws?

CECE MCDONALD

CeCe McDonald is an artist and prison abolition activist. She is also a Black trans woman who was wrongfully convicted. In June 2011, in Minneapolis, while walking to the neighborhood Cub Foods with her young Black queer friends, they passed a bar with patrons outside. The white patrons started yelling anti-gay and anti-Black insults at CeCe and her friends. The insults escalated. One white woman smashed CeCe in the side of her face with a glass full of alcohol, gashing CeCe's cheek. CeCe and the woman grabbed at each other, and the patrons started hurling bottles.

When CeCe and her friends moved quickly away, the woman's ex-boyfriend, inked with a swastika tattoo, ran after CeCe. CeCe grabbed the only defense she had: fabric scissors from her purse. She was a fashion design student. CeCe held the scissors up as a warning. When the man lunged at her, CeCe stabbed him. Wounded, he turned to walk back to his crew. CeCe and her friends ran in the other direction.

CeCe, bleeding, waved down a police car. The police officers promptly arrested *her*. CeCe was the only person arrested that night. The man, Dean Schmitz, collapsed and died outside the bar.

When police arrested CeCe they did take her to a hospital to get stitches. But then they took her to the jail, interrogated her, and put her in solitary confinement. CeCe would wait two months in jail before receiving a doctor's visit for her injuries. She had been targeted and survived a hate crime and hateful violence, but when she defended herself—legally so under the law—she was charged with murder.

CeCe's judge wouldn't let her have an expert testify about how transgender women are disproportionately victims of hate crimes, and trans women of color even more so. The judge allowed the prosecutors to exclude Dean Schmitz's past criminal and assault history, any images of his swastika tattoo, and the toxicology report showing he was amped up on cocaine and meth.

As the jurors were selected, CeCe made a difficult decision. Right before the trial began, she accepted a guilty plea to manslaughter. CeCe would serve time, despite being legally innocent. As she told the court during plea hearing, she was giving up her legal claim that she acted in self-defense. She told the court how Dean Schmitz grabbed her and pulled her toward him while she had the scissors in her hand. But she pled guilty to avoid potentially eighty years in prison if she had been found guilty at trial.

The prosecutors got their guilty conviction, against a hate crime survivor. CeCe was sentenced to forty-one months in a men's prison. While straight people can still defend their actions with a "trans panic" defense, trans people cannot even use self-defense. As Mara Keisling, executive director of the National Center for Transgender Equality, told the press, "People are being killed out there, and CeCe is being punished for not being killed."

PROPOSED SOLUTIONS FOR TRANS VICTIMS OF VIOLENCE AND OF WRONGFUL CONVICTIONS

We must support trans people who are survivors of the criminal legal system, and those who are victims of other people. Trans women of color are assaulted and murdered each year. Many of these murders go unsolved.

Some prosecutor offices actively liaise with LGBTQ+ nonprofits to investigate crimes against LGBTQ+ individuals. These prosecutor offices are frequently in jurisdictions that no longer allow the "trans panic" or "gay panic" defense. This means that if prosecutors charge someone for killing the victim, the defendant cannot be absolved by arguing they acted on their "instinctual" homophobia or transphobia.

Within the innocence community, innocence projects and Conviction Integrity Units can partner with LGBTQ+ nonprofits to identify and assist LGBTQ+ people who are victimized by the legal system and wrongfully convicted. These partner organizations could include Black and Pink, which supports queer and HIV+ people in prisons, Who Speaks For Me?, which centers incarcerated LGBTQ+ women of color and recognizes the "trauma-to-prison pipeline," the Sylvia Rivera Project, which challenges the criminalization of queer people, and Lambda Legal Defense and Education Fund, a broad team of lawyers for LGBTQ+ rights.

These partnerships are necessary if innocence work is to recognize and encompass discriminatory charges against queer defendants, as well as represent more innocent queer defendants. Given the low number of openly LGBTQ+ individuals on the National Registry of Exonerations, and the high rate of over-incarceration of queer people, this is a vital call to innocence litigators to step up.

WRIT OF CORAM NOBIS—REVERSING A CONVICTION AFTER SERVING A PRISON SENTENCE

Innocence litigators have tools for manifesting justice. One is the writ of coram nobis.

Through coram nobis, a formerly incarcerated individual can still challenge their conviction. The challenge is either based in law—a violation of constitutional due process—or on mistakes of fact. The writ of coram nobis is seen as the counterpart to the writ of habeas corpus, similar except for people who are no longer incarcerated.

The U.S. Supreme Court has held that the writ of coram nobis is available to remedy "errors of the most fundamental character." It is also a path to challenge convictions for "crimes" that are no longer criminalized or for wrongful convictions.

CORAM NOBIS AND MANIFEST INJUSTICE: FRED KOREMATSU AND GORDON HIRABAYASHI

Fred Korematsu and Gordon Hirabayashi were ordered to Japanese American incarceration camps, in the United States, during World War II. They lived in California, a state that at the time demanded all free Japanese Americans be incarcerated or excluded from the state under military order. As American citizens, Korematsu and Hirabayashi refused. They were criminally charged and convicted for violating the orders to leave their homes on the West Coast to live in Japanese Internment Camps as far east as Arkansas and Louisiana. People of Japanese ancestry numbering 120,000 were forcibly relocated and incarcerated in camps. Of them, 62 percent were U.S. citizens.

The convictions of Korematsu and Hirabayashi formed the basis of a now-disgraced Supreme Court decision in 1944, *Korematsu v. United States.* The *Korematsu* decision condoned overt racial discrimination against Japanese Americans and affirmed the exclusionary orders of the government and the military. Constitutional law scholars identify the *Korematsu* decision as an example of what our constitution is *not.* In that way, *Korematsu* is similar to *Dred Scott v. Sandford,* another disgraced opinion where the 1858 Supreme Court declared that enslaved people were not U.S. citizens. These cases signal how laws and the creators of laws can reinforce the boundary between haves and have-nots: by making racial and gender bias neutral and legal.

Forty years later, Korematsu and Hirabayashi used coram nobis to challenge their convictions. They argued their convictions should be vacated due to government misconduct. They had violated the law, but their convictions for that violation were a miscarriage of justice—manifest injustice.

In 1980, a congressional commission issued a report finding that racial prejudice, not military necessity, drove the incarceration camps. Without review or evidence against them, citizens and resident aliens were excluded, removed, and detained by the United States. In Korematsu's case, prosecutors failed to disclose key information about the order, not even to the Supreme Court. The general who ordered the exclusion had issued a justification report that contained "willful historical inaccuracies and intentional falsehoods," according to the Department of Justice. The prosecutors, however, told the Supreme Court that the orders of exclusion were beyond judicial oversight because they related to security and defense. The prosecutors refused to disclose how unsubstantiated the orders were in reality.

In 1984, through the writ of coram nobis—because neither Korematsu nor Hirabayashi were in custody or prison at that point—they were able to vacate their convictions. The vacating court explained that coram nobis was an appropriate remedy both for the miscarriage of justice and for the prosecutorial impropriety. The writ of coram nobis "'strikes at the veracity of the government's representations to the court' and is appropriate *where the procedure by which guilt is ascertained is under attack.*"

The court in Hirabayashi's case recognized that the military orders and subsequent criminal convictions were based on racial prejudice, and that "the orders caused needless suffering and shame to thousands of American citizens." Although Korematsu and Hirabayashi were legally and "properly" convicted of violating the laws, vacating the convictions would, in the court's opinion, "make the judgements of the courts conform to the judgements of history." The federal court vacating Fred Korematsu's individual conviction said the reversal was in the public interest and to do otherwise would result in manifest injustice.

ASSISTING QUEER PEOPLE WRONGFULLY ON THE SEX OFFENDER REGISTRY

A claim of manifest injustice in habeas or coram nobis petitions can challenge convictions for decriminalized behavior. As the Supreme Court said in *Davis v. United States*, "conviction and punishment . . . for an act that the law does not make criminal . . . results in a complete miscarriage of justice." When an act is no longer criminalized, incarcerated people and formerly incarcerated people have a right to argue their convictions be vacated.

The writ of coram nobis can legally assist people, for example, who are free but still on sex offender registries and cannot expunge their now wrongful convictions for consensual adult sodomy. Even though the Supreme Court decriminalized consensual sodomy between adults in 2003, queer people previously convicted were still registered as sex offenders. As recently as 2018, people with lingering felony convictions for "unnatural intercourse" had to register as sex offenders with the Mississippi Sex Offender Registry.

Both writs of habeas corpus and coram nobis can be used to challenge unjust convictions. CeCe McDonald could challenge her conviction as a manifest injustice through coram nobis; Darnell Wilson could challenge their conviction as a manifest injustice through habeas corpus. The U.S. Supreme Court has held that the writ of coram nobis is available to remedy all "errors of the most fundamental character." The scope of the writ of habeas corpus includes convictions that "constitute[] a denial of fundamental fairness shocking to the universal sense of justice."

For Leigh and Tami, the next step was a writ of habeas corpus, to petition the court to reverse their wrongful convictions. The only question was what evidence could convince the court that these convictions were wrongful, and that Leigh and Tami were innocent.

CHAPTER 19
Undisclosed Evidence

Even after Leigh and Tami went to prison, their mothers never gave up. Mama Sheila and Mama Sandi bonded through their daughters' wrongful convictions, and both fought to free their daughters. They would not accept a forty-four-year sentence for such bogus charges.

PRIVATE DETECTIVE JOE KEY

The mamas weren't going to wait for justice through the courts. They hired Joe Key, a private detective and paralegal. Joe was shocked when he first read the trial transcript. Then he became angry, indignant, and determined.

Key's deep dive into the transcript unearthed significant questions. Why had the defense attorneys never asked about Kim's personal journal in police possession? Kim had left her "Fourth Step" Alcoholics Anonymous journal in Leigh's truck, and Leigh and Mama Sheila dutifully turned it over to the police. It was Leigh's sister, Lori, who insisted they make a copy of it first, just in case. That was smart—the police and prosecutors never again gave them or their defense attorneys access to the journal.

At Cady Hill, the social workers required everyone to keep a Fourth Step journal. The journal was simultaneously an opportunity for reflection, and a means for the social workers to evaluate and assess the person. Kim shared her attraction to both men and women, and most relevant to the charges against Leigh and Tami, she wrote about enjoy-

ing rough sex and participating in group sex. This was important since
Dr. Moak's initial diagnosis was that Kim's injuries were due to rough
sex from two to four days before she was admitted to the hospital,
when she was at Cady Hill.

The amount of sexual shame in the courtroom over Leigh and
Tami as lesbians would have been head-spinningly duplicated by this
information. For Leigh and Tami, it would further show their innocence. But for the prosecutor who had his hands on that journal, it was
damning of both his timeline and his victim.

He couldn't risk exposing that Kim was attracted to women. Dunn
Lampton may have wondered if, on that fact alone, jury members
would even still consider Kim a victim. How could he ask jury members to empathize with a woman who had a drug addiction and also
had been sexually intimate with women? Particularly when he asked
those same jurors to dehumanize and stereotype the defendants based
on the exact same identity? This was the prosecutors' motive for the alleged assault—that Leigh and Tami wanted sex and drugs, as vicious
addicted lesbians. They had no other motive.

Among Lampton's final words to the jury were these: "Ladies and
gentlemen, when you look at all the evidence, you'll realize that while
it's a circumstantial evidence case, these two women who were living
together, were lovers, whether because of the drugs or the alcohol or
their lifestyle, viciously attacked Kimberly Williams for no reason and
tried to cover it up."

For no reason—except that they were queer and used drugs. For
Lampton, it was a winning strategy: shame people as outsiders and
present experts who testify that people are violent based on who they
want to have sex with.

But if all the women are queer, the shame loses its power. There has
to be the outsider, the person so different that they would bite off a
woman's labia just because they want to. If everyone is queer, then
everyone can be written off—then perhaps biting labias is just what
happens among sexual deviants.

The journal would have undermined that there was an assault, undermined that any sex was nonconsensual, and taken the wind out of
focusing on Leigh and Tami as perpetrators of violence. The jury

never heard about Kim's own sexual identity, never heard about group sex and rough sex, and Joe Key was right—the prosecutors never gave that journal back to Mama Sheila or the defense attorneys. No one asked Dr. Moak about his initial diagnosis and timeline at trial, and this particular shame was buried.

Homophobia and Jurors

I know many people who were homosexual and God saved them . . . they will tell you they lived the life of sin . . . The fact of the matter is the pro-homosexual perspective undercuts God's authority as our creator to tell us how we are supposed to live. —Dr. James White, director of Alpha and Omega Ministries

But God made them homosexual and they don't have any alternative to suicide. —Pastor Rick Shaeffer
—Talk show *The Dividing Line*, "Gay Christianity Debate," May 26, 2001

Joe Key was unearthing shames. He was the first to openly talk about how the prosecutors exploited the lesbian identities of Leigh and Tami and how that led to their wrongful convictions. He looked closely at how the experts and closing statements encouraged the jurors to build on their own homophobic biases and take the next step: that queer people are inherently violent and vicious and able to commit gross acts of violence. For a basis of that homophobia, Joe looked at the largest religion in the community: Christianity.

Joe discovered that in 2000, there were 90 churches in Brookhaven serving a population of 13,028 people. A church for every 145 people.

Eight years after Leigh and Tami were convicted, the Williams Institute on Sexual Orientation Law and Public Policy at UCLA issued a report, Homophobia in the Courtroom: How to Identify Gay-Biased Jurors. The report was based on a survey of 7,800 mock jurors between 2002 and 2008 from across the United States. According to the report, while jury bias against gay men and lesbians had decreased since the early 1990s, it still existed among juries. Nationally, the most anti-gay biased jurors were people living in the South and people who tried to attend church regularly, or who said that religious beliefs were important in their daily lives. The study asked questions ranging from whether jurors believed queer people should be free from discrimination in the workplace, to being permitted to marry and adopt children, to whether they'd feel comfortable living next door to a queer couple, or how they'd feel if their child's teacher was queer.

The strongest predictors of anti-gay bias were being politically conservative, religiosity, and whether or not the jurors had gay or lesbian friends.

From 2003 to 2008, 45 percent of the jurors in this national spread viewed homosexuality as an "unacceptable lifestyle," the report said. Forty percent of the jurors believed that lesbian and gay people could change their sexual orientation and become heterosexuals if they really wanted to.

Tami's attorney, McNees, had briefly made an attempt to ask the jurors about homosexuality and religion before trial.

"There may be some testimony here regarding *deviant or lesbian behavior*," he began. "Can you, in your religion, or otherwise, can you promise Tami Vance and Leigh Stubbs that you will try them only for what they are indicted and not based on your own personal morality, just what they have been indicted on? Can you do that?"

McNees looked closely at the jurors. "If I were to ask you right now, could each of you vote my client not guilty, what would you vote? Right now? Could you vote my client not guilty?"

And with that, two jurors admitted that they would vote Tami and Leigh guilty before the trial had even begun.

The judge was furious—at Tami's attorney.

"I don't appreciate what you're trying to do," Judge Smith declared. "You ask them if they can listen to the evidence and then, based on the evidence, they decide. You're trying to confuse them."

"Your honor, I didn't know that was wrong," McNees apologized. "I've never done this before. I'm sorry."

"You be specific," the judge admonished McNees.

And that was it. Jurors' beliefs about "deviant or lesbian behavior" could not be discussed.

The Williams Institute report, released eight years too late to do Leigh and Tami any good, recommended strategically useful questions to identify anti-gay bias in jurors:

Would you feel bothered if a gay or lesbian couple moved in next door to you?

Do you think employers should be able to refuse to hire someone because of his or her sexual orientation?

Would you feel bothered if you had to work closely with someone who was gay or lesbian?

According to the study, 10 to 20 percent of the people queried between 2003 and 2008 nationally were likely to answer yes to these questions.

FBI Involvement

Joe Key also keyed in on the reference in the transcript to the FBI. A random remark by Dunn Lampton: "Those are the photographs that the FBI blew up off the videotape."

It was a throwaway line that apparently was missed in the midst of trial. But now on reading the transcript, it jumped out. The FBI? But Dr. West had testified that he was less expensive than the FBI and could do their same work on his own home computer. How was the FBI involved? And why had no one heard anything about it?

Joe Key went through defense attorney Bill Barnett's trial file. He found a copy of a letter from co-prosecutor Jerry Rushing to the FBI, requesting the FBI examine the Brookhaven Comfort Inn surveillance video. But there was no response from the FBI in the file.

Sheila and Sandi learned what to do. They filed a Freedom of Information Act (FOIA) request with the FBI, for any and all information on the case of their daughters.

Backbiting

In 2005, Sheila reached out to another forensic odontologist, Richard Souviron. Dr. Souviron was one of the most respected forensic odontologists in the profession. He had testified as an expert witness against Ted Bundy.

Years later, evidence would show that for all of Dr. Souviron's expertise, he had been wrong at least twice. He had testified against

Robert DuBoise. DuBoise was an innocent man in Tampa who spent thirty-seven years in prison for a crime he didn't commit until DNA evidence exonerated him. Souviron also testified against Gary Cifizzari in Worcester, Massachusetts, providing the key evidence that convicted him. Thirty-five years later, Dr. Souviron recanted his testimony, and DNA evidence also set Mr. Cifizzari free.

If anything, this shows the unreliability of odontology.

Dr. Souviron was primarily a prosecution witness. But he also had no love for Michael West. He buckled to Sheila's pleas and agreed to look at Leigh and Tami's case.

First, Souviron made clear that Dr. Rodrigo Galvez was not a forensic odontologist and should not have testified to bite marks. Second, he chastised Dr. West's shoddy and false work.

"Dr. West's statements are not accurate and are extremely misleading," Dr. Souviron concluded. "Another term would be a 'snow job.' I viewed the videotape and my comment is that I see exactly what Dr. West did and I doubt seriously that there is a bite mark in the area which he laid a pattern of teeth over."

Souviron declined to blame the prosecution. "The prosecutor certainly has no reason to doubt what Dr. West says unless someone were able to point out the spin, inconsistency and outright errors in Dr. West's qualifications . . . Based on the video, it is my opinion that there is no bite mark in the area that Dr. West is placing teeth."

OLE MISS

In 2009, I was new to Mississippi, the South, and small-town life. Little did I know then that I'd spend the next ten years advocating for criminal justice in rural parts of our country. Then, it was all new to me—especially the traditions at Ole Miss, where I was an adjunct professor of law while working at the Mississippi Innocence Project. About the time of Leigh and Tami's trial, the school had stopped unfurling a massive confederate flag across the field at each football game. But the confederate flag was still part of the state flag and still waved at every game. The state flag would finally change to a beautiful magnolia blossom, representative of the trees young and old across the state, in 2020. But in 2009, the band still played Dixie before each game, gathered in the Grove on the Ole Miss campus, where white Ole Miss fans would erect red and blue tents, lay out massive spreads of food, and set up televisions before the game.

I'm from the Midwest. I was used to tailgating at Purdue football games when I was a kid, hanging out in the parking lot with my parents and their friends with coolers, wearing our Boilermaker sweatshirts in the crisp Indiana autumn.

Ole Miss was completely different, and I would have been sorely out of place in an Ole Miss sweatshirt. Instead, women wore dresses and heels even in the grassy lawn and mud of the Grove. Men wore blazers and polo shirts. I couldn't believe they were actually going to a football game—this was not the Midwestern casual culture I was used to.

I gradually learned more about the history of the Grove, and why I rarely saw Black people there except for at the faculty and staff tent. The Grove was a welcoming place to white people and white traditions. Setting up in the Grove was no small thing, and before the civil rights movement, white game-goers had tents with chandeliers, and full meals served by Black people. In 2009, the tents had big screen televisions, women wore designer clothes, and the school band played Dixie, while the predominantly Black football players ran through the "Walk of Champions" arch, the Grove, and the gathered fans on their way to the stadium. The final line in the Dixie medley, incorporating the unofficial anthem of the Confederate States of America, was a chant "the South will rise again."

In the three years I was at Ole Miss, the band would stop playing Dixie. The Ole Miss mascot of Colonel Reb, a white male mustachioed plantation owner, was officially eliminated in 2003 and finally replaced with another mascot in 2010. But the team was still the Rebels, and the Klan came to protest the ending of Dixie, appearing near the Grove at a football game. While confederate monuments appear prominently on campus, the statue of the first Black student, James Meredith, was garnered with a noose by fraternity members in 2014. White people so opposed the enrollment of James Meredith in 1962 that President Kennedy sent the national guard to Mississippi, and two people died in the violent protests. Established in 1848 for the sons of plantation owners and slaveholders, Ole Miss history continues alongside efforts to evoke change.

The nickname "Ole Miss" was adopted during the Jim Crow era, when a white woman proposed the name as a connection to the antebellum status of the state. The state institution was allegedly nicknamed with the enslaved person's caricatured honorific for the white mistress of the plantation, "ole miss." Old Southern families continue to make their donations to the school contingent on keeping confederate emblems. A Tiffany stained-glass window depicts the University Grays, students who fought for the Confederacy in the Civil War and were killed or wounded. Although some vocal Black alumni have encouraged the nickname New Miss, Ole Miss remains.

When I came to the school in 2009, I thought the student council proposals to bring back Colonel Reb were the extent of the protests. I soon realized that a state senator introduced a bill each year to require Ole Miss to keep Colonel Reb and to play Dixie before every ballgame. This was similar in my eyes to a proposed bill to create a license plate with Nathan Bedford Forrest on it—a famous Confederate general, a Mississippian, and also the first grand wizard of the Ku Klux Klan.

But there were many things to love about Mississippi. Southern literature beyond William Faulkner and the Oxford Square: Barry Hannah's *Airships,* Larry Brown's *Big Bad Love,* and Jesmyn Ward's *Salvage the Bones.* I was figuring out the difference between hill country blues and delta blues, and fife and drum—which is its own beautiful contribution. My community garden plot would bloom in the Spring with okra and zucchini, and I shared a wall with my eighty-nine-year-old neighbor Mrs. Mize (or Ms. Dorothy). She became my perpetual anti-planner "I might die before tomorrow" friend, who had taken to giving me hugs.

I was learning how to be appropriately feminine in a Mississippi courtroom. How to not appear like a dyke, or a Northerner. Gone were my power black pantsuits from D.C. and being a prosecutor. I found suits in shades of pastel and beige, always with a skirt.

Yet I was reminded how I still didn't quite get the culture of Southern femininity when I attended the law school dedication for University of Mississippi's new building. The stage was lit up with speakers, venerated older white men. I had been told the event was suit attire—professional. What I was not told was that it was suit attire for men. My feminine skirted suit didn't work, and I stood out among the frilly and flowery dresses. By that time, I was used to it. I enjoyed my personal happy moment of heading home after the event, throwing on a casual T-shirt, and heading to the town veggie potluck with some homemade banana ice cream. I had found a community.

THE MISSISSIPPI INNOCENCE PROJECT INVESTIGATES

Attorney Tucker Carrington opened the doors of the George C. Cochran Mississippi Innocence Project in 2007. I learned, when I joined the project in 2009, that from the very beginning, Mama Sheila and Mama Sandi had been contacting Tucker. They sent him everything that Detective Keys had uncovered.

During his testimony, Dr. West had bragged, "Ten years ago, I would have to send photographs off to the FBI . . . [and it would] cost us $20,000 to get them back and enhanced . . . Now you can sit at home, with your own computer, with $1,000 software and do enhancement that used to be only NASA could do . . . and that's what we did in this case."

Inspired by that testimony, Joe Key contacted someone at NASA, who was disinclined to believe Leigh picked up a body from the toolbox. The person in the video easily picked up the item from the toolbox and jumped down from the truck bed, leading the NASA expert to believe the item was relatively light. At a minimum, the item was much lighter than a person who was Leigh's same height and weight.

Joe Key also found a picture of Kim Williams from the time she was at Cady Hill. Her hair was only shoulder length.

The Mississippi Innocence Project's first staff attorney, Will McIntosh, began investigating the case. When he went to the Brookhaven courthouse to look at the filings, Leigh's file was twice as thick as Tami's. Tami's trial attorney only filed a perfunctory, one-page motion to suppress the evidence and a one-page motion for a new trial. Leigh's attorney, Bill Barnett, on the other hand, filed numerous in-depth motions for relief.

Will reached out to Detective Nolan Jones.

In his younger days, Nolan Jones had been a prizefighter. He was not a big man, but he was scrappy. He fought informal bareknuckle matches for cash, until a particularly brutal fight left him blind in one eye. Nolan had become a police officer, then a detective, and served the community for many years. Even today he is the jury commissioner for the Brookhaven courthouse, to make sure all proprieties are observed when they draw jurors for the panel.

Nolan Jones was certain that Leigh and Tami were guilty. Leigh and Tami themselves admitted that they were the only people with Kim in the time when Nolan believed Kim was bitten—after she left her boyfriend's home in Summit. Based on this time window, Nolan was convinced they did it.

Nolan Jones also told Will that in the thirty years he had worked in law enforcement, he knew that he had never sent an innocent person to prison. He could "go to bed with a clear conscience every night."

But there were plenty of unanswered questions. If Kim had these severe vaginal injuries, why didn't the paramedics note them when they were inserting the catheter? Why did the paramedics describe her breasts as normal instead of raw and chewed like Kim's mom testified at trial? And how come no one identified a head injury until long after Kim had been admitted, revived and bathed at King's Daughters hospital and then transferred the hour-long drive to the hospital in Jackson? What about Kim's grand mal seizures?

Will also talked to Mama Sheila, about Tami.

"Tami is one of the sweetest girls I've ever known," Mama Sheila said. "She'd give you the shirt off her back, literally. She's had it tough, she moved out of her home when she was thirteen or fourteen. She's made it on her own."

On August 31, 2008, Mama Sheila and Mama Sandi finally got their long-awaited response from the FBI. The packet was thick: twenty-nine pages of documents. They soon discovered they had hit the jackpot.

Every document was about the hotel surveillance video—the recording that allegedly showed Leigh carrying Kim out of a toolbox. This video had clinched the convictions against their daughters. The date of the FBI report jumped out to them. The FBI report and worksheet about the Comfort Inn video were dated September 11, 2000. That was nearly a year before their trial in 2001.

The FBI also disclosed letters that had been sent back and forth between prosecutors Jerry Rushing, Dunn Lampton, and the FBI lab. There was a chain of custody document; a worksheet; fifteen pages of a log and notes; and a shipping invoice for three CD-ROMs sent to the district attorney's office in Brookhaven.

The chain of custody record showed the FBI had received the Comfort Inn surveillance video from the Brookhaven prosecutors at 2:00 P.M. on April 18, 2000, by priority mail. But what had happened to the FBI's analysis? Why had Sandi and Sheila never seen it before?

CHAPTER 20
The Innocence Movement

If you're feeling helpless, help someone.
—Aung San Suu Kyi

I have never—not once—had a prosecutor agree to DNA testing without going to court. Yet a prosecutor can test any evidence they want at any time. Prosecutors have a state crime lab, usually controlled by the police. A prosecutor can test a discarded cigarette at a remote crime scene for DNA, then run the DNA profile through a national database—CODIS—that includes all people incarcerated in the United States and many people who were simply arrested. A police officer can give an alternate suspect a soda to drink, keep the can, test it for DNA, and see if the DNA profile matches DNA at a crime scene.

A defense attorney can't run a DNA profile through CODIS, and they must be careful collecting DNA from suspects. Chris Mumma, director of the North Carolina Center for Actual Innocence, inadvertently took a plastic water bottle from a suspect's family member. She then decided to test it, to see if the family profile matched DNA at the crime scene. The DNA didn't match. Mumma ultimately discovered other evidence that exonerated her client, Joseph Sledge, who had been imprisoned for almost forty years for a double homicide he did not commit.

After the exoneration, the prosecutors officially complained about Mumma's behavior testing the water bottle. The North Carolina legal bar held a hearing on whether Mumma violated the rules of professional responsibility. Mumma—now with a defense attorney of her own—argued that County District Attorney Jon David spent more time investigating her than investigating Sledge's claims of innocence.

The North Carolina bar admonished Mumma but allowed her to keep her bar license. As another of her exonerated clients, Dwayne Dail, stated, "Chris Mumma has had a target on her back since she started this work. Out of all of the years that Sledge was in prison wrongfully, Chris Mumma is the only one being held in any kind of way responsible. And I just think that's ridiculous."

The first hurdle for innocence litigators has always been finding the DNA evidence and then being able to test it. If prosecutors or judges grant defendants' request to test DNA evidence, the court system can uncover whether someone is innocent or guilty. They can even identify the true perpetrator. A swab collected from a rape kit may have DNA from sperm to identify the assailant. Or in a struggle, the victim may have the assailant's skin DNA under their fingernails. Even cigarette butts next to a victim may unlock who was present at the rural scene of death.

But innocence litigators must have permission from the local prosecutor or local court to test DNA crime scene evidence for a defendant. This tremendous battle in the 1990s and early 2000s led to actual policy reform. Now, every state has a statute that provides the *possibility* for DNA testing of evidence forgotten in police lockers, or musty on courthouse shelves.

Just because defendants can ask for testing, however, doesn't mean a prosecutor or judge will grant it. They frequently adhere to the story of finality, and that their role is to oppose any further work on a case after a conviction.

Or maybe they just don't want to be proven wrong.

I've heard prosecutors say that DNA testing dishonors the memory of the victim. Yet when a victim asks a prosecutor to lessen the charges or advocate for a lighter sentence, prosecutors respond that they don't represent victims. When victims ask for mercy for the perpetrator, prosecutors generally ignore them.

A day before Mississippi officials would execute Henry Curtis Jackson, a Black man, the living victims met with the Mississippi governor. These victims were Henry Jackson's sisters. He had murdered his own nieces and nephews. Pleading with the governor, Henry's sisters Regina Jackson and Glendale Kyoto proclaimed what they had said for years to government officials: do not kill him in our name. Regina, who was stabbed five times by her brother, told Governor Phil Bryant that executing her brother would only bring more pain. Henry's death would not bring back her children. This close to the execution, the governor was the final official who could put a stop to the killing.

The State of Mississippi executed Henry Curtis Jackson on June 5, 2012. No one in a position of power in the government stopped the execution for the victims.

Despite every prosecutor standing up in court saying something along the lines of, "Valena Beety, on behalf of the people of the United States," "the people" means only the government.

But we the people can affirmatively support reform, not the status quo. To affirmatively support defendants instead of the government, for example, people can organize community bail funds, act as court-watchers, and join participatory defense teams. These challenge the prosecutor narrative of de facto representing the community interests.

Exculpatory DNA can also identify when police and prosecutors rely on false information to convict an innocent person, again changing the status quo.

As DNA exonerated innocent people, we crucially learned how our criminal legal system gets it wrong and relies on false information. DNA showed that innocent people plead guilty. Innocent people accept a plea as the best calculation, instead of a lengthy sentence or the death penalty. DNA showed that innocent people falsely confess to crimes they did not commit, like the young Black teenagers called the Central Park Five. People will confess when police use coercive interrogation tactics—whether that confession is true or not. DNA showed that eyewitnesses, positively certain they have identified the perpetrator, can frequently be wrong. Current police practices exacerbate the problem. DNA showed that forensic evidence analysts, looking at bite marks or comparing bullets or hairs, can be overconfident and sweepingly inaccurate in their testimony. DNA showed that informants working for police or prosecutors lie with frequency. They are also simply acting in their own best interest.

Prosecutors and police gather evidence to show a jury and judge that the defendant is guilty, that is their storyline. They rely on the confession, the eyewitness identification, the jailhouse informant, the fingerprints. In other cases they hide exculpatory evidence, they ignore alibi witnesses, and they miss alternate leads by focusing only on the named defendant. We learn all this when DNA proves the defendant was not the perpetrator of the crime.

Over the past thirty years, many people have worked in good faith to improve our criminal legal system based on these now recognized hallmarks of wrongful conviction. Police have adopted alternative methods of interrogation based on social science instead of coercion; police have adopted protocols for making eyewitness identifications more reliable; and the federal government has funded more studies and research support for the forensic science fields. Tremendous research on memory, coercion, and tunnel vision has bolstered the work of advocates in both challenging the current measures and implementing new practices for police and prosecutors.

HISTORY OF THE INNOCENCE MOVEMENT AND DNA CASES

In 1987, Kate Germond saw a news story that changed her life and thus changed many others. The story described the first organization in the world to investigate and advocate for wrongfully convicted and incarcerated people: Centurion Ministries. Jim McCloskey, a seminary student, started Centurion Ministries in 1980, after ministering to incarcerated men at Trenton State Prison. Appropriately for a new pastor, the name came from the Roman centurion who said "surely, this one is innocent" at the foot of the cross. When McCloskey got *New York Times* press coverage for his success freeing innocent men from prison, Kate saw the article. She called him up and asked for a job. Jim gave Kate a volunteer position. Together, they built and grew the first innocence organization, located in Princeton, New Jersey. They reversed convictions based on false forensics including faulty bullet matching; they got confessions made "under hypnosis" tossed; and slowly they grew the attention to wrongful convictions.

Media played a crucial role as Centurion began to take cases nationally alongside death penalty cases in the 1980s. One such case was that of convicted murderer Joyce Ann Brown in Dallas, Texas.

On May 6, 1980, two Black women robbed Fine Furs by Rubin in Dallas. During the robbery, the women shot the owner, who died from the wound. They spared the life of his wife who was also working in the store. The women rushed out, piled the stolen furs into a rental car, and drove off.

The initial evidence pointed to Joyce Ann Brown.

The day after the robbery, police found the getaway car. A woman named Joyce Ann Brown had rented it. Furthermore, police had discovered a Black woman named Joyce Ann Brown worked at another fur store in Dallas. The police included a photo of Joyce Ann Brown in a lineup, and the surviving wife, a white woman, picked her out. Police arrested Brown and prosecutors then charged her with murder and robbery. The judge set her bail at $1 million. Brown, unable to pay the bail, spent months in jail until her trial.

At trial, the wife identified Joyce Ann Brown, who was sitting in the courtroom behind the defense table, as the perpetrator. Then the prosecution called a surprise witness: Brown's cellmate in jail. Her cellmate shared how Brown had confided in her. Brown had told her she committed the robbery and the murder. An all-white jury in Dallas, Texas, heard the evidence and quickly made their decision: Joyce Ann Brown was guilty. The judge sentenced Brown to life in prison.

The jailhouse informant who testified against Brown walked out of prison a free woman a month later at the behest of the Dallas district attorney. The district attorney wrote to the Texas Board of Pardons and Paroles saying the witness's five-year sentence for attempted murder should be reduced. The board agreed, and the governor ordered the informant released immediately.

In 1989, Centurion Ministries discovered what police and prosecutors had known all along. The Joyce Ann Brown who rented the getaway car was from Denver, Colorado, not Dallas, Texas. Indeed, the police had contacted the Joyce Ann Brown in Denver before trial. That Joyce Ann Brown told police that yes, she had rented the car. She had done so for a friend who was also in Denver, Renee Taylor.

Police searched Renee Taylor's Denver home and found the stolen furs, and the murder weapon. They didn't find Taylor. And thus, the state continued with the prosecution of Dallas Joyce Ann Brown.

The prosecutor also knew that his jailhouse informant witness had a previous conviction for lying to police. At trial, the cellmate denied having any prior convictions, and the prosecutors never disclosed the conviction to the court, the jury, or the defense attorney.

Months after Joyce Ann Brown's conviction, the police found

Renee Taylor. Facing the death penalty, she pled guilty to the fur store robbery and murder. She also made a statement that Dallas Joyce Ann Brown was not her accomplice. Neither police nor the prosecutor told Dallas Joyce Ann Brown about the statement.

Joyce Ann Brown remained in prison for the next nine years.

By the end of the decade, Centurion started investigating Brown's case. The pivotal coverage of Brown's conviction on *60 Minutes* in October 1989 critically led to her exoneration just weeks later, on November 3, 1989.

Joyce Ann was convicted based on what we now identify as "hallmarks of wrongful conviction": mistaken eyewitness identification, a jailhouse informant, and prosecutorial and police misconduct. Her case involved a mistaken eyewitness making a cross-racial identification. The only other civilian witness to testify against Brown was a jailhouse informant who in exchange was released from prison. Police and prosecutors knew and failed to disclose the informant's past conviction, as well as the exculpatory information that they had the wrong Joyce Ann Brown.

But the other underlying causes of Joyce Ann's incarceration are more sinister and more pervasive. They are not identified as "hallmarks of wrongful conviction" but are just as damning against innocent and guilty defendants alike. Joyce Ann was a Black woman, identified by a white female victim, and judged by an all-white jury. She was only "found" by police and put into an initial photo lineup because she had a prior misdemeanor arrest. And despite her alibi of being at work, with only a thirty-seven-minute break the day of the robbery, she was painted as a criminal. Finally, no one in the government ever questioned Brown's conviction or even told her about Renee Taylor's statement and guilty plea. Renee Taylor pled guilty to committing the exact same robbery and murder and in writing denied that Dallas Joyce Ann Brown was her accomplice—yet this was never disclosed.

These are the hallmarks of mass incarceration: racism, discrimination based on prior involvement with police and the court system, and no avenues for relief after conviction. These are the hallmarks of manifest injustice. The damning of an individual for their race and gender, the condemnation for having any criminal record, even a simple arrest, and the refusal to free people after they have been convicted, no matter the evidence that arises nor the injustice.

These are the hallmarks this book discusses. All of these hallmarks have also been confirmed and identified by DNA evidence, the crucial development that established the innocence movement.

Media coverage and citizen advocacy were pivotal to early wrongful conviction cases before DNA evidence, like Joyce Ann Brown's. Neither Kate Germond nor Jim McCloskey at Centurion were journalists or lawyers. Instead, they were determined advocates and they partnered with journalists and lawyers. Errol Morris's now infamous documentary *The Thin Blue Line*, released in 1988, led to the exoneration of Randall Adams from death row for a murder in Texas. And then an explosion of coverage to the potential of DNA evidence came from the case of the century, the trial of O.J. Simpson.

DNA is a "genetic fingerprint," unique to each individual and passed down through families. Now mass-marketed through "personal genetic DNA tests" by testing companies like 23andMe, or AncestryDNA, DNA can identify relatives or paternity. In the 1980s, police first used this breakthrough of DNA profiling to match blood from a suspect to blood at a crime scene. Barry Scheck and Peter Neufeld, two defense attorneys, challenged the ad hoc collection of blood and evidence even if the testing itself was reliable. While Centurion Ministries was investigating innocence cases in New Jersey, Scheck and Neufeld, across the river in New York City, were litigating DNA evidence—challenging whether it should be admitted against defendants in court.

In 1990, three members of the Hell's Angels motorcycle gang were charged with murder. In their defense, Scheck and Neufeld argued a novel issue: whether a federal court should allow DNA evidence to be admitted in court. The FBI sought to admit blood evidence from the defendants' van that matched the murdered individual. Scheck and Neufeld argued that the FBI's methods of testing were not peer-reviewed and criticized the testing procedures.

Judge James G. Carr of Toledo, Ohio, would prize his decision in this case more than most in his long career. His former clerks, myself included, gifted him with a bobblehead of our boss riding a motor-cycle. He ruled for the FBI. Judge Carr admitted the DNA evidence, evidence that was novel at the time, "new scientific evidence," laying the groundwork for courts nationally to do the same.

Four years later, in 1994, DNA evidence was broadly accepted and admissible in courts. Police collection of DNA evidence, however, was still ad hoc and potentially unreliable. Nothing broadcast this disso-nance more than the murder of Nicole Brown Simpson in Los Ange-les, and the investigation and arrest thereafter of her famous football star, actor, and celebrity ex-husband, O.J. Simpson. Nicknamed "The Juice," Simpson's flight from police in a white Ford Bronco SUV on the Los Angeles freeway was nationally broadcast, live. So was his later trial for the murder of Nicole and her friend Ronald Goldman.

Barry Scheck and Peter Neufeld joined Simpson's "Dream Team" of defense lawyers to interrogate how police gathered the DNA evi-dence. The police officer who scaled the wall of Simpson's home to find evidence, Mark Fuhrman, was recorded using derogatory lan-guage for Black people and boasting about planting evidence and falsi-fying reports to imprison Black men. When asked if he had planted any evidence at Simpson's home, Detective Fuhrman invoked the Fifth Amendment—his right to remain silent. But his statement "we could have murdered people and got away with it. We were tight. We all knew what to say" was damning of the Los Angeles police response to all Black men, not just Simpson. The jury acquitted O.J. Simpson of all counts.

The O.J. Simpson trial brought tremendous attention to DNA evi-dence and to Barry Scheck and Peter Neufeld, along with their Inno-cence Project in New York. The case challenged how DNA evidence is collected, and Scheck and Neufeld used the opportunity to advocate for more regulated testing and gathering of evidence. They also advo-cated that DNA evidence was a tool to identify innocent people who were wrongfully convicted. In 1996, the National Institute of Justice created a report on wrongful convictions at the behest of then Attor-ney General Janet Reno, the first female U.S. Attorney General. In the NIJ report *Convicted by Juries, Exonerated by Science*, Scheck and Neufeld identified wrongful convictions as systemic and widespread.

The duo shared their policy vision for innocence work: to examine systemic weaknesses in police interrogations and prosecutor methods, exposed by DNA evidence of innocence.

In 1992, Barry Scheck and Peter Neufeld founded the Innocence Project as a clinic at the Cardozo Law School in New York City. While Centurion started as a nonprofit model taking cases, the Innocence Project started as a clinic, focusing on DNA cases and policy reform. From the beginning, the project looked at how DNA could prove innocence as well as identify the causes of wrongful conviction. They started the project with a team of women, including three attorneys who became leaders in innocence litigation: Nina Morrison, Vanessa Potkin, and Aliza Kaplan.

INNOCENT PEOPLE ON DEATH ROW

The year 1993 was explosive. In January, the Supreme Court affirmed the death sentence of a Texas Latino defendant who proclaimed he was innocent in *Herrera v. Collins*. Lionel Herrera had been convicted of murdering two police officers. In post-conviction, Herrera provided affidavits of his innocence and that another person had committed the crimes. He argued that executing someone who is innocent is cruel and unusual punishment, which violates the Eighth Amendment to the U.S. Constitution.

The Supreme Court decided that Herrera's professed innocence did not invalidate his death sentence. The Constitution guaranteed a process—due process—not innocence or guilt. As long as Herrera had a constitutionally fair trial, then the conviction and sentence were appropriate, despite his evidence of innocence. As Justice Scalia stated years later, "This Court has *never* held that the Constitution forbids the execution of a convicted defendant who has had a full and fair trial but is later able to convince a habeas court that he is 'actually' innocent." In the innocence community, Scalia was notably remembered for valuing expediency and finality above proof of innocence and exoneration proceedings.

However, contrary to Scalia's statement, Justice Rehnquist's opinion against Herrera did entertain a free-standing claim of actual innocence, separate from constitutional rights. *Herrera v. Collins* opened the door for claims of actual innocence. But Rehnquist found that

Lionel Herrera had not presented the overwhelming evidence that would be necessary to establish such a claim.

On May 12, 1993, four months after the Supreme Court opinion, Texas government officials executed Herrera. With Herrera's dying words he proclaimed, "I am innocent, innocent, innocent . . . I am an innocent man, and something very wrong is taking place tonight."

Little did Rehnquist know when he wrote the opinion against Herrera that, within months, DNA evidence would begin exonerating people from death row through scientific evidence.

Kirk Bloodsworth became a free man on June 28, 1993. Proven innocent by DNA, he was the first death row exoneree. In October, the Death Penalty Information Center released a report on *Innocence and the Death Penalty: Assessing the Danger of Mistaken Executions*. Released only months after Lionel Herrera was executed and Kirk Bloodsworth was exonerated, the DPIC report powerfully exposed how courts sentence innocent people to death in the U.S. criminal legal system. Ever since, the Death Penalty Information Center tracks and monitors who is exonerated from death row.

By 1996, Illinois alone had nine death row exonerees. In 1998, Chicago hosted a National Conference on Wrongful Convictions and the Death Penalty with exonerees, lawyers, death penalty activists, investigators, journalists, and professors. At the time, there were only three legal innocence organizations: Barry and Peter's Innocence Project, Jacqueline McMurtrie's Innocence Project Northwest in Seattle, and Keith Findley and John Pray's Wisconsin Innocence Project. In the 1990s, the role of investigative journalism was instead paramount to innocence work. Yet many litigators attended that conference and then began innocence projects in their respective states, like queer women Cookie Ridolfi and Linda Starr with the Northern California Innocence Project, and Theresa Newman with the Duke Wrongful Convictions Clinic in North Carolina. Other women attendees later went on to lead innocence projects, like Shawn Armbrust and the Mid-Atlantic Innocence Project. In 2000, ten innocence projects gathered for another meeting in Chicago, and informally created what would become the Innocence Network. The meeting became annual, and the projects formalized an Innocence Network Steering Committee in 2003, with Cookie and Theresa as the founding presidents of this national organization of affiliated innocence projects. In 2004, the Innocence Project in New York hired Madeline DeLone as their executive director as they expanded and became an independent nonprofit. Maddie was a prisoners' rights attorney and advocate who directed the Innocence Project until she retired in 2019.

Today, the Innocence Network is guided by an elected executive board of innocence organization directors, and has a Network Support Unit, led by founding director Meredith Kennedy. The Network is a loose affiliation of innocence organizations, with every member organization as an independent entity. Affiliated member organizations are clinics at law schools, independent nonprofits, and some are connected with public defender offices. Since its founding, the Innocence Network has now spread internationally, supporting innocence work globally, with region specific networks for South and Central America, Asia, and Europe.

In 2000, then Governor George Ryan of Illinois imposed a moratorium halting the death penalty, the first moratorium nationally. At the time, Illinois had exonerated more people from death row than the state had executed since the reinstatement of the death penalty in 1976. Before leaving office, Governor Ryan commuted the sentences of the people on Illinois' death row, facing harsh blowback from many prosecutors. The criminal charges that prosecutors later brought against him may have even been connected to his opposition of the death penalty. In his memoir, Ryan reflected on his motivation to impose a moratorium: "That belief—that feeling—has not subsided in me. If anything, after five years as a prisoner of the criminal prosecution system, I have an intimately better understanding of the fundamental reforms that are needed and the consequences of leaving things as they are."

The innocence movement accomplished many policy successes in the 2000s. These include the passage of the Innocence Protection Act in 2004, for access to post-conviction DNA testing by federally incarcerated individuals. The Act also funded state DNA testing programs named after Kirk Bloodsworth. In the 2000s, every state in the nation ultimately adopted a post-conviction DNA testing statute.

Policy work that began at the national federal level has spread to state-level reforms, including laws for access to DNA testing in all fifty states, reformed eyewitness identification police procedures, recording of interrogations, and compensation statutes for wrongfully convicted individuals. Each year, the Innocence Network and member innocence organizations nationally support state-level legislation to create systemic change in individual jurisdictions.

In 2012, journalist Maurice Possley worked with professors Sam Gross and Rob Warden to create the National Registry of Exonerations, to track exonerations in the United States. Armed with this data, more researchers analyze what factors lead to innocent people being convicted.

The Innocence Project in New York has branched into strategic litigation, focusing in part on recognizing and excluding false forensic evidence from trials.

These are but some of the ongoing innocence efforts today.

The vision for the innocence movement by the Innocence Project and Innocence Network has been nothing less than transformational. Their work validates a crucial criticism of the criminal legal system as a whole: our system convicts innocent people and our prisons incarcerate innocent people. The creation of mass incarceration and the proliferation of prisons in the 1990s was based on fear about crime, alongside the profit and seeming economic advantages of building prisons. Fear and profit coupled with exploiting and blaming people of color broadly and Black people in particular for crime, and then restricting their freedom. In this way, America continued the legacy from slavery to convict leasing to present-day prison labor and hyper-incarceration.

Innocence work challenges our current system and ultimately encourages reforming our system for everyone—not only innocent people. Manifesting justice, advocating against unjust convictions even without concrete proof of factual innocence, is in my opinion the next step.

CHAPTER 21
Exculpatory Evidence
from the FBI

A letter from Prosecutor Jerry Rushing to Dr. Richard Vorder Bruegge at the Federal Bureau of Investigation lay at the top of the FBI file. Dr. Vorder Bruegge had been with the FBI since 1995 and performed forensic analyses of video and photographic evidence. Mama Sheila and Mama Sandi had never heard of him. Yet Vorder Bruegge was not only an imaging expert, he was Rushing's point person for Leigh and Tami's case. Rushing had sent Vorder Bruegge the VHS Comfort Inn surveillance tape to analyze.

In this follow-up letter, Jerry Rushing included Dr. West's own timeline of events for the video.

The letter appeared to follow up on a previous conversation between Dr. West and Dr. Vorder Bruegge. Further down the pile of FBI documents, Dr. West had documented the conversation in a letter to Dunn Lampton and Detective Jones. In this letter, Dr. West encouraged Lampton and Jones to send their video analysis request to Dr. Vorder Bruegge's forensic program. Dr. West said he would continue to work on his copy, while the prosecutors and police sent a version to the FBI. And it became apparent they did exactly that.

THE FBI REPORT, SEPTEMBER 11, 2000
The FBI conclusion for the prosecutors was brief: the video quality was too poor to see anything. They couldn't tell what the object lifted from the toolbox was. They also couldn't identify the person who lifted it.

The FBI detailed how they came to their conclusion. An FBI expert had enhanced the video, but the quality was so poor that the specialist could only see "an object or objects" carried by an unidentifiable figure.

This was damning of the prosecution's case. But it was the mailing slip, showing the prosecutors' office received the FBI report before trial, that sealed the deal for Sheila and Sandi.

Dr. Vorder Bruegge's final written analysis report was mailed to the Brookhaven district attorney's office on September 11, 2000. Included with the analysis was the original videotape, an FBI-enhanced copy of the videotape, and photo stills from the enhanced video. The FBI labeled and addressed the package to Mr. Jerry L. Rushing, Assistant District Attorney, Fourteenth Circuit Court District in Brookhaven, Mississippi.

The FBI report documented how they had communicated with the district attorney's office initially on April 13, 2000. Then Jerry Rushing sent the video to Dr. Vorder Bruegge who received it on April 18, 2000. Four and a half months later, Dr. Vorder Bruegge had evaluated the video, identified as Lab number 000418251 HD, and returned it to prosecutor Rushing's office.

After receiving the packet of materials from the FBI, prosecutors Lampton and Rushing turned over the enlarged photo stills to the defense attorneys. But the defense attorneys never received the FBI findings, that the video did not show Leigh removing a body, let alone Kim Williams, from the toolbox in the back of her pickup truck. No one did.

Instead, the prosecutors, in spite of the FBI analysis, went ahead with Dr. West's version of events. They presented to the jury Dr. West's interpretation of Leigh in the video as "anxious" and exhibiting "fight or flight" behavior; Dr. West's testimony that Leigh lifted the victim's body out of the toolbox; his testimony that although the video time ticker said only one second, perhaps there was something wrong with the tape and it was actually on fast forward.

Sheila and Sandi gave the FBI report to Will McIntosh, who started investigating why the prosecutors had failed to disclose the FBI report to Leigh's and Tami's attorneys. One major problem: Bill Barnett and Ken McNees were deceased.

Will reached out to Leigh's original attorney who had bowed out under pressure and health problems: John Ott. Ott was still practicing near Brookhaven and still taking cases, though rarely criminal ones. He was the one who had received the initial discovery from the prosecutors.

Before the trial, Ott received a copy of an overture letter. In the letter, prosecutor Jerry Rushing asked the FBI to review the hotel surveillance video in the case. Ott had also received the photo stills taken by the FBI from the hotel surveillance video. But he never got anything else. He wasn't told much about the FBI involvement, aside from the photo stills. Years later, he still believed Leigh was innocent, and he had heard nothing more about the FBI's involvement.

Next, Will contacted Tami's lawyer on appeal, Walter Wood. Walter Wood had met Tami while she was held in the Lincoln County jail, shortly after the jury convicted her. When he accepted the case, Wood had received McNeese's file. He, like Ott, said he had never seen or received any FBI reports or results. Neither McNees, Bill Barnett, nor even Tami Vance, ever told him the FBI had drafted their own findings about the videotape.

A POST-CONVICTION PETITION

Armed with new evidence, the Mississippi Innocence Project filed a petition for post-conviction relief for Leigh and Tami on April 5, 2011. The 59-page petition was a team effort. And then we waited. Leigh and Tami's case and convictions were almost ten years old. We couldn't just reopen the case and get a new trial, we had to ask permission of the Mississippi Supreme Court for a hearing. If they granted us permission, then the original trial court would hold a hearing to consider our newly discovered evidence.

We made three claims for why the Mississippi Supreme Court should let us have a hearing to reexamine the convictions. First, the newly discovered and exculpatory FBI report was withheld from the defendants. Second, the prosecutors put on testimony by Dr. West that they knew was false or at least contradicted by the FBI report. And third, Leigh's and Tami's attorneys failed to object to Dr. West as a video expert and object to the testimony and statements about Leigh's and Tami's sexual orientations. We argued that the State hadn't turned over exculpatory evidence in violation of *Brady v. Maryland*, a 1963 U.S. Supreme Court decision that required prosecutors to disclose evidence favorable to a defendant prior to trial. We also argued that the defense attorneys were ineffective. As a result, Leigh and Tami were wrongfully convicted.

The current state prosecutors opposed the motion for a hearing. For support, they referenced the case of Eddie Lee Howard, a man condemned to death row. In 2006, the Mississippi Supreme Court had denied Howard a post-conviction hearing on new evidence relating to Dr. West. The Supreme Court held that the trial court had appropriately accepted Dr. West as an expert in bite mark identification. The opinion read:

> In support of his post-conviction claim, Howard has offered numerous expert affidavits and other documents which attack Dr. West, his testimony, and bite mark evidence in general. These affidavits and other documents point out how many times Dr. West has been proven wrong and they discuss how unscientific his methods are . . . *[j]ust because Dr. West has been wrong a lot, does not mean, without something more, that he was wrong here.*

The prosecutors argued Dr. West appropriately testified to the bite marks in Leigh and Tami's case.

For the videotape analysis, the prosecutors contended that Dr. West wasn't testifying as an expert, he was simply testifying as a lay witness. The prosecution noted that during West's day and a half of testimony, he had at one point said, "I just want to allow people to look at the video and come to their own conclusions, do they see this or not." That was their proof that West was a lay witness rather than an expert.

The prosecutors also claimed that the FBI findings weren't anything new—indeed, they're what the defense attorneys had argued. The defense attorneys told the jury in closing that Leigh was moving a trash bag with clothes, not a body. So, the prosecution argued, they had said the same thing that an FBI agent would.

The prosecutors supported the bite mark evidence, as well as Dr. West's other testimony. In their response to our petition, they argued that "there was evidence that Stubbs smoked. The area of damage to the nipple was consistent with the pattern which would have been created by a burn from the end of a woman's narrow cigarette." In total, the prosecutors spent nineteen pages arguing that Leigh and Tami hadn't shown any prejudice against them, hadn't shown any new evidence that would have changed the verdict, or any evidence that was exculpatory.

Post-conviction motions for relief are generally time-barred after three years in Mississippi, and the Mississippi Innocence Project filed this petition nearly ten years after the conviction. So, by that measure, Leigh and Tami were too late.

However, there is an exception to the three-year limitation. Proving actual innocence tolls the three-year time limit. Leigh and Tami argued their innocence.

Now it was up to the Mississippi Supreme Court to decide if we could have a hearing and present our evidence—a crucial first step.

I continued to visit Leigh and Tami, and on a Tuesday in July I made the drive down to the women's prison in Rankin. Before I went in, I had to leave everything in my car except my documents, notepad and pen, and my ID and car keys that I would give to the guard. I checked my phone one last time. Tuesdays were opinion days. The Mississippi Supreme Court always released their decisions on that day, so I regularly checked the docket online.

When I saw Leigh and Tami's case listed, my heart started pumping wildly. *Please, please, give me good news to tell them today,* I silently implored.

There, in the parking lot of Central Mississippi Correctional Facility, I got the most joyful optimistic news that Leigh and Tami had had about their case in ten years.

I rushed inside, my face flushed, hardly patient with the guard who took my keys and ID and then led me to the bathroom to search me. When I came out, I could see another guard escorting Leigh in handcuffs to the room where we were to meet. Through the two glass double doors, operated by the control room to open one and not open the second until the first had closed, I saw her. She couldn't hear me, but I yelled anyway, waving dramatically, "We got good news! Good news!"

A look of panic spread across her face. She knew something was going on, but could she even dare to hope? I saw her face go red before she was walked out of sight to the meeting room. Now I waited, pacing, for the guard to walk me from the outside visitors waiting room, through the glass double doors, to the inside of the prison. I went to that small cinderblock walled room with a metal table, where I'd met with the two of them again and again.

Tami was already in the room when the guard let me in. Leigh came soon after.

"We got the hearing! The Mississippi Supreme Court just decided!" We all hugged and let out cheers of happiness.

The first hurdle was down. We were going to have a hearing in Brookhaven, back in that same courtroom as the trial. But we had a different judge this time: Judge Michael Taylor.

INVESTIGATING DR. WEST

Judge Michael Taylor took the bench at the Brookhaven Circuit Court in 2005. He had already been a part-time youth court judge for nine years. His wife was from Brookhaven, while he harkened from eastern Mississippi originally. He'd easily confide that he wasn't the country club type, saying "I don't have golf clubs, and no one in my family has owned a tennis racket." Instead, in August he'd get a limited permit to go alligator trapping in the nearby swamps of Wilkinson County.

Because Leigh Stubbs and Tami Vance had been granted a hearing, they could ask the district attorney's office for records—documents and evidence known as "discovery." We asked for a copy of the prosecutor's file. Judge Taylor granted it. The district attorney's office turned over their communications with the FBI, and their material relevant to Michael West in particular.

We were surprised by what we found inside.

On November 23, 2007, the Innocence Project in New York sent a letter and memo to Mississippi Attorney General Jim Hood. Vanessa Potkin at the Innocence Project was representing Kennedy Brewer and Levon Brooks—two men wrongfully convicted in part due to Dr. West's bogus bite mark findings. Vanessa and Peter Neufeld, the co-founder of the Innocence Project, had set out to prove Dr. West's lack of credibility and the unreliability of bite marks. To do so, they performed a sting operation.

They hired Dr. West to evaluate whether a suspected murderer's teeth matched bite mark photographs. Dr. West issued a nineteen-minute video, concluding that the "teeth did create that mark" and that the odds that anyone else made the bite were "astronomical."

In reality, West had evaluated a random set of teeth from an innocent man and matched them to the photographs. There was no way there could be a match. The true perpetrator had already been properly charged and convicted based on DNA evidence.

By March 25, 2008, the Mississippi attorney general's office was conducting its own investigation into Dr. West, led by Chief Investigator Karl Pree and the Public Integrity Division. Investigator Pree had already reached out to Dunn Lampton about cold case files involving West.

Internally, the investigators couldn't determine if Dr. West had committed a crime. Investigator Keith Milsap pulled the court transcript for Leigh and Tami's case and looked at Dr. West's testimony. Milsap didn't think any criminal charges were applicable. Thus, he recommended sending the file to the Ethics Commission. Milsap forwarded his recommendation, along with the case file for *State of Mississippi v. Vance and Stubbs*, to Pree. The date was over a year later—September 15, 2009. Nothing ever came from the internal investigation into Dr. West, and Dunn Lampton never mentioned that the Public Integrity Division had contacted him about Leigh and Tami's case. By this point, Lampton had challenges of his own; he was paralyzed from his bruised spinal injury in 2007, and he resigned from his post as U.S. Attorney of the Southern District of Mississippi in 2009.

MORE BITE MARK EXPERTS

To prepare for the hearing, I reached out to Mary and Peter Bush, two experts on analyzing and challenging bite marks. Dr. Mary Bush was and is a dentist and professor of Dental Medicine at SUNY Buffalo. From 2011 to 2012 she was the president of the American Society of Forensic Odontology and a fellow of the Odontology Section of the American Academy of Forensic Sciences. Her academic focus and writing are on Forensic Dentistry. Together with her husband Peter Bush, director of the South Campus Instrument Center at SUNY Buffalo and also a member of the American Society of Forensic Odontology, they coauthor papers on bite mark analysis research. Dr. and Mr. Bush agreed to write and submit an affidavit on their bite mark research for Leigh and Tami's hearing.

First, they noted how the 2009 National Academy of Sciences report on forensic science had specifically called out bite marks, saying that the uniqueness of bite marks had not been scientifically established. Then, in their own research between 2009 and 2011, they analyzed dental shape in large populations, and the distortion of bite marks inflicted on human cadaver skin. In their research they discovered that human skin is not an accurate "recording medium." The same teeth marks could look wildly different on different bodies and skin. Their research also found a large possibility for false positives, where dental molds that weren't the creator of the imprint were the best "match" or fit. Together, their research findings created a stir in the community and raised concern over the use of bite mark evidence in legal proceedings.

We filed the affidavit of their research with the court as soon as we could.

TRYING TO DEPOSE DR. WEST

We sent a notice to take Dr. West's deposition. He refused to attend unless we paid him.

He demanded $3,600 to render his "expert opinion" on whether Leigh and Tami were guilty or innocent. Perhaps it was not surprising, considering that Leigh and Tami had been ordered to pay his expert fees the first time around.

Dr. West went so far as to file a motion on his own behalf that he shouldn't be forced to participate in a deposition, particularly not unpaid.

At the time, Dr. West was the head of the dental clinic at the South Mississippi Correctional Institute. Occasionally, Mama Sandi was asked to work in that very dental clinic. She always refused. It was stunning that Dr. West, who put people in those prisons with his junk science, somehow had the confidence to be a prison dentist.

But we were deposing Dr. West not as an expert but rather to review his trial testimony in the case. We additionally asked for West's reports on the Brewer case, the Brooks case, and other cases that West discussed in his testimony at trial. These people had now been proven innocent. In two of the cases, the actual culprit was apprehended.

Fortunately, once a criminal case is challenged post-conviction, it becomes a civil case where different rules apply. In the purportedly even playing field of civil cases, everything is disclosed. This transparency is very different from the rules of criminal procedure. In the 1930s, when the rules were created, Southern prosecutors successfully argued that criminal rules should be different because the focus is on the trial, while civil cases focus on the facts and the science and the information before trial. The heavy burden on the prosecution at a criminal trial—proving the defendant is guilty beyond a reasonable doubt—allegedly balanced out how little information prosecutors must share with the defendants.

But in the United States, 95 percent of defendants plead guilty. If defendants choose to go to trial, they are punished with a more severe sentence. This is known as the "trial penalty." The faulty reasoning that a trial balances the power between the parties only benefits prosecutors.

In post-conviction, however, the proceedings become civil and former defendants are entitled to discovery. We could depose Dr. West.

When Judge Michael Taylor held a hearing on Dr. West's motion to be paid for the deposition, Judge Taylor reminded him that the court rules set forth a witness fee: $25 a day. That's how much jurors are paid per day, and that's how much witnesses compelled to attend and give testimony in a case are paid.

"Dr. West, people aren't free to set their own rates," the judge said. "You're not entitled to whatever amount of money you want. You're not even entitled to what you regularly make for testifying. But you can be compelled to testify."

"Your honor, I regret to find out I'm a slave," West exclaimed. "As far as I'm concerned, strike everything that I have ever testified to and cut them loose, have a new trial. I don't remember, I ain't got the evidence, and I ain't got a dog in the race."

Silently, the courtroom reeled.

Dr. West continued, "I quit. Cut the girls loose. Everything I've said, I don't remember. I don't care anymore. What do you want from me? I get accused of being a criminal. And I take it personal."

Judge Taylor instead ordered him to attend the deposition.

"I'll be there," Dr. West said. "Or I'll go to jail. They've got good food and you can get dental care and health care. What the hell."

Dental care from the likes of Dr. West.

We set a date for the deposition.

CHRISTMAS IN MISSISSIPPI

That November 2011, I got a letter from Tami. She said that since the holidays were coming up, she didn't expect she'd hear from us for a while. She wanted to thank us for all of our work on her case.

It didn't seem right. Family holidays in prison without outside family.

I went to a greeting card store we had in our small town and got cards for all of us at the Mississippi Innocence Project to sign and send to our clients. It was a tradition I continued every year. Sometimes ours was the only card our clients received.

Finding the right message was difficult. "Hope you appreciate the warmth and closeness of friends and family this season" seemed cruel; "your light brightens and makes the world a better place" could be accurate or downright taunting. Dancing gingerbread men chanting "Merry Christmas!" seemed juvenile and too focused on Christmas.

Finally I found a UNICEF card. On the outside it read: "Peace, Joy, Love." Inside the words were poignant: "the same simple wishes . . . each year with a new hope."

I bought all of them.

CHAPTER 22
Imagining Dickie's Mother, Helen Ervin

In this chapter I envision what Helen Ervin thought and felt. Helen has died, so I have no way of knowing. Therefore I want to make clear that I'm imagining this, unlike the rest of the book, which is factually based.

HELEN

She had looked after all of her kids, but the ones she tried to hold the closest, the ones who stayed at home with her, had left her arms and this world even while she tried to hold them tight.

She was still in this old house. She'd thought it charming, a needed change of old world when she bought it in the 1990s and it was already almost one hundred years old. Her husband James Ervin Sr. was from Pike County, Mississippi, and they moved back from Louisiana. She didn't realize he'd pass on so soon, in 1999. She didn't realize the old ghosts and shadows that came with the house, the house that now welcomed the ghosts of her husband and sons of the same name.

Sitting on the broad porch, she faced the slow cars on Robb Street. The only time the street was busy was on Sundays, with cars pulling in to First Baptist Church across the street. All these years later, her home was still next to the Star Drive-In and the Piggly Wiggly down the street. She had always liked the small town of a thousand people, coming there from Louisiana. From her front porch, she could see the one red stoplight at the end of Robb Street, before hitting Highway 51.

More shadows were on the porch now. She suddenly saw them, the girls whispering on the porch. It was dark outside, but she saw their heads together. Then they disappeared.

Dickie's life had fallen apart after sweet Kim overdosed. That sweet kind girl. A breath of fresh air in their old house. She came and went as she wanted, but Helen never minded. Seeing Kim when she came back, some healthy weight on her, that hug and kiss for Mama Helen. She was back.

Except she wasn't—this was her last return to this house. This house that needed her.

They never talked about it, but she could see Kim weighed on her son. She had hoped the young girl would settle down with Dickie, give him motivation. She remembered the Christmas when Dickie told her Kim was going into rehab. Good, she thought. That would get things back on track.

Sometimes Helen would go into her work as a receptionist at the medical center and think she saw a glimpse of Kim in a hospital room. Of course she didn't, she'd remind herself. But just as the ghosts of her sons stayed with her, those images of Kim did as well. Kim, in a hospital bed, with tubes connecting throughout her body. Her naked skin amplified by the glowing projector in the dark courtroom. Then Kim was there, live in the courtroom, present though not really, not any more than she was on the screen. Helen saw her on a bench outside the courtroom with her mom, slumped. Her dark hair was in a short bob, a cane by her side.

That was one of Helen's hardest days. Getting on the stand, answering those prying questions. She had practiced her answers with the prosecutor, Dunn Lampton, the U.S. Attorney, the rising star. Back then, he had failed at getting into Congress twice, but everyone knew he was going places. He'd been the district attorney for twenty years. All those years he had been striving, telling the people of Pike County that he put away drug dealers, stopped welfare fraud. Sometimes, Helen wondered if he was talking about her family. That didn't seem right.

Then right after Kim's case and those girls got locked away, George Bush Jr. became president. Dunn was off, he got the U.S. Attorney position.

But then Dunn became like her son, Dickie. Like Dickie, he was in a car accident in Pike County, and damaged his spinal cord. He was on his private muscadine farm, but nonetheless. Like Dickie, Dunn was hurt. But unlike Dickie, the pain pills were not enough to make him walk. Dunn was in a wheelchair the rest of his shortened life. He was buried now, in Pine Bluff Cemetery, not too far down the road.

When they found Dickie, hanging, Helen's heart broke. He chose such a difficult way to leave this world. They took his body to the same funeral home in McComb as his father, James Ervin Sr. Dickie killed himself just two years after that trial, that last time they saw Kim.

Those questions.

"Now, tell us a little bit about the physical condition of your son James or Dickie?"

The memories.

"Well, he's a cripple. He has multiple things wrong with him. Mainly his spine. He's had several operations."

"What caused those injuries?"

As if she hadn't been asked that a million times. What's wrong with your son?

"An automobile accident, then operations that didn't work."

And then the pills always talking about the pills. The drinking. The DUIs. They had told her the FBI even had a number for Dickie.

"Isn't it true that Kim had tried to get James to go to a recovery center, as well, for some help?"

"Not that I know of. It could be true but I didn't know it."

"Would you call James a—of course I realize he is your son, ma'am—but would you call him a truthful and believable person?"

Just because he was a cripple. Just because of those drugs. He needed them. Sure he'd been in some trouble, but none of this was his fault.

"As far as I know, yes."

"Might he take some drugs illegally? Would he do that?"

"He wouldn't tell me if he did."

"Isn't it true that your son James smoked marijuana on a regular basis?"

"You could say that, yes."

The police. Dickie had been arrested at least four times for possession of marijuana and selling marijuana. Thankfully Dickie had never served any time, the charges were always dropped. It was Peanut who got in real trouble, Peanut with his blond hair and blue eyes that kept him in trouble but out of punishment. Until the punishment was unavoidable, and they didn't have the money to keep him out of it. Peanut, convicted of attempted murder when they all lived in Louisiana. Peanut,, who was charged a $10 fine and to serve a year of weekends at the jail. He was only seventeen, they had waited until his eighteenth birthday to sentence him. He had been a kid in her eyes.

But then Peanut violated his probation later that year with the hit and run, where he gave a fake name. After that he was arrested on armed robbery, auto theft, and felon in possession of a firearm. For that, he served time in Elayn Hunt Correctional Center in Louisiana. After that, Helen and James Sr. had moved the family and both boys to Summit, Mississippi, seeking a return to small town life for her boys, even though they were now adults. Even though they would soon be ghosts.

Helen tried to calm herself, questioning why she was remembering so much tonight. This house had always been full of shadows. That dark night, with the girls whispering on the porch. The darkness starting.

Inside, the lights on, she saw it again. Kim sweeping through like a beautiful tumbleweed, hair spinning as she turned and moved and looked throughout the house, happy, bustling, and then she disappeared into the back room with Dickie. He needed her. Helen had smiled to herself, then turned to talk with the girls, while Peanut eagerly helped them look for the tent. Peanut, who died only a few years after Dickie. Of her five children, only her daughters survived.

It all ended so quickly. Kim running out and jumping in that truck. Peanut running after them, chasing in his own car. Helen, standing on the front porch, watching Peanut's taillights as they sped to the red stoplight. They stopped, and turned, and the street was in darkness.

CHAPTER 23
A Post-Conviction Hearing

DEPOSITION OF DR. VORDER BRUEGGE, FBI ANALYST

In January, we deposed Dr. Vorder Bruegge. We did it over the telephone, the Mississippi attorneys meeting in Merrida "Buddy" Coxwell's office in Jackson. Buddy was now representing Tami while the Mississippi Innocence Project represented Leigh. Dr. Vorder Bruegge was in Quantico, Virginia, with an FBI attorney listening on his end.

Dr. Vorder Bruegge was a senior photographic technologist at the FBI who examined questioned photographic evidence—images from film, but also digital—for fifteen years. In 2000, he was already a photographic technologist. He used professional quality video equipment, and a video production studio.

In 2000, Dr. Vorder Bruegge received a request for assistance from the Brookhaven district attorney's office. The letter from Prosecutor Rushing arrived soon after, along with Dr. West's timeline and the VHS tape. Dr. Vorder Bruegge set to work. He completed a report, which he sent to the Brookhaven district attorney's office, along with a cover letter, the original videotape and copies, and two envelopes of photographs from the video.

Dr. Vorder Bruegge never talked with any defense attorneys on the case. Not until his deposition in 2012.

The key document in question was the chain of custody log. The log documented who communicated between the FBI and the district attorney's office, when, and why. The chain of custody log along with the activity and communications of the analyst notes were solely in the FBI file and custody of the FBI. Mama Sheila and Mama Sandi had brought this document to light through their Freedom Of Information Act request to the FBI.

This two-page document confirmed that between April 18 and September 11, 2000, the FBI had analyzed the tape, written a report, and told the prosecutors about it.

But the prosecutors never told Leigh and Tami. Or the jury that judged them. No one called Dr. Vorder Bruegge as a witness at the trial.

In his notes, Dr. Vorder Bruegge specified how he tried to bring out as much detail as he could from the images and the surveillance video itself. Indeed, he used the best technology available at the time to do so. But much of the video was corrupted or degraded, so that there were lines of static roll down the screen—meaning no one could see anything on the video at those moments. Reviewing the enhanced segments, Vorder Bruegge ultimately determined that they were "unsuitable for use."

"Were you able to determine whether or not two people moved a body from the toolbox on the back of the truck and carried it into the hotel room?" Buddy Coxwell asked.

"I was not able to determine that," Dr. Vorder Bruegge responded.

"Were you able to determine whether or not a person slammed the toolbox top down on a person lying in the toolbox?"

"No, I could not see anything to determine that happened."

"Your notes at 10:47:23 read: 'garment individual observed in rear of truck, behind truck, with dark object in possession (?)' What does the question mark mean?"

"It basically means I can't tell what I'm really seeing at that point. It could be a dark object or not," Dr. Vorder Bruegge clarified.

Buddy continued. "Your notes at 10:48:30 read 'Individual in light shirt picks up dark object from box.' Did you attempt to focus in on that dark object?"

"Yes, but it isn't possible to see any detail."

"Were you able to determine whether that object was a bag, or a piece of luggage, or a human body?"

"No, I could not."

Buddy asked, "You could make no determination whatsoever what the dark object was?"

"That's correct," Dr. Vorder Bruegge answered. "I'm pretty sure it is actually a physical object because I believe it moved with the individual."

"On page 1 of 15 of your case activity log, it says 'called' and there's a box 'concerning needing case information,'" Buddy said. "Do you know who is the person you called?"

"The name listed is Detective Nolan Jones."

So now we knew. Nolan Jones also had been in touch with the FBI about analyzing the video and creating a report.

"So you called Nolan Jones?"

"Yes. That would be standard procedure—you contact the individual who submits the request to let them know it has been received."

Dr. Vorder Bruegge also called Nolan Jones when he was sending back the video, along with his report and the still photos.

"One last question," Buddy said. "Dr. Vorder Bruegge, is this examination and looking at the videotapes—I don't know a scientific way of putting it—does it just boil down to a matter of interpretation of what you think you see?"

"When conducting an examination like this, the way reports get written here is we try to make it as objective as possible," Dr. Vorder Bruegge replied. "So interpretations about a body being moved or two different people—we try to restrict ourselves to the facts only. That's why there are terms like 'dark object.' If I can't tell that it's a human being with arms, legs, and a head, for example, I have no basis for saying that. That's a long-winded way of saying there can be a lot of interpretation, but you're not going to get it out of me or this laboratory."

Dr. Vorder Bruegge had spent sixteen days working on the videotape at the FBI.

DEPOSITION OF DR. WEST

On Saturday, February 11, 2012, on Main Street in Hattiesburg, Will McIntosh and Tucker Carrington of the Mississippi Innocence Project and Buddy Coxwell interviewed Michael West. Marvin Sanders from the attorney general's office was there as well. He was representing the state in its effort to uphold the convictions.

I was not. After drafting the questions and gathering materials for Dr. West's deposition, I had received a scholarship for a meditation class for that very same date. And after months of working on this case, I was going to take a break.

What a mistake. That deposition would be used by attorneys against Dr. West for years to come. My being there wouldn't have made a difference about how Dr. West answered—I was right about that—but I wish I had heard those answers myself.

I drafted deposition questions about Levon Brooks and Kennedy Brewer, and their wrongful convictions due to Dr. West's testimony—along with Johnnie Bourn's dropped case, and the cases of Mark Oppie, James Earl Gates, Larry Maxwell, John Ross, and Anthony Keko. The list went on. I had questions about Dr. West's suspension and dismissals from governing boards in his field, about Dr. Vorder Bruegge and the surveillance tape, and of course holes in Dr. West's own testimony.

The deposition went way off the rails, and West made stunning claims—even for him. I could not possibly have prepared for what unfolded.

Dr. West defended his testimony from the trials against Kennedy Brewer and Levon Brooks. West argued that he had testified how each defendant bit each respective girl when she was alive. He never testified that Levon Brooks or Kennedy Brewer raped or killed the girls, "only that at some time prior to the girls' death, they had been bitten—physical child abuse."

"I still to this day believe Kennedy Brewer bit Christina Jackson and Mr. Brooks bit his victim prior to their kidnapping and murder," Dr. West said in our deposition. "They haven't been exonerated in my mind. Nothing—no new evidence has been brought to make me think those teeth did not make this mark."

But first, Dr. West refused to answer any other questions about Levon Brooks and Kenny Brewer's cases—or any of the other wrongful conviction cases where he had testified "indeed and without doubt" that the defendant bit the victim. West refused to talk about his testimony against Anthony Keko, for example, except to say, "I got a call a couple months ago Mr. Keko had died, and before he died—well, it wasn't a confession. It was a brag to his friend that he thought it was going to take thirty minutes to kill his wife but it only took him nineteen. I remember that. I don't have any independent recollection of [my] testimony."

Anthony Keko was wrongfully convicted in Plaquemines Parish, Louisiana. The prosecutor exhumed the victim's body fourteen months after burial, and Dr. West testified that he found a bite mark on her shoulder and matched it to Keko. That was the only evidence against Keko.

Anthony Keko is still alive today.

As a general question, Tucker asked, "Is it fair to say that your conclusions in the Stubbs and Vance case with respect to the bite mark, you're as sure about them today and as confident about them today as you were when you made them back in 2000?"

Dr. West's answer was a shock.

"No. I no longer believe in bite mark analysis. I don't think it should be used in court. I think you should use DNA, throw bite marks out."

Tucker didn't miss a beat. "And does that opinion include this case?"

"Yes. Throw the bite marks out."

"Are you withdrawing your testimony about the bite mark identification in this case?" Tucker pushed.

"When I testified in this case, I believed in the uniqueness of human bite marks. I no longer believe in that," Dr. West declared. "And if I was asked to testify in this case again, I would say I don't believe it's a system that's reliable enough to be used in court."

Dr. West leaned back in his chair. He then described how three forensic odontologists, who he respected tremendously, had mis-identified bite marks. The DNA from the saliva on the bite mark had excluded the person that each reputable odontologist had identified as the biter.

"Now," Dr. West continued, "when I have three men that I really respect their opinion in odontology to be proven incorrect, I either have to assume that these three men are idiots or the system they're using to deal with is flawed. And I've come to the opinion that the system of bite mark analysis is flawed. It's nowhere as exact as we thought it was. And for that reason, I no longer conduct those."

Dr. West paused. "I can no longer rely on bite marks as a truth . . . whether or not I can say this guy bit this person, to which degree of certainty that the court may require, I don't know if I can do that anymore. You have a system, to me, that's better than bite marks, and that's DNA. We didn't have that technique available to us at that time. Go with your best evidence."

Tucker asked, "Have you at any point made this change of opinion known to any law enforcement in Mississippi?"

"I've had some call me," Dr. West said. "I told them I wouldn't waste my time. I've been wrong in the past. I'm human. I make mistakes. I know my first wife kept a list."

"You say you've been wrong," Tucker continued. "Have you been wrong with respect to the past in your bite mark identifications?"

"I made bite mark analysis that turned out to be wrong, yes."

As astonishing and seemingly show-stopping as that testimony was, Tucker had more work to do. He asked Dr. West questions about the Comfort Inn surveillance video.

"Detective Nolan, when we got this tape, he showed it to me," West explained. "I told him, 'Send that tape off to the FBI and have them enhance it.' Three or four months go by, and he calls me up, says, 'Look, the FBI sent the tape back. Said they didn't have the hardware, software, or equipment to work it. Could you give it a try?' I said, 'Yeah, I will give it a go.' He gave me the VHS tape."

West said he worked on his home computer. "It was a regular old computer. That was the thing that stunned me. I said, 'The FBI don't have these computers?' And they told me no, they didn't. And that kind of stunned me. I thought they had, you know, great super computers. And they didn't have laptops."

"Were you aware "—Tucker caught himself—"Ever made aware that the FBI was, in fact, able to engage in an analysis of the same surveillance videotape?"

"I was told they couldn't do anything with it," West responded. "Dunn was kind of, you know, 'The FBI can't do it. Mike, can you?' I said, 'Yeah. Hell, take it to the TV station.' He said, 'Okay. Do it.' And

I'm going, 'The FBI can't afford $300 for Adobe Premier?' But they didn't have it in their budget, didn't have a computer, whatever. We were both kind of stunned about the inability of the FBI to do anything."

Buddy took over the questioning.

"Do you remember Jerry Rushing?" he asked.

West responded, "Oh yeah, I don't know what his title was, but he was always with—Yogi and Boo-Boo, Dunn and Jerry."

Buddy ignored the comment. "The video enhancement you did, where did you get your training on that?"

West looked blank-faced. "What training?" he puzzled.

"Your training in video enhancement."

"Self-taught."

In 2003, Leigh and Tami had appealed their initial convictions, arguing that the court should not have admitted Dr. West's testimony about the surveillance video because he wasn't an expert and was not qualified to be giving opinions. The Mississippi Supreme Court denied relief, saying that since the defense had not objected to Dr. West's testimony on the video at the time of trial, the issue had been waived and Tami and Leigh couldn't bring it up on appeal. But the Supreme Court did say that a different record would have likely led to a different result—a reversal of their convictions.

Back to the bite marks.

"Are you now saying that you would not render testimony in the Stubbs and Vance case on the uniqueness of any bite mark testimony?" Buddy asked.

"In today's climate, no, I wouldn't. Michael West don't believe in bite marks—uniqueness of bite mark anymore."

"So, it's not reliable?"

"Not to Mike West. Have I made mistakes on any of my opinions? I could have. Have I tried my darndest to minimize and double-check and triple-check? Yes. Am I confident in the opinions that I've rendered in other cases in Mississippi in federal and state courts? Yes, I am."

What kept coming up was that Dr. West was being sued civilly for his false testimony in the Brooks and Brewer cases.

"I feel I've been forced out of the profession by the Innocence Pro-

ject," Dr. West complained. "I've been accused of being a criminal by
several members of the Innocence Project. When I go into a courtroom and render an opinion, it lays me open to savage attacks by un-
scrupulous men. You're going to need a big shotgun to get me in court
to render an opinion again because you can't protect me from this
scum."

Tucker chimed in.

"Let me follow up. As you know, my name is Tucker Carrington,
right? And I work with the Mississippi Innocence Project."

"I don't know. You say it is."

"All right. Would you—when you characterized these people as
scum, just to be clear, am I included in that definition?"

"No."

COMPARING DR. WEST AND THE FBI'S FINDINGS

It's September 2000, more than nine months before Leigh Stubbs and
Tami Vance's trial. Prosecutors Dunn Lampton and Jerry Rushing
hold in their hands two conflicting opinions on what happened in the
parking lot of the Brookhaven Comfort Inn.

One opinion was by a dentist, "self-taught" in video analysis, working on his home computer. He had repeatedly testified for Dunn and
other prosecutors across Mississippi. As a defense attorney once told
me, Dr. West was like a snake-charmer with juries. He would testify
confidently that Kim was put in the toolbox on the back of Leigh's
truck, and then either Leigh or Tami took Kim out of that toolbox and
carried her unconscious body into the hotel room. He would testify
that the video caught the act: even under the cloak of darkness and
with Leigh looking repeatedly out the door, the video had captured
Kim's legs and her long hair hanging down, as Leigh quickly and ner-
vously grabbed Kim from the toolbox and carried her inside.

The other opinion was by an FBI analyst, trained in video analysis.
He had worked on the video for sixteen days, making blow-ups, documenting his work with his notes, and creating copies of enhanced
videos to send to the prosecutors. In the two seconds during which
Dr. West said he saw Leigh pick up Kim from the toolbox, the FBI analyst saw only a dark object. He never identified a body, legs, jeans,

hair, or any part of a person. Whereas Dr. West didn't see the truck being unloaded, Dr. Vorder Bruegge saw between 10:15 and 11:00 P.M. that an individual carried objects back and forth between the truck and the hotel fourteen times.

Dr. Vorder Bruegge and Dr. West agreed on a few things: whatever was taken out of the toolbox was taken out between 10:47 P.M. and 47 seconds and 10:47 P.M. and 49 seconds. They also both identified that parts of the video were missing and were completely unusable. Dr. Vorder Bruegge, however, thought some of those crucial moments were distorted as well.

The FBI remained unable to discern the figures and details that Dr. West attributed in his viewing of the videotape.

Faced with a choice, the prosecutors elected to go with Dr. West.

ARGUING QUEER BIAS

In our office at the Mississippi Innocence Project, we knew the argument about Leigh's and Tami's queer identities was a nonstarter. But when Leigh and Tami finally had their post-conviction hearing to challenge their wrongful convictions, I was determined to bring up the lesbian bias even if there was no hope of winning on that point. If Leigh and Tami had been made to feel ashamed of their sexual orientation, and criminalized for it, then I would do what I could to make the court feel ashamed for allowing that to happen.

I reached out to the Williams Institute at UCLA School of Law for research. A new book had just come out by Joey Mogul, Andrea Ritchie, and Kay Whitlock, *Queer (In)Justice: The Criminalization of LGBT People in The United States.* Joey, a civil rights attorney in Chicago, had represented people convicted based on their queer identities. She thankfully took some of my questions when I asked for advice.

Joey recommended I ask whether Professor Ruthann Robson, a professor at CUNY Law School and an expert in sexual orientation discrimination, particularly against lesbians, would testify as an expert witness. I asked. Ruthann ultimately couldn't testify on the days of the hearing, but she did write an affidavit for the court. Her words were powerful:

Neither Dr. West nor Dr. Galvez were experts in sex, sexuality, lesbianism, or criminal behavior. Based upon my knowledge, including 30 years of research into lesbians and crime, there is *absolutely no empirical evidence* to support a statement that lesbians are more likely than other people, including other women, to be violent or commit violent crimes or to be especially brutal when committing crimes. Additionally, there is also *absolutely no empirical evidence* to support a statement that lesbians are more likely than other people, including other women, to "bite" during an assault or during sexual activity.

While it is not based upon any empirical evidence, the notion that lesbians are especially brutal has gotten traction because it is a frequent negative stereotype of lesbians in popular culture. While the situation by 2012 has improved, the stereotype of the "killer lesbian" endures. According to a Report from GLAAD, the Gay and Lesbian Alliance Against Defamation, the depiction of lesbians on television and movies was "almost uniformly negative," citing as an example that in 1991 "out of a total of the four lesbians appearing on series television last season, two were portrayed as murderers, and one as a murder victim in which the other lesbians are under suspicion for the murder." The Report concluded that in summary, "lesbian images in film and television depict us as man-hating, society-destroying, sex-driven or sexless creatures who have no hearts, homes, families, values, or reasons to live."

Likewise, although not based upon any empirical evidence, the notion that lesbians are especially prone to bite is believable for some because it is consistent with the stereotype that lesbians possess animal sexuality or are vampires. As women's studies scholar Bonnie Zimmerman has observed, the lesbian vampire myth has a long history in literature, legend, and film. Professor Zimmerman observes that contemporary films, television plots, novels, and stories draw on two sources: "One is the Countess Elisabeth Bathory, a sixteenth century Hungarian noblewoman who was reputed to have tortured and murdered 650 virgins, bathing in their blood in order to preserve her youth. The second source is Joseph Sheridan LeFanu's *Carmilla* (1871), an intensely erotic novella recounting the story of the Countess Millarca Karnstein, who lives through the centuries by vampirizing young girls." The lesbian Dracula, a woman who bites other women because she must do so to survive, is a stereotype, often unconscious or not fully articulated, that permeates popular culture.

The convictions and harsh sentencing of Leigh and Tami were based upon the logical structure advanced by the prosecutor and supported by the opinions advanced by non-experts: all lesbians are sadistic, brutal, and sexually violent; the defendants are lesbians; therefore the defendants are guilty of the brutal attack on the victim.

What is not based in logic or empirical evidence is the premise that all lesbians are sadistic, brutal, and sexually violent. Instead, it is based on mere prejudice.

Doctors, attorneys, jurors and even judges can be biased and unthinkingly accept outdated stereotypes that lesbians are brutal sexual torturers with a propensity to bite. But courts can also act to remedy such prejudice.

And with that, we were ready for the hearing.

THE POST-CONVICTION HEARING

In February 2012, the hearing finally began. Leigh and Tami were brought in from Rankin Prison. They saw the sunrise from outside the prison walls for the first time in ten years. The courtroom filled with supporters for the two women. The lawyers paced in the front talking and preparing.

We had the burden to show that with this new evidence, a jury would more likely than not have come to a different conclusion at trial.

Jerry Rushing took the stand. He said he didn't think the FBI report was exculpatory. The FBI report had been conspicuously missing from the prosecutors' file, just like it had been missing from the defense attorneys' files.

Buddy Coxwell noted for the court, "I'm not accusing Mr. Rushing of saying, okay, I got this report, I've got to hide it from the defense in this case. I don't know what happened. And I wouldn't want to say that to him. But *Brady* and *Giglio* [*Giglio v. United States*] and all of the cases that the U.S. Supreme Court has come down with apply, regardless of good faith or bad faith. These documents have to be put in the hands of the defendant."

I was next.

"Jerry Rushing, when he testified, said that Dr. West was simply presenting the video," I said. "But Dr. West was doing more than that—he was providing a running commentary for the jury, encouraging them to imagine, to see what he saw, a woman's body. Far beyond what a lay witness or a fact witness could do, yet he wasn't qualified or experienced as an expert to give the scientific testimony that he did."

I took a deep breath. And then, I began on the issue most important to me.

"We see throughout the transcript of this case that there are homophobic portrayals made of Leigh Stubbs and of Tami Vance," I said. "But all of this begins with Tami Vance's own counsel in voir dire of the jury equating 'lesbian behavior' with the word 'deviant.' That's where it begins. That alone would be ineffective. But it goes beyond that. Because counsel never objects to the multiple times that sexual orientation is brought up.

"Now, the state may argue sexual orientation was relevant. But it was not relevant in the way it was used. It was used to show that Leigh Stubbs and Tami Vance had a greater likelihood of committing this type of aggravated assault because they were lesbians, that they had a propensity even, to commit an aggravated assault. It was used to inflame the jury, to show that they are not just average people, that they are different because of their sexual orientation. That's not permissible.

"If it had been probative or relevant to have their sexual orientation brought forward to the fact finder, then defense counsel could have stipulated yes, they're lesbians. But they didn't. That's ineffective. And that is coupled by the fact that because they didn't stipulate, we see these multiple questions.

"And what we know about this is that juries at that time were much more likely to be homophobic and, frankly, repulsed by deep discussion about homosexual behavior. We even see Dr. Galvez himself, the defense case-in-chief, he testifies that these are repulsive cases. And he makes these claims about finding bite marks in lesbian rapes, that homosexual crimes are very sadistic. None of this should have come in.

"We see this on the State side, with Dr. West saying that he would expect to find bite marks in a homosexual rape case. Where he has the qualifications to say that is questionable. He says that on one hand, Galvez says it on the other, and those are used to the detriment of these clients in many ways.

"I think one of the most hard and fast ways you can see the detriment is in the sentencing. We see the judge at sentencing specifically saying, because of Dr. Galvez's testimony about homosexuals being dangerous, I'm sentencing them to the max. They're getting a twenty-year sentence for possession of Oxycontin. Even if it's a first-time offense, they're getting a twenty-year sentence. And that's because of the testimony about them being homosexuals," I said.

"We see that the prosecutors say this was a brutal assault, that it was like torture. And they close by saying, 'When you look at all the evidence, you'll realize that while it's a circumstantial evidence case, these two women who were living together, were lovers, whether because of the drugs or the alcohol or their lifestyle, viciously attacked Kimberly Williams for no reason and tried to cover it up.'

"One of the reasons why all of this is so damaging was that fact-finders at that time and juries at that time, as we see from studies in Professor Robson's affidavit, in 1998, potential jurors were more than three times as likely to themselves say that they couldn't be fair or impartial to a gay or a lesbian defendant than if the defendant was from another minority group, such as African-American or Latino."

Judge Taylor interjected. "I saw that statistic. And does that say anything other than what it says? It doesn't say they're more fair now, it just means they're less likely to say they can't be fair now. So what do we do with that information?"

"That may be correct, Your Honor," I replied. "But in the present we work to limit that kind of bias. And you're right, there might be the same reactions from juries today. I wouldn't be surprised if there is."

"Well, I understand all she says is they're less likely to say it now," the judge responded.

"They did say it then," I pointed out. "And relevance is at the time of this trial. Now if there were a retrial in this case, I think there would be a stipulation that they're lesbians and that there would be objections to testimony about kissing, to behavior, and particularly to people opining about sadistic lesbian rape when they're 'experts' and when they really have no qualifications to say that."

I continued. "What you're referring to also from the affidavit from Professor Robson is where she says that for her thirty years of research, there's absolutely no empirical evidence to support a statement that lesbians are more likely than other people to be violent or commit violent crimes. She also said there is absolutely no empirical evidence to support a statement that lesbians are more likely to bite during an assault or during sexual activity. Your Honor is correct in pointing that out. The studies point to what the jury would have been like in the first place, and how all of this information would have, could have, and, I would argue, did negatively influence the perception that the jury had of the defendants in this case.

"The final point on that is just there should have been objections. The sexual orientation was not relevant, it didn't show that they had a greater propensity to commit an aggravated assault, but it was used that way. And it was a key component in their harsh sentence, as we see from the sentencing judge's comments. This is why it's ineffective assistance of counsel to fail to counter these statements at all."

I took a deep breath and finished.

"Finally, briefly, Your Honor, I'd like to go into why we are asking this Court to make a factual finding of innocence for the petitioners. If we take out the false evidence, if we take out the bite marks, if we take out the false testimony about the videotape, if we bring in the exculpatory evidence from the FBI, we have a completely different case with a completely different tone.

"In that case, we have three girls who are together. One of them overdoses and the other two respond in completely normal ways. They call nine-one-one, they perform CPR, they assist the EMTs. The circumstantial evidence actually goes to their innocence."

"We have the crime lab report that shows no blood from the victim in the trunk or in the toolbox, that there are no hairs in the toolbox that match the victim. We have Leigh Stubbs who has no prior convictions. She took a drug test immediately after Kim Williams went to the hospital. She came back clean. And we know from testimony at trial that Kim Williams took the drugs from her boyfriend.

"We know, even from the closing from the State, that the only proof of a conspiracy was Mrs. Ervin's testimony that Stubbs and Vance were whispering on the porch. The State even says in their closing that's the only proof of the conspiracy. There's no independent evidence to support the larceny charge. And it all points to neither one of these women stole the drugs from James Ervin, and they didn't conspire to.

"And if you take West out of the other charges, we have an internal investigation done by the attorney general's office into West's testimony in this specific case as to whether criminal charges can be brought against Dr. West because of his testimony in this specific case. We have the deposition from February 11, 2012, where Dr. West no longer believes in his own methodologies or the validity of bite mark evidence."

I continued. "These women would not have been convicted without that evidence and without the inflammatory comments made about their sexual orientation. Without the bite mark, without the videotape, there's no plan and there's no motive. There's no motive here. Circumstantial evidence points to innocence. They did what they could to help their friend, Ms. Williams, who overdosed on drugs.

"I'll just close, your honor, that the lifestyle became the motive. As Ruthann Robson's affidavit points out, when you have a circumstantial evidence case, the impact of bias becomes heightened.

"Now, the State called this a senseless crime. They couldn't find a motive behind it. But the sexual orientation became the motive. That created the plan. Without West, it's girls responding to a friend in crisis.

"They are innocent, Your Honor, and we ask for a factual finding to that end. Thank you."

Behind me, someone briefly applauded. At least someone had heard what I said.

Tucker closed out our arguments. He pointed out that the prosecutors affirmatively knew or should have known they were presenting false evidence when they put Dr. West on the stand to testify about the surveillance video. Dr. West wasn't qualified to testify to the surveillance video as an expert. And the prosecutors knew or should have known that—they did, after all, go to the FBI.

When the FBI said the video was garbage, the prosecutors went back to Dr. West. And they knew or should have known they were putting on false testimony when they called Dr. West to the stand. When Dr. West brought up the FBI at trial and said the FBI couldn't analyze the video, the prosecutors had a duty to correct him and make the record clear to the jury.

Tucker then referenced Dr. West's deposition statement to "throw the bite marks out." A jury hearing that at the time of trial wouldn't have convicted Leigh and Tami.

The State's assistant attorney general, Jeff Klingfuss, gave his closing argument to defend the conviction.

"As far as Mr. Coxwell's argument into the *Brady* violation, the State would like to bring to this Court's attention the case of *Howard v. State*, a Mississippi Supreme Court case. We would say there has not been enough evidence presented of a *Brady* violation. But even under the holding [in *Howard v. State*], it's still not a *Brady* violation to which would entitle them to a new trial in this case."

The reference was to the case of Eddie Lee Howard who was convicted and sent to death row due in large part to the testimony of Dr. West, who found bite marks on the victim and matched them to Howard. The prosecution couldn't know that in August 2020, the Mississippi Supreme Court would reverse Howard's conviction. In 2021, he would finally be exonerated.

Judge Taylor interjected. "Let me ask you this, just for the sake of argument. It wouldn't undermine your confidence in the outcome of the trial if you discovered that the FBI had looked at this and said there was no evidence on it, it wasn't capable of being enhanced? Assuming, arguendo, there is a *Brady* violation, you just said it wouldn't be of a magnitude and it still wouldn't warrant relief?"

Klingfuss responded, "We collectively have the opinion, as would Mr. Rushing, that we don't think there was anything exculpatory. In the facts we have here, we had more than one witness. We had Detective Nolan Jones. He was the first witness at trial. He looked at the tape. It was in his testimony where he talked about being able to see someone carrying a body. Of course, he was privy to other facts, the people that had seen them coming and going, had some statements. Whereas I don't think the FBI knew of all those things."

Exactly! Detective Jones couldn't shield himself from being biased, he couldn't look at the video impartially.

Klingfuss added, "We also feel that the statements of one of the defendants that she was going to be carrying something out of the truck into the motel—don't worry, they're not dead, they're just passed out, I'm going to be carrying someone in—that it's not exculpatory."

Klingfuss continued. "As to ineffective assistance and the surveillance tape, for strategic reasons maybe that wouldn't have been used. It could very well have been trial strategy."

Judge Taylor wasn't finished. "Let me ask you. What possible strategy, what possible strategy, could be furthered by the defense attorneys keeping from the jury the fact that the FBI disagreed with the State's witness? What possible strategy could that further?"

Remarkably, Klingfuss responded, "We don't necessarily think that the FBI disagreed with what Dr. West testified to."

Judge Taylor continued, "Well, he didn't see what Dr. West saw, did he? What possible strategy would have been furthered by not highlighting disagreements between the FBI and the State's witness with regard to the tape? I'm saying, just imagine and help me understand what possible strategy defense counsel, knowing of the FBI's disagreement over inconsistencies with the videotape, what possible strategy could have been furthered by not bringing that out?"

Klingfuss punted.

"There's a presumption that trial counsel was effective," he said. "And I'm afraid my mind does not always work in a defense attorney mode, coming up with things on those arguments and what strategies could be used.

"Furthermore, it's the position of the State that there was no fraudulent testimony brought forth," added Klingfuss.

Buddy Coxwell got up to rebut. He told the court how the three women had loaded up the back of the truck with their things from the rehab center, luggage and black bags. Leigh raised this with the front desk, specifically asking for a room near a surveillance camera in order to not have her belongings stolen.

"You know, the people who founded this country never worried about the State being short of power. The Bill of Rights and the constitutional rules that apply, apply to all accused people.

"Mississippi has ethical opinions for all lawyers to say if you see a falsehood go in before a court you are under an affirmative duty to correct it. And when West said, well, used to be we had to send these to the FBI, somebody should have said, 'Can we approach, Judge; Judge this did go to the FBI.' And I guess had that happened we would know 100 percent whether the defense lawyers knew about it."

But that hadn't happened.

Tucker made one request. "Your Honor, I request in open court—I'd move Your Honor for a motion for bond in this case and just submit it on the evidence."

"I'll deny that," the judge said.

The hearing concluded.

Leigh and Tami took the two-hour drive back to Rankin. It was their first time out of prison walls in ten years. Now they would go back there to wait—for how long, no one could know—for Judge Taylor's ruling on whether they would spend the next thirty-four years of their lives in that same prison.

CHAPTER 24

Prosecutorial Misconduct

I became a prosecutor because I wanted to fight for a noble cause. I believed that incarcerating offenders would stop cycles of violence against vulnerable people. Prosecutors and police are often drawn to their work by a noble cause of protecting victims.

But believing in my own noble cause also led to shortcuts: the ends justify the means. I focused on achieving my goal of public safety through incarceration, isolation, and containment. I focused on protecting survivors of violence at any cost. And I defined victims as the select people for whom society allows itself to experience compassion.

DUNN LAMPTON AND NOBLE CAUSE CORRUPTION

Dunn Lampton, District Attorney for the Fourteenth Circuit Court District, worked his way up from a town prosecutor to district attorney. Lampton's drive to obtain higher political office was well known, and indicated by his multiple attempts to win a seat in Congress.

At the time of Leigh and Tami's trial, President George W. Bush was considering appointing Lampton as the U.S. Attorney for the Southern District of Mississippi. Less than three months after Lampton convicted the two women, on September 7, 2001, President Bush appointed him as U.S. Attorney. He was only fifty-one years old at the time.

The ideal noble cause of being a prosecutor was another one of

Lampton's motivations. He was best known for prosecuting Ku Klux Klan member James Ford Seale.

In May 1964, Seale kidnapped and murdered two young Black men in Meadville, Mississippi: Henry Hezekiah Dee and Charles Eddie Moore. Seale was a working-class white man and, along with his brother and father, an active member of a militant KKK organization called the Silver Dollar Group. Seale abducted Dee and Moore when he saw them walking along a road. He forced the two men into his car by telling them that he was an FBI agent.

Seale called up other white men in the Silver Dollar Group and together they beat the men, kidnapped them in the trunk of a car, and drove over one hundred miles to the Ole River. At the riverside, the group of white men chained Dee and Moore to an engine block and to sections of railroad track rails. While Dee and Moore were still alive, the white men rowed them in a boat to the middle of the river. Then they pushed Henry Dee and Charles Moore into the water and watched them drown.

The KKK members brutally murdered Henry Dee and Charles Moore. However, when Dee's and Moore's bodies were exhumed from the river, the FBI was searching instead for three civil rights workers who went missing in Meridian, Mississippi: Michael Schwerner, Andrew Goodman, and James Chaney. Dredging the rivers of Mississippi could reveal unknown horrors of violent white supremacy.

When the FBI investigated the murders of Henry Dee and Charles Moore in 1964, Seale and his fellow Klan member Charles Edwards *admitted to the crime.* Yet in 1965, the local district attorney, Lenox Forman, filed motions to dismiss the charges against the Klansmen "in the interest of justice." This same tool of dismissal that can be used to free Black and Brown people today was used by this prosecutor on behalf of violent white Klansmen.

Nearly forty years after Moore's murder, his brother Thomas Moore fought to reopen the case. Thomas, together with journalist Jerry Mitchell, the cofounder of the Jackson Free Press Donna Ladd, and documentarian David Ridgen re-investigated the murders. Thomas had served in the Army with Dunn Lampton, who was by now the U.S. Attorney for the Southern District of Mississippi, and brought their newly discovered evidence to him. In 2007, Lampton charged Seale with kidnapping and conspiracy in the murders of Moore and Dee. A jury convicted Seale in 2007 after his codefendant Charles Edwards testified against him in exchange for immunity from prosecution. Seale was sentenced to three life terms.

A noble cause motivated Lampton to prosecute James Ford Seale for murdering innocent Black men. It also drove him to prosecute innocent queer women for an assault that never occurred seven years earlier.

Lampton was both hero and villain. These terms clarify little.

Days after the Seale verdict, Lampton was in the Jeep accident on his muscadine grape farm that would leave him paralyzed for the rest of his life.

CARCERAL FEMINISM

I had long identified as a victims rights advocate. In college, I was on call every month for twelve-hour shifts as a Rape Victim Advocate. Armed with a pager, I'd respond to the alert that a sexual assault survivor had arrived at one of my assigned hospitals and I needed to go and be their advocate.

Sometimes the police would begin interrogating the survivor, and I had to advocate for the survivor's personal decision of whether to talk with the police or not. Sometimes the doctor or nurse, who at that time weren't all properly trained, would ask inappropriate questions or pressure the survivor. Sometimes the survivor would be a man, who felt ashamed of the assault and feared people would think he was gay.

Most of the time "my" survivor just wanted someone to hold their hand, to listen without judgment. The first and foremost thing we were taught was to tell the survivor, "It's not your fault. You did what you had to do to survive."

In the early 2000s, prosecuting and punishing rapists was seen as a form of social advocacy. Survivors had suffered through being disbelieved and ignored. Punishment was a response. When I worked for a summer in the Office of the Prosecutor in the International Criminal Tribunal for Rwanda, I felt like I was doing righteous work by assisting one of the first prosecutions of rape as genocide. This was adding weight and seriousness to assaults that were belittled or dismissed every day.

I was a carceral feminist. I thought assailants should be punished and thus deterred and prevented from ever harming someone again. Incarceration was the tool to accomplish that end.

But there's a difference between a response and a solution.

Sociologist Elizabeth Bernstein coined the term "carceral feminism" to describe the late twentieth-century growing commitment "to the carceral state as the enforcement apparatus for feminist goals." Among these feminist goals was acknowledging and protecting people who were sexually or physically abused by arresting and incarcerating alleged perpetrators. To this day, if I look to many sex crimes and domestic violence prosecutors, I see prosecutors who also oppose the death penalty, who oppose the war on drugs, and who oppose mandatory minimum sentencing. I know many of them well. They see horrible crimes that they consistently have to plead down in order to obtain any kind of conviction. But they also see how the system still ignores many survivors, and how its solution of incarceration is often only a temporary one.

PROSECUTORS AS WHITE SAVIORS

As a young prosecutor, my savior mentality was my shield from criticism. I would protect survivors from their assailants and abusers by incarcerating the perpetrators—for as long as possible. I firmly believed that I, as a prosecutor, should have all tools at my disposal. This included doing what I could to persuade survivors to testify against the defendant, including arresting survivors to guarantee they'd be at the trial. This included having total access to police and crime lab information. I decided what to disclose to the defendant and what to keep to myself.

As a prosecutor, I had the power to make some sort of accountability stick, and I thought both the rules and the survivors should bend toward my kind of accountability. Carceral accountability.

Furthermore, as a prosecutor, the idea of a defendant having equal access to crime lab information, a defendant able to see DNA results and search in a DNA database, talk with "our" lab analysts, or even ask to interrogate "our" witnesses infuriated me. As the old saying goes, when you're accustomed to privilege, equality feels like oppression.

The governing court rules made sure there was not equality in the courtroom. The governing rules of criminal courtrooms are rooted in Jim Crow.

In the 1930s, the federal government created rules to govern civil cases and criminal cases. The rules of criminal procedure were originally drafted to be just like the rule of civil procedure, with open disclosure and discovery for both parties, the ability to interrogate witnesses before trial, and both parties could discover additional information and compel any party—including the government—to disclose that information.

But the civil courtroom was mainly white litigants, while the criminal courtroom was disproportionately people of color. Southern prosecutors proposed changes to the rules of criminal procedure, concerned about ensuring their convictions of Black male defendants. They proposed and passed the rules we still have eighty years later: prosecutors can decide what information to reveal and keep hidden.

I, as the prosecutor, also had more leeway with whether to abide by the court rules. I could be late with my pleadings or filings; I could push the boundaries. I saw my control and power as natural and not worth commenting on, except to defend against any challenge. I fought against changes that would "uneven the playing field" by diminishing the power of the prosecutor. I fought to preserve the status quo in furtherance of my noble cause ideal.

PROSECUTORIAL MISCONDUCT AND NOBLE CAUSE CORRUPTION

In pursuit of a noble cause, we have a natural human tendency to lock in on how to accomplish our goal and block out all conflicting information. It's called tunnel vision. Anyone can be susceptible to only acknowledging evidence that confirms their own idea or belief, and being unwilling to change their belief even in the face of contradicting evidence. But tunnel vision can turn into noble cause corruption.

Noble cause corruption leads to wrongful convictions. Noble cause corruption can drive prosecutors to bend the rules in their favor. One third of exonerations involve misconduct by prosecutors. Over half of exonerations involve some form of official misconduct generally. The most common form of misconduct is when police and prosecutors hide exculpatory evidence from the defendant, called a *Brady* violation.

A perverse incentive exists for prosecutors to commit misconduct. Prosecutors can obtain a conviction by hiding evidence, and there's little risk that they'll be found out.

There's even less risk that prosecutors will face any consequences. If a court finds out, the judge frequently dismisses a prosecutor's failure to disclose evidence to the defendant as harmless error, or rules that the hidden evidence wasn't "material."

When Brandon Bernard was about to be executed, neither the U.S. Supreme Court nor President Donald Trump commuted his sentence in the final days of December 2020. Brandon was a Black teenager sentenced to death when he was eighteen years old for participating in a horrible felony murder. In her dissent from the Supreme Court's denial to stay Bernard's execution, Justice Sotomayor wrote, "If the prosecution had not committed the *Brady* and *Napue* violations Bernard alleges, there is a reasonable probability Bernard would have been spared a death sentence." Instead, the prosecutors were not held accountable, and the federal government executed Bernard—at the same time that all state governments had suspended executions because of COVID-19.

When prosecutors can hide evidence, and their noble cause corrupts their actions without check, we undermine any integrity in our system. We must ask more from prosecutors, because their duty is not to win convictions but to seek justice.

CHAPTER 25
Freedom

When you look at all the evidence, you'll realize
that while it's a circumstantial evidence case,
these two women who were living together, were
lovers, whether because of the drugs or the alcohol or their lifestyle, viciously attacked Kimberly
Williams for no reason and tried to cover it up.
—Dunn Lampton, closing argument.

I kept working on other cases. On my bad days, I wondered if my time
in Mississippi would end in apathy or in overload. A number of our
clients at the Mississippi Innocence Project were on death row. My
local community was regularly organizing vigils for the onslaught of
executions at Parchman Farm, the maximum security prison that
houses Mississippi's death row. Three executions were carried out in
2010, two more occurred in 2011, and then in the spring of 2012, the
pace accelerated. Between February and June, Mississippi executed six
men, some of them over the objections of family members of victims.

I was teaching my Prisons and Civil Rights class at the law school.
We read David Oshinsky's *Parchman: Worse Than Slavery*, then
"toured" the prison, including the execution chamber. Even the sani-
tized tours were always eye-opening. My biggest hope was for my students to learn, to engage, and to realize their own strong voices.

By this time, I had applied for a job to found and direct an innocence project in West Virginia—and I'd gotten it. No more death row
cases, West Virginia had eliminated the death penalty in the 1960s.
West Virginia became its own state during the Civil War, separating
from Virginia when it joined the Confederacy. The mountain people
of West Virginia broke away, petitioning to Lincoln to become an independent state and remain part of the Union. Their state motto then
and now is "Mountaineers are always free."

But how could I leave when my clients couldn't? Part of me would remain in Mississippi. Just as Parchman was an old plantation, just as the state mental institution was built on a penal colony, these histories and cycles of exclusion and suppression and control stemming from slavery would always be with us. Mississippi would always be with me, the joy and the pain.

As James Baldwin said, "History is not the past. It is the present. We carry our history with us. We are our history. If we pretend otherwise, we are literally criminals."

It was June in Mississippi, and I would be moving to West Virginia in July. The eleven-year anniversary of Leigh and Tami's trial and conviction was coming up. Tami had told me her dream, her long-standing premonition, that she and Leigh would serve ten years and then be free. One more week and another dream would be crushed.

I was ruminating, as I often did, on the plea offer to Leigh, right before her trial: ten years for a guilty plea. Should she have taken it?

Just then, an email alert popped up—from Judge Taylor's clerk, Laurie. It had an order attached.

I didn't even have to read it through, the title told me everything.

"Order Setting Aside Conviction and Sentence," June 27, 2012.

The ruling came eleven years to the date of the opening of their trial. They were convicted June 30, 2001.

I would read the full order later. Right now, I had to let Leigh know. Immediately.

I called the prison, asking to be put through to her counselor. I couldn't help pacing, gesturing at the phone, yelling to her, "I have to talk with Leigh! The judge reversed her conviction!"

"You know you can't talk with her; she has to set up a phone call to call you."

"Please!" I nearly shouted. "She's going home! We just found out!"

"Okay, let me see . . ."

Leigh told me later that she heard the guards calling her name to come out, and she started tucking her shirt in and putting away her things. They told her to hurry and she said she had to put stuff away in her cell or else she'd get written up. The guards smiled. *You don't have to worry about that, you're going home.* They rushed her to the room with the phone and circled her while she took the call.

Smiling giddily at her, they encouraged her to pick up the phone while they waited around her.

"Leigh, the judge reversed your conviction!" I exclaimed. "You're going home!"

"What?!"

She was stunned.

"You're going home!"

"Oh my God, oh my God!"

And after those few short words, the guard took the phone and ended our conversation. But that was all we needed—those few moments to tell her those precious words. You're going home.

Leigh and Tami were scheduled to be transported to the Brookhaven jail the very next day. The jail stood next to the courthouse where they had been convicted and also where Judge Taylor held their post-conviction hearing. They would be released to freedom from that jail in Brookhaven. Judge Taylor decided against a hearing to reverse their convictions. They could simply go home.

Bright and early that next day, all of us drove to Brookhaven in our different vehicles along the Mississippi roads. In the waiting room, we gathered: Will McIntosh and Carol Mockbee from MIP, MIP students, our MIP fellow K.C. Meckfessel and her fiancé, Mama Sandi and her husband, Mama Sheila and Papa Stubbs, Leigh's sisters Lori and Kristi, and Leigh's brother-in-law Steve Wade. They had all worked so hard for this moment.

I remembered the last time I had been in that jail, meeting with Leigh and Tami behind the bars before the post-conviction hearing. Now I was on the outside with the family, waiting for Leigh and Tami to be processed out.

A large white man in bib overalls waited with us—the bail bondsman. Leigh and Tami's family had to post bond for the two of them, and Tami had received special permission to leave the state to finally live with her mama in Louisiana. Leigh was going to live with Mama Sheila and Papa Stubbs.

Hours passed. A reporter for the Brookhaven *Daily Leader* arrived, the same paper that had covered the trial almost eleven years earlier. He waited with the family, the students, and all of us from the Mississippi Innocence Project.

Sheila and Sandi held hands as they waited next door to the courthouse, the place where they had seen their daughters taken away all those years ago. Now, they waited for them to come back.

Sandi clutched something else—shoes. She'd brought the shoes Leigh and Tami wore when they went to prison—the shoes they had to leave on the outside.

Sandi had visited Tami two Sundays every month for ten years. The drive was eight hours round-trip, but still she went. She'd see Sheila and Pete there too, and often Leigh's sisters.

Tami had lived in Pearl before she was incarcerated there. She went to Pearl High School and got her GED in nearby Brandon. She'd worked for nine years in the North Hill Square Apartment Complex, and her former employer, Kathy Loveall, also visited Tami on the regular visiting days.

Now, Sandi wanted her daughter home in Dry Prong. She remembered helping her daughter years ago in New Orleans, and she was ready to do the same again, wanted to, needed to for herself. Her husband made sure they had a comfortable life with his off-shore work, and Sandi had a job lined up for Tami, working at the dental lab. It was going to be a new start.

Now she waited with the shoes. All these years later, Sandi had them as a memento and would reunite them with Leigh and Tami. The plain tennis shoes that were meant to be worn in a different life.

We waited. How could it possibly take this long? Did something go wrong?

Finally, the guards announced that Leigh and Tami were coming out. The mamas lined up, waiting for their daughters by the door. Mama Sandi, then Mama Sheila, then Papa Stubbs.

Leigh and Tami came through the doors into their arms, dressed in civilian clothes.

There was hugging and crying. As the reporter snapped photos, they signed the paperwork for bond. Tami asked Will to buy her a

Dr Pepper from the vending machine, her first in eight years. Then Leigh and Tami were both eager to leave the jail far behind and do something so normal yet forbidden to them for a decade: get in a car with their family for a drive.

Will and I drove to Mama Sheila's home to celebrate. When we got there, neighbors and family were already coming over and stopping by. Their beautiful home was vibrant with lights, people, and joy. I stayed into the evening, and when I left, Will was still celebrating with the Stubbs family, who were reunited with their daughter at last.

AN ORDER FROM JUDGE TAYLOR

"The issue before the court is the evidence *not* admitted—the FBI report."

Judge Taylor's opinion focused on the undisclosed report. He found that the prosecutors were required to disclose the FBI report because it directly contradicted Dr. West and his testimony. The report was material and exculpatory. "The State's discovery violation effectively denied the defense the information necessary to challenge the admission of Dr. West's video enhancement testimony."

The prosecutors argued at the hearing that the report probably was disclosed, yet no report existed in either their file or in the defense attorneys' files. The argument did not prevail.

"It is worth noting," the order read, "that a simple system of documenting the materials produced to the defense in such a case would have given the State a way to prove what had been produced in discovery." Ultimately, Judge Taylor said that if the report had indeed been disclosed, and defense counsel failed to object to Dr. West's testimony or use the document in any way at trial, then defense counsel were ineffective under *Strickland v. Washington*. That U.S. Supreme Court decision defines whether a trial was unconstitutional because of the inadequacy of defense counsel.

The convictions were reversed.

But today was not the day when bite mark evidence would be thrown out. It was not the day when prosecutors would be chastised for their arguments against Leigh and Tami as lesbians. The order acknowledged those arguments and made its decision on the other grounds.

ALFORD PLEAS

The next few weeks were a whirlwind of pictures, texts, and calls from Leigh. The Stubbs drove down to the beach, and the daughters took family photos together, all in white. Leigh adopted a dog she named Taylor, and a cat she named Tucker. Summer was beautiful and the days of freedom were fresh.

On August 6, Leigh and Tami were re-arraigned on the same initial charges: conspiracy, drug possession, and assault. A new prosecutor charged them again.

This was sadly no surprise. Even when DNA evidence identifies the actual assailant, the prosecutor's playbook is usually to refile the charges and pressure the person to plead guilty.

This tactic is more successful than one might think. Almost every single one of my clients has been in this situation. We fight for their conviction to be reversed, but the prosecutor simply refiles the same charges. Then the prosecutor offers them a special plea deal.

An Alford plea.

An Alford plea means that the defendant can plead guilty while maintaining their innocence. In the plea, the defendant is saying I'm not guilty, but the prosecutor has enough evidence that they could convince a jury that I'm guilty. I don't want to risk going back to trial, and I don't want to risk a new prison sentence.

The deal is take the plea, have a conviction on your record, and your sentence is time served. You don't have to go back to prison.

Many of my clients take these pleas. They've already been wrong-fully convicted by a jury, and there's no assurance a jury won't find them guilty again. As Judge Taylor asked me, "What's really going to be different about homophobic bias in 2012 instead of 2001, except that people might not as readily admit to it?" An Alford plea is an incarcerated person's chance to walk free and never go back to prison again, and maintain their innocence.

But they'll also have a conviction on their record, which they'll have to reckon with every time they apply for a job, an apartment lease, child custody. One of my former clients has done extremely well as a carpenter; another still struggles at job interviews.

One of my biggest criticisms of prosecutors is that they refile these charges. Defendants have met an exceptionally high standard in order to convince a court to reverse the conviction. The original charges are for serious crimes, where defendants originally were sentenced to decades if not life in prison.

Yet now the prosecutor is offering this person an opportunity to walk out of prison free if they simply plead guilty. The process suggests that prosecutors don't actually believe the defendant committed the offense. If they truly believed the defendant was guilty, then wouldn't they demand a prison sentence similar to what the defendant originally had?

Maybe they're perceptive of the fact that prison frequently doesn't make people on the inside or outside safer. Maybe they're experienced enough to know that a person sentenced to probation for a violent crime instead of prison is generally *less* likely to commit another violent crime, as antithetical as that may sound.

But I think that instead, they just want the conviction for their own prosecutorial records. The conviction doesn't further safety for the community, and it damages the life of the defendant even if there is no prison time. It's simply in my eyes a cruel mechanism where the prosecutor doesn't have to admit that they made a huge mistake.

After the prosecutors recharged Leigh and Tami, we filed a motion to quash their indictment as unreliable. The prosecutor simply recycled the same indictment from 2000. That grand jury in deciding whether to indict Leigh and Tami relied on the findings of Michael West. Now, Dr. West admitted that false evidence was presented to the grand jury.

Our argument failed—the old indictment stood and Leigh and Tami were newly charged.

The prosecutors no longer had any witnesses on their side. Michael West wouldn't testify for them, the FBI would testify against them, and everything else had been circumstantial about the case.

So, they offered a plea deal they thought Leigh and Tami couldn't refuse. The plea offer was to plead guilty to felony possession of the Oxycontin pills and get a sentence of time served.

Under the law, Leigh and Tami could be prosecuted and potentially convicted for possession of Oxycontin pills. Even though Leigh had never imbibed any of the pills, and Tami hadn't taken or held on to the pill bottle, they could be charged with "constructive" possession. This is a common legal argument by prosecutors. Leigh and Tami didn't ever have to physically possess the pills or pill bottle. As long as the bottle was in their "domain or control" and they knew about it, a jury could find them guilty. That's what the court had instructed the jury at their first trial. The bottle of pills was in Leigh and Tami's domain when they were all in the truck together, once they knew that Kim had taken Dickie's medicine bag.

People are convicted and serve time in prison every day for constructive possession. A friend left marijuana in your car, and it gets pinned on you. You can say you didn't know about it, but the prosecutor will argue to the jury that you did.

Leigh and Tami had spent nearly eleven years in prison. They were ready to move on with their lives. Leigh had been in community college when she went in; she wanted to go back to school. Tami wanted the freedom of making her own choices, and she had a job lined up.

They took the plea offer.

EXPUNGEMENT AND THE NATIONAL REGISTRY OF EXONERATIONS

Leigh wanted to go back to school to become a nurse. But with a felony conviction, even a nonviolent drug possession felony, she couldn't be licensed as an LPN or an RN in Mississippi. This was one of the "collateral consequences" of having a criminal record, and one she couldn't have anticipated.

But there still was hope.

In Mississippi at the time, she could petition the court for her conviction to be expunged, if it was a first offense. It didn't matter that it was a felony as long as it was nonviolent. When the required time had passed, Leigh and Tucker petitioned for an expungement; the prosecutors did not object. In 2016, Leigh finally had a clean record and could put the case behind her. She was headed back to school to become a nurse, starting that fall.

The National Registry of Exonerations tracks all known exonerations in the United States. On November 12, 2018, after Leigh's expungement, Leigh and Tami and their cases were finally posted on the National Registry of Exonerations. Their case was categorized as a no-crime wrongful conviction.

LIFE AFTER

Judge Taylor went on to be particularly attentive to forensic science cases, and to preside over drug court proceedings. He still sits on the bench, and is next door neighbors with Dr. Moak. Nolan Jones appears in Taylor's courtroom from time to time in his role as jury commissioner. Brookhaven was and is a small community.

Judge Taylor recalls his decision in Leigh and Tami's case as one of his most personally meaningful moments on the bench. Nevertheless, when I asked him for his perspective years later, he responded, "The most spiritually dangerous thing for me, as a judge, is to talk about when I was right. I'd rather talk about when I was wrong." He continued. "The great thing about the law is that it is self-correcting—it presupposes we get the wrong answer. The whole mechanism is premised on the idea that I, as a judge, could be wrong. What other discipline is set up to correct itself?"

In June 2019, Leigh texted her graduation certificate to me—she was now a registered nurse. She was working in a hospital near her hometown in the emergency room, helping people in crisis. She was helping people, and where she was meant to be.

She sent the nursing certificate to Judge Taylor as well, along with a note.

The note was simple: "Thank you."

CHAPTER 26
Alternate Paths to Freedom and Restorative Justice

For innocent people in prison, most pathways to freedom do not include a vindication of their innocence. Freedom can be a reality riddled with shame and no public reckoning of the wrongs against them.

Strangers or even loved ones may still believe you committed a serious crime. Your hope is to use your freedom to rebuild your life and your reputation, to lean on the people who know you well and know your truth. Sometimes that is the best the world can offer, the ongoing struggle but with a reclaimed voice.

My clients have been released from prison through Alford pleas, where they pled guilty to a crime they didn't commit; through executive clemency where their sentence was shortened and they were set free; through parole, where a panel decided they had served enough time; and through re-sentencing, where a court shortened their time in prison.

With all of these paths to freedom, the wrongful conviction remained on their criminal record. Their painful time in prison also stayed with them.

Change, growth, and well-being are not the purposes of prison. They cannot successfully be the purposes of an institution that detains people in small, unsanitary, surveilled, and violent cages. Prison does not unravel the root causes of substance use disorder, a leading cause of incarceration. Prison does not counteract the mental health crises that lead to crimes, even though over 50 percent of people in prison report having mental health issues.

Instead, prisons punish people in closed spaces, upheld by law and away from public view. The law sustains and mutes the violence and suffering in prisons. It is simply policy.

WE ARE ALL LAWBREAKERS

Every year in class I hand out a worksheet. The worksheet lists criminal offenses, crammed in small font across four pages. The students don't have to show me their answers, but they must fill out the worksheet. They must self-identify if they've committed any of the listed offenses.

The criminal offenses range from using someone else's Netflix account, to cutting through a neighbor's yard, to getting in a fight, to smoking marijuana, or getting a beer for someone who is underage. Then the students calculate, based on the state criminal code, what their sentence would be if they were arrested, charged, and convicted.

Most of my students have never been convicted of a crime. If they have been, the state legal bars make it very difficult to be admitted to practice law and be a lawyer. A person with a conviction could pay for three years of law school, graduate, and still not be able to practice law because of a conviction—even a misdemeanor.

Although most of my students have not been convicted of crimes, almost every one of them has broken the law. Most of us have. There are far more lawbreakers than there are criminals.

It is the punishment that creates the "criminal," the class of convicted people.

We may have a social view of someone with a conviction as a particularly harmful person. My parents have siphoned off of my TV-streaming accounts for years, yet they would not see themselves as criminals, nor would I. Somehow a convicted person is different from us other lawbreakers who never have to think about our offenses or pay for them. The government decides who is surveilled, who is arrested for breaking a law, and then who is prosecuted. They decide who is deemed a criminal.

But there are alternative ways for prosecutors' offices to function, and alternatives to criminal punishment.

A HORIZON OF CHANGE

Two solutions arise. The first is reforming our system, a plea that has been ongoing for decades, and which I advocate for with habeas law. The second is to create an alternative to state-sponsored punishment for violence. This is the creativity of the movement for abolition.

The prison and police abolition movements advocate to change who we pay to keep us safe, through our county, city, state, and federal budgets. Instead of solely funding police and prisons and exclusively using criminal law to control behavior, funding could be additionally provided to housing, health care, education, and employment—all of which have a better likelihood of changing behavior than arrests and incarceration. The abolition movements also advocate creating safety outside of financial payment systems and establishing more community control over how to define public safety.

SEEKING SAFETY AND ACCOUNTABILITY

I've interviewed over seventy cisgender women leaders in innocence work—lawyers, social workers, activists, and exonerees. One of the key things we discussed was abolition and restorative justice. Another way to prevent wrongful convictions is to not rely on the criminal legal system so much.

At our current rate of 1 percent decarceration a year, it will take sixty-five years—until 2085—to cut the U.S. prison population in half. In 2085 we won't be back to 1980 rates of incarceration. Over two million people live in prisons and jails in America on any given day.

Yet societally, prisons have not brought a sense of safety. Those who are safe do not feel safe. People who most fear being a victim of crime often experience low levels of actual victimization. Crime survivors, alternately, are frequently not protected by the criminal legal system and incarceration.

It's calculated that police arrest a suspected culprit in only 10 percent of major crimes, and prosecutors convict a suspected culprit in less than 2 percent of major crimes.

Danielle Sered, the founder and director of Common Justice, informs us that less than half of the survivors of a crime in the United States call police. Common Justice is a restorative justice "alternative-to-incarceration and victim-service program" that focuses on violent felonies in adult courts. They estimate that 75 percent of survivors opt out of the criminal legal system. Of the 25 percent of survivors who engage with the criminal legal system, Common Justice reaches out to these survivors of serious violence. Ninety percent of these survivors choose Common Justice, a survivor-centered, accountability-based, safety-driven, and racially equitable restorative justice alternative to traditional criminal prosecutions.

According to Sered, these survivors choose restorative justice because they want accountability and safety. They don't want the defendants to harm anyone else. And they want that person to take responsibility.

PROSECUTORS CREATING ACCOUNTABILITY WITH RESTORATIVE JUSTICE

Common Justice believes that prison creates a barrier to accountability. Accountability requires taking responsibility for one's actions, rather than simply being punished in prison. Instead of accountability, prison imposes structural harms that generate further violence: shame, isolation, exposure to violence, and inability to have economic security. Certain people—largely poor people of color—are incarcerated for harms that far more people commit. And certain victims—namely middle class white straight women—are treated fairly and with respect by the system. Race and class cultivate attention and accrue value for certain survivors within the criminal legal system, not all survivors.

Jennifer Henry, the Former Chief Prosecutor of the Navajo Nation, said in my interview with her that all victims need to be respected—including victims who have at some point committed offenses themselves. In her words, "[W]e really get to know our defendants, their families, the victims, the witnesses, our partners. So often a defendant today is a victim tomorrow, and a victim yesterday is a defendant tomorrow . . ." This is a similar message as the organization Survived and Punished, which focuses on incarcerated women and their experiences of domestic violence, rape, and gendered violence. In some women's prisons, nearly 94 percent of the incarcerated women have a history of physical or sexual abuse *before* being incarcerated.

The Navajo Nation Office of the Prosecutor affirms a restorative justice framework in addition to traditional prosecution. Other prosecutor offices are doing the same. For example, the prosecuting attorney's office in King County, Washington, works with community partners in a pre-filing diversion program. In their Community Diversion Program, the prosecutor does not bring charges against a person facing their first nonviolent felony case. Instead, the person can be assessed by a public health specialist and matched with a community partner organization for services and support. The program also includes a Victim Restoration Fund for harmed parties in these cases.

In Arlington, Virginia, Parisa Dehghani-Tafti is the Commonwealth prosecuting attorney. She is also a former innocence litigator.

Prosecuting Attorney Dehghani-Tafti believes her experience with restorative justice and working with victims in innocence cases make her a better prosecutor. "Victims only sort of start healing after convictions, based on the way that the system is currently set up."

Dehghani-Tafti believes in incorporating restorative justice in her office, alongside traditional case management. "Normally with most people, once they see the harm that they've done, and once they have a chance to learn that and do the work to help heal the victim or survivor, then they will actually be in a better position to not do that harm again."

I asked her about the roles for prisons and restorative justice, as a prosecutor who seeks accountability.

Dehghani-Tafti answered thoughtfully. "Bringing in a restorative process actually can help bring about the kind of accountability that we pretend that prison does. I think that the people who have those kinds of thought processes are having them in spite of the way that the system is set up, and not because of the way that the system is set up."

She continued. "And it's okay to admit that we sometimes need to use prison as a tool of incapacitation and punishment. But I think it's not okay to pretend like that is true accountability."

HEALING FROM A GENOCIDE WITH RESTORATIVE JUSTICE

State legislatures can incorporate restorative justice as an option in the criminal code. In 2018, Massachusetts passed legislation codifying restorative justice as an alternative to criminal charges. For certain cases, rather than incarceration the remedy can be "an offender's acceptance of responsibility for their actions . . . as they make repair to the victim or community in which the harm occurred."

But while restorative justice may be new to the U.S. criminal legal system, it is not new.

In 1994, over 1 million people in Rwanda were harmed or killed by other Rwandans, split along ethnic lines of Hutu and Tutsi. The United Nations established international, legal, and distant criminal trials of the few designated leaders of the Rwandan genocide.

The Rwandan government, instead, adopted a traditional form of restorative justice to address thousands of smaller individual harms of the genocide. Rwanda created community circles called Gacaca. A guiding principle of restorative justice community circles is that collaboration and empathy can come from shared trauma, as well as the will to move beyond it.

Gacaca across Rwanda listened to community members speak about harms they suffered. Gacaca also heard from the offenders who committed these harms. Ultimately, Gacaca decided on actions for the offender to take responsibility and compensate the victim, in a way that was meaningful to the victim and the community.

The UN International Criminal Tribunal for Rwanda heard the cases of fewer than one hundred people over the span of twenty years. By contrast, 12,000 community-based Gacaca heard nearly 1.2 million cases related to the 1994 genocide. In Gacaca, the focus was on reconciliation—by attempting to recognize and hold the harms suffered by Rwandans at the hands of other Rwandans.

Restorative justice is a series of practices based on international traditions and customs that bring together offenders, survivors, and their communities, where they work together to make reparations and help each other heal. Some mediums include guided victim-offender mediation, community conferencing, and sentencing circles.

Restorative justice asks a different set of questions than a criminal legal system. A legal system asks what law was broken, who broke the law, and what punishment is deserved. Restorative justice instead asks who was harmed, what are their needs, and whose obligation is it to meet those needs.

Within restorative justice, crime is a violation of people and relationships rather than the law and the state. That violation creates obligations and a responsibility on the offender to repair the harm.

HEALING JUSTICE FOR EXONEREES AND SURVIVORS

What about when the offender is the criminal legal system itself? Exonerees and crime survivors in a wrongful conviction share a lot in common: they have both been victimized by the criminal legal system.

Healing Justice hosts restorative justice circles for exonerees of wrongful convictions and survivors of the original crime. Founder Jennifer Thompson is a sexual assault survivor who was re-traumatized when police and prosecutors convicted the wrong person for her assault. Director Katie Monroe is the daughter of an exoneree and former director of the Rocky Mountain Innocence Project. Their message is that the criminal legal system has wronged both survivors and exonerees, and they can empathize with each other as no one else can.

When a wrongful conviction is exposed, survivors are frequently blamed for causing it.

Yet it was a system of legal actors that brought the charges, investigated the case, and wrongfully convicted the defendant. Director Katie Monroe told me, "There should never be a moment where a crime victim or survivor is made to feel guilty about a wrongful conviction. It can never be their fault . . . I've been astounded by the way the criminal justice system treats crime victims and survivors, and about how we in the innocence community forget about them."

Jennifer Thompson spoke with me about the lack of space for people to sit with each other, listen, and share in grief. "In true restorative justice, the questions are, How are you harmed and what do you need? And whose obligation is it to fix that?"

She continued. "In wrongful convictions, we know how we were harmed. Some of us know what we need, but whose obligation is it to fix it? It's the person who breaks it. The person who breaks it in a wrongful conviction is first and foremost the perpetrator, but rarely do we know who that person is. Second, it's the system. And the system wasn't stepping forward and claiming any responsibility, and certainly wasn't looking to fix the harm. So I continued to watch people be broken and they had no place to sit and unpack. And I certainly was broken. I hadn't unpacked my harm either."

Thompson touched on the social difficulty of addressing the true harms and pain of violence and punishment. "We are uncomfortable to sit with somebody and just hold their hands as they grieve. We want to say, 'Now it's time to move on, it's time to get over it."

"The hardest parts of our story are not the day of the trial or the day of an arrest," Thompson persisted. "The hardest part of our story is when an exoneree's child dies and they're in prison and no one can warn them. The hardest part of our story is when our families refuse to talk to us about the rape of our body. And we are isolated with our own heads and hearts. The hardest parts of our stories are the grief and the losses."

While wrongfully convicted individuals may never have their innocence legally restored, and may always carry a wrongful conviction on their record, Healing Justice provides a space where they can heal from the harms of prosecution and incarceration. Restorative justice may also provide a space of healing—in wrongful convictions and traditional offenses alike. It is one alternative to our current system, and one path to manifesting justice.

CHAPTER 27
Tami Vance in Her
Own Words

Tami's voice on the phone was the same voice—I would have recognized her anywhere. I could picture her face, her squinting eyes and kind smile. Her gift to not take things too seriously and pepper the conversation with "I'm blessed."

She told me about her friends who are still on the inside, Tasha Shelby, Amy Wilkerson, Karrie Glen. That in the COVID-19 pandemic she had lost six people in her family, and lost her daddy in May 2019, her grandmama at Christmas that year. She had moved up from Louisiana to Rankin County to take care of her daddy and of her brother who had a stroke.

She told me that Mama Sandi was still working in the dental office, and still running her wedding business. "She does beautiful things."

"You know, my mama went to prison the same day I did. She just served her time on the outside. Families do the time too. Families get punished too," she told me.

She remembered the trial judge, who told her and Leigh in chambers that they deserved to spend their lives in prison because they loved each other. And that he would make sure they did. Forty-four year sentences.

I talked with her about our LGBTQ+ community.

"A lot of people commit suicide. But we just don't know because they're still in the closet. Can't get counts of suicide for being queer." She said when she started to get tired of it, when she was in prison, she told herself, "Don't give a fuck what anybody else thinks of you, just what you think of yourself."

A friend of hers and Leigh's, Cory, killed himself while they were away in prison. Cory lived with his grandmother and he couldn't tell anyone that he was gay. "Out of respect," Tami said. He'd bring Leigh over to be his girlfriend in his grandmama's house.

Tami almost killed herself when she realized she was gay. She was eighteen years old, married to a man since she was sixteen. She was relaxing on her front porch in Jackson, sitting with her best friend, and it struck her out of nowhere. "Why am I more attracted to my best friend than my husband?"

She didn't know what to do. "I ran. I was scared. I filed for divorce the next day and went to New Orleans."

She left everything behind, left her home. In New Orleans, she started using heroin.

"I almost killed myself, because I thought I was a freak. It was the late '80s, and I thought I can't tell nobody else. I didn't understand it. I didn't know what to do with my feelings."

"I couldn't tell anyone; I didn't want to fuck up anyone else."

After six months in New Orleans, she decided to live, not die. Tami went to Mama Sandi, who took her to the hospital and she went through withdrawal. "That got me five years of sobriety." And Tami is still with us today.

EPILOGUE
The Future Innocence Movement

The history of the blues is closely entwined with prison-plantations in the South. I'd listen to blues greats like Bukka White, Leadbelly, and Son House while driving to Columbus in the East, or through the Delta on my way to Parchman Prison. Creative power and creative people aren't always stopped by prisons. I remember a debate among friends in Mississippi about who had the greater influence on America, who changed history more, Bob Marley or Dr. Martin Luther King? The lawyers said Dr. King; the artists said Bob Marley.

Son House's Death Letter Blues frequently played on repeat in my now-defunct gray Saab's CD player. "I got a letter this morning, I say how you reckon it read? It says, 'Hurry, hurry! The gal you love is dead.'"

Kim didn't die, but her life paused. Caught in that moment of clinical death, before Narcan brought her breath rushing back in, she was suspended. Her friends, Leigh and Tami, hurried to save her, but their actions only sealed their own fate.

That moment.

We've created change that could have led their lives down a path far from prison. We now have medication for people who can't control their drug use, and medication so that people don't overdose and die. We now have Good Samaritan laws, including in Mississippi, to protect people from criminal charges if they call paramedics when a friend overdoses. We now know bite mark evidence is far less reliable than we thought it was, and we have more research on the reliability of other forensic disciplines.

But most important for this book, we as a society can step away from the criminal legal system as the only answer to harms. Most major crimes of violence remain unsolved by police and prosecutors. We know wrongful convictions occur, especially when additional pressure exists to find a culprit. And we know once the wheels of a conviction are in motion, how difficult it is to reverse that conviction.

This book provides tools to reverse convictions, to rethink justice, and to free more people from prison. Prosecutors and judges don't have to accept the story of finality, and claims of manifest injustice are one step of the path to freedom. The rest must be taken before the conviction, before the charge, and among far more people than just lawyers.

Lawyers alone cannot be a movement. Lawyers alone cannot create a movement. It takes a community.

I wrote this book trying to bring together storytelling with justice and explain one path forward for people touched by the criminal legal system. While I hope lawyers use this in court, I hope individuals use it far outside of the courtroom as well.

Innocence litigator Karen Thompson shared with me her view that innocence work is an awareness. There is hard work needed to address racism in wrongful convictions, and to center people who are wrongfully convicted and community activists in the work. She believes innocence work can evolve, and grow, and ultimately with courage and openness become a movement. As Thompson said, "I can't wait to meet and show up for the innocence movement."

Me too. I'll see you soon.

CHECKLIST OF TOOLS FOR MANIFESTING JUSTICE

A goal of this book is to challenge the criminal legal system to be just; here are some tools discussed throughout.

War on Drugs
- Recognize substance use disorder as a physical addiction, not a moral failing.
- Treat opioid use disorder with medication like methadone or buprenorphine; move away from abstinence only treatment models.
- Expand Good Samaritan laws to protect people who report overdoses from being charged with possession of a controlled substance as well as distribution of a controlled substance.
- Use prosecutorial discretion to treat drug possession as a public health issue instead of a crime.
- Elected prosecutors can educate their offices with medical experts, who explain the basics of substance use disorder and treatment, and local harm reduction experts, who share the consequences of drug convictions alongside different types of interventions.
- Prosecutor offices can hold forums for community members to share how office policies and actions help and harm survivors, drug users, and the safety of community members.
- Implement "second look" sentencings, and resentence and release people who are serving long sentences for drug-related offenses; potentially release them to receive treatment, through a post-incarceration drug court model like that established in Baltimore with the Baltimore City Office of the State's Attorney.
- Treat drug use by pregnant women as a public health prob-

lem not a crime, thus encouraging women to seek appropriate treatment without fear of prosecution and incarceration.

Habeas Law

• Encourage Congress to reform the Anti-Terrorism Effective Death Penalty Act (AEDPA): eliminate the one-year filing deadline for federal habeas petitions; change deference to state court decisions by allowing federal courts to review state court decisions *de novo*; eliminate procedural default for not raising a claim in state court first.

• Encourage federal courts to review post-conviction petitions by looking at the "evidence as a whole," an AEDPA requirement: consider evidence from original and successive petitions, review evidence excluded at trial, evidence submitted in prior unsuccessful post-conviction proceedings, and any newly discovered evidence.

• Encourage state courts to review habeas petitions with a "confluence of factors" review, like Massachusetts, Kentucky, Illinois, and Connecticut, instead of looking at individual errors in isolation and as harmless error: consider all factors and claims including those previously brought, and rule based on the aggregate influence of errors from investigation through post-conviction. This can be similar to "cumulative error," which sometimes applies on direct appeal of a conviction.

• Using a "confluence of factors" review, encourage courts to reverse convictions based on a manifest injustice or miscarriage of justice standard, rather than actual innocence. The question becomes not whether a person is proven to be actually innocent, a standard too high for many innocent and wrongly convicted people, but instead whether the conviction is a manifest injustice.

• Bring coram nobis petitions to challenge convictions after a person is released from prison, like Fred Korematsu who was convicted for refusing to go to a Japanese American internment camp during World War II, and had his conviction reversed nearly forty years later.

Bias in the Criminal Legal System

- Using confluence of factors review, courts acknowledge racism and bias as factors in a wrongful conviction, like an associate justice of the Massachusetts Superior Court did in reversing the wrongful conviction of Frances Choy.
- Legislatures pass state laws to end the legacy of *McCleskey v. Kemp* and allow defendants to challenge charges, convictions, and sentences based on racially disparate impact, like the California Racial Justice Act.
- Recognize ableism as a cause of wrongful convictions, and urge greater training of police interacting with differently abled civilians, including initial stops and interrogations.

Forensic Evidence Reform

- Urge local governments to fund pre-trial forensic experts for defendants as well as prosecutors to stop bad science coming in at trial, like the State Board of Oregon funding the statewide Forensic Justice Project.
- Enact statewide reviews of a particular type of faulty evidence, like the statewide review of arson convictions in Texas in the wake of Cameron Todd Willingham's wrongful execution.
- Draft and pass "Junk Science Writs" for defendants to challenge their sentences post-conviction when the state used false or faulty evidence at trial, like the writ in Texas that resulted in freedom for Steven Chaney, who was wrongly convicted by bite mark evidence.
- Have state crime labs release scientific findings directly to prosecutors and defense attorneys, not just prosecutors, like the practice of the Houston Forensic Science Center.

Women in the Criminal Legal System

- End state sanctioned sexual assault by ending group strip searches of incarcerated people, particularly as drills, like those at Lincoln Correctional Center in Illinois.
- Recognize misdemeanor and felony wrongful convictions that impact women and queer people, notably prostitution

charges, and charges where Black girls are treated as adults and their behavior criminalized.

• Increase and expand Safe Harbor laws to support sex workers and trafficked people to leave dangerous situations.

• Pass laws for courts to vacate prostitution related convictions of underage teenagers, which are legal wrongful convictions.

• Recognize the criminalization of trans people and urge courts to dismiss pre-trial charges in the interest of justice and to reverse convictions that are influenced by bias as manifest injustice, like the conviction of Darnell Wilson for stealing bras, resulting in a life sentence under Mississippi's Three Strikes Law.

• Free Tasha Shelby, wrongly convicted due to a false diagnosis of Shaken Baby Syndrome.

Clemency and Expungement

• Organize with community participants to petition for clemency by writing and gathering letters, amplifying cases on social media, and working with news outlets, as many people did for Jamie and Gladys Scott resulting in Mississippi governor Haley Barbour granting the sisters' clemency petition.

• Enact legislation to expand expungement laws, so peoples' lives aren't captive to the hundreds of collateral consequences that occur as a result of a conviction.

Prosecutorial Reform and Restorative Justice

• Recognize noble cause corruption and tunnel vision as important influences on prosecutors and police who wrongfully arrest, charge, and convict individuals.

• Follow the American Bar Association Resolution from February 6, 2017, on Alford pleas, to discourage prosecutors from pressuring wrongly convicted individuals to plead guilty to new charges as a condition of their long-fought freedom. Remember Michelle Byrom who was forced by prosecutors to remain incarcerated until her new trial unless she took an Alford plea—which she ultimately did.

- Encourage prosecutors to acknowledge wrongful convictions, rather than seek a conviction for conviction's sake.
- Affirm speedy trial rights for defendants facing re-prosecution. Remember Kennedy Brewer whose conviction was reversed, and then he spent five years in jail waiting for the prosecutor to re-try him.
- Prosecutors prioritize safety and accountability rather than convictions, and recognize we are all lawbreakers in some way.
- Prosecutors explore creating accountability with restorative justice, instead of prisons.
- Incorporate restorative justice alternatives into the criminal legal code, diverting certain individuals from trial and conviction.

ENDNOTES

2 This is their story: I have used pseudonyms throughout the telling of this story.

3 My clients were not: Where possible, I use the term "survivor" instead of "victim."

5 Through manifest injustice, courts can: If the court determines that such relief is necessary "to avoid manifest injustice." *State v. Olish*, 164 W.Va. 712, 715 (1980).

5 Through manifest injustice, prosecutors can: California and Indiana.

5 Courts can acknowledge: Travis S. Hinman, *Varying Degrees of Innocence? Expanding the McQuiggin Exception to Noncapital Sentencing Errors*, 94 N.C. L. Rev. 991 (2016). Available at: scholarship.law.unc.edu/nclr/vol94/iss3/5.

5 Courts can recognize a confluence: Confluence of errors has been used post-conviction. On direct appeal, defendants can raise a claim of cumulative error—that the errors combined violate the defendant's due process right to a fair trial under the 5th and 14th Amendments. Approximately half of states have adopted a cumulative error claim for direct appeal review. *See, for example, People v. Ka Yang*, 67 Cal. App. 5th 1 (2021), as modified on denial of reh'g (Aug. 24, 2021) ("When the cumulative effect of errors deprives the defendant of a fair trial and due process, reversal is required"); *State v. Tully*, 293 Kan. 176, 205 (2011) ("In a cumulative error analysis, an appellate court aggregates all errors and, even though those errors would individually be considered harmless, analyzes whether their cumulative effect on the outcome of the trial is such that collectively they cannot be determined to be harmless."); *Valdez v. State*, 124 Nev. at 1172 (2008) ("The cumulative effect of errors may violate a defendant's constitutional right to a fair trial even though errors are harmless individually.").

5 The idea of manifest injustice: As bell hooks opines in "Theory as Liberatory Practice," *Teaching to Transgress: Education as the Practice* *of Freedom* (1994), theory can challenge our assumptions of what is "natural"—and only "natural" because it is a "routine social practice."

5 Like manifest injustice: *See* Valena E. Beety, "Judicial Dismissal in the Interest of Justice," 80 *Missouri Law Review* 629 (2015). California can dismiss charges post-conviction.

6 Judges dismissed charges: Valena Beety, "COVID-19 Dismissals in the Interest of Justice," *Chicago Law Review Online* (Nov. 16, 2020).

6 Courts can grant coram: *United States v. Taylor*, 648 F.2d 565, 571 (9th Cir. 1981) (referencing *coram nobis* writs).

15 In an extensive interview: (Stubbs Clerk File p. 110).

15 But then, he said he figured: In the interview and ultimately Statement of James Ervin, Jr., the interview was conducted by Detective Nolan Jones, Chief McKee, and Assistant Chief Henderson.

15 Dickie would also tell: (Trial Transcript, pp. 326–27).

16 He told police that: (Stubbs Clerk File p. 128).

16 But some of the words: "They had the accent, it was more coon ass and you may have a drawl with it but some of the words they use are, you know they're coon asses. Like dis, dat, dose, dem and de udder. They always say the th's are d's and they didn't have the drawl like I imagine people in North Mississippi have. I know they weren't from like around here." (Stubbs Clerk File p. 126).

20 Worse yet, there's more: Jennifer Oliva, "Policing Opioid Use Disorder in a Pandemic," *University of Chicago Law Review Online* (November 11, 2020). Available at: lawreviewblog.uchicago.edu/2020/11/16/covid-oliva/comment-page-1. The Drug Abuse Treatment Act (DATA Act), legalized outpatient prescription of buprenorphine to treat opioid use disorder, and 60 percent of such prescriptions are dedicated to white patients. Access to methadone, which is cheaper and more traditionally prescribed to people of color, continues to be restricted to federally sanctioned methadone clinics and still cannot be legally prescribed in the outpatient setting. Additionally, buprenorphine is classified as a schedule 3 drug while methadone is a schedule 2 drug.

20 "Vice"—drugs, alcohol: Muhammad, Khalil. *The Condemnation of Blackness: Race, Crime, and the Making of Modern Urban America*, 2 (2019). Available at: www.hks.harvard.edu/publications/condemnation-blackness-race-crime-and-making-modern-urban-america.

20 Prosecutors now have: Rebecca Neusteter & Megan O'Toole, Vera Inst. of Justice, Every Three Seconds, Unlocking Prison Data on Arrests: Emerging Findings (Jan. 2019). Available at: www.vera.org/publications/arrest-trends-every-three-seconds-landing/arrest-trends-every-three-seconds/findings.

20 The United States spends: Jeffrey Miron, CATO Inst., "The Budgetary Effects of Ending Drug Prohibition," *Tax & Budget Bulletin* No. 83 (July 23, 2018). Available at: www.cato.org/sites/cato.org/files/pubs/pdf/tbb-83.pdf.

20 A recent national study showed: Megan S. Wright, Shima Baradaran Baughman, Christopher Robinson, "Inside the Black Box of Prosecutor Discretion," *University of California Davis Law Review* (2022).

21 Indeed, a majority of: Megan S. Wright, Shima Baradaran Baughman, Christopher Robinson, "Inside the Black Box of Prosecutor Discretion," *University of California Davis Law Review* (2022). The hypothetical case was as follows: "a man at a train station was arrested for, in the words of one arresting officer, 'yelling obscenities, stopping patrons for money, and brandishing a knife.' The man was emotionally distressed from a recent break up with his girlfriend and needed money for a train ride, but when no one gave him any money, he became more upset. One witness reported that the man, while holding a knife, had grabbed a woman's arm after she refused to give him money, but did not hurt or threaten her. Although people at the train station were scared, no one was physically hurt. The man submitted to an arrest without incident."

21 That can change: Institute for Innovation in Prosecution, *A New Approach: A Prosecutor's Guide to Advancing a Public Health Response to Drug Use* (2021). Available at: www.prosecution.org/publichealth.

21 Nearly one in four people: "To Safely Cut Incarceration, States Rethink Responses to Supervision Violations," *Pew Charitable Trusts* (July 16, 2019). Available at: www.pewtrusts.org/en/research-and-analysis/issue-briefs/2019/07/to-safely-cut-incarceration-states-rethink-responses-to-supervision-violations.

21 Oregon, through a ballot: Tatiana Parafiniuk-Talesnick, "Starting Monday, Oregon Spearheading Drug Decriminalization: Here's What You Need to Know," *Register Guard* (Jan. 31, 2021).

Available at: www.registerguard.com/story/news/2021/01/31/faq-measure-110-goes-into-effect-feb-1-need-know-drug-decriminalization/4235674001.

21 Three elected prosecutors: Garrett Andrews, "District Attorneys Disagree on Measure to Decriminalize Some Drugs," *Bulletin* (Oct.14, 2020). Available at: www.bendbulletin.com/localstate/crimeandjustice/district-attorneys-disagree-on-measure-to-decriminalize-some-drugs/article_ac505a80-0e69-11eb-aa25-f7e2fb72f885.html.

21 Other states are decriminalizing: State-by-State Laws, Drug Policy Alliance. Available at: drugpolicy.org/decrim/laws.

24 The front desk clerk: (Trial Transcript, p. 338).

27 We are socialized: Patricia Williams, *The Alchemy of Race and Rights* (1992).

27 We ignore any reality: Erving Goffman, *The Presentation of Self in Everyday Life,* 167–68 (1959).

28 This can be achieved: This is similar to a claim of cumulative error on direct appeal. *See, for example, State v. Parker*, 301 Kan. 132 (2014) ("The test used in a cumulative error analysis is whether the totality of the circumstances substantially prejudiced the defendant and denied him or her a fair trial.")

28 Black Americans have always: Jackie Wang, *Carceral Capitalism*, at 118 (2018).

29 The writ of habeas corpus: Victoria Romine, "Habeas Corpus Reform and Black Lives Matter: A Historical Perspective," 57 *Criminal Law Bulletin* 5 (2021). Victoria Romine expanded my own view on the history of race and habeas law as my student and now colleague.

30 Yet before the Civil War: Justin J. Wert, *Habeas Corpus in America: The Politics of Individual Rights* (2011).

30 Federal courts could review: Victoria Romine, "Habeas Corpus Reform and Black Lives Matter: A Historical Perspective," 57 *Criminal Law Bulletin* 5 (2021); LeRoy Pernell, "Racial Justice and Federal Habeas Corpus as Postconviction Relief from State Convictions," 69 *Mercer Law Review* 453, 522 (2018).

30 Those accused of being: LeRoy Pernell, "Racial Justice and Federal Habeas Corpus as Postconviction Relief from State Convictions," 69 *Mercer Law Review* 453, 522 (2018).

30 In the 1857 case: 60 U.S. (19 How.) 393 (1857).

31 The Court ruled that: Lea Vandervelde, "The *Dred Scott Case* in Context," 40 *Journal of Supreme Court History* 263, 263–64 (2015); *Scott v. Sandford*, 60 U.S. 393 (19 How.) at 493 (1856) (Campbell, J., concurring).

31 These citizen's arrest laws: *See, for example,* South Carolina Code § 17-13-20 (allowing for the arrest of Black people "by such efficient means as the darkness and the probability of escape render necessary, even if his life should be thereby taken"). Roger M. Stevens, "A Legacy of Slavery: The Citizen's Arrest Laws of Georgia and South Carolina," 72 *South Carolina Law Review* 1005 (2021).

32 This meant that federal: Diana P. Wood, "The Enduring Challenge for Habeas Corpus," 95 *Notre Dame Law Review* 1809, 1812 (2020).

32 The Fourteenth Amendment: Diana P. Wood, "The Enduring Challenge for Habeas Corpus," 95 *Notre Dame Law Review* 1809, 1812 (2020).

32 In *Gideon v. Wainwright*: 372 U.S. 335 (1963).

33 Fast forward to present day: Monica C. Bell, "Police Reform and the Dismantling of Legal Estrangement," 126 *Yale Law Review* 2054, 2057–58, 2059–61 (2017).

33 Unprotected by law enforcement: Monica C. Bell, "Police Reform and the Dismantling of Legal Estrangement," 126 *Yale Law Review* 2054, 2057–58, 2059–61 (2017). Scholar Monica Bell's research reveals how poor people of color often see themselves not just as "subjects of a carceral state" or "second class citizens" but as themselves essentially stateless.

33 The narrative of finality: Allegra M. McLeod, "Prison Abolition and Grounded Justice," 62 *University of California Los Angeles Law Review* 1156, 1211–12 (2015).

34 Even the Supreme Court lauded: *Herrera v. Collins*, 506 U.S. 390 (1993) (finding "the very disruptive effect that entertaining claims of actual innocence would have on the need for finality:").

34 If someone is innocent, even if they have been convicted: Allegra M. McLeod, "Prison Abolition and Grounded Justice," 62 *University of California Los Angeles Law Review* 1156, 1214–15 (2015).

34 Our federal statutes: Nancy J. King, "Non-Capital Habeas Corpus After Appellate Review: An Empirical Analysis," 24 *Federal Sentencing Reporter* 308, 317 (2012).

34 Finality removes this moral: Allegra M. McLeod, "Prison Abolition and Grounded Justice," 62 *University of California Los Angeles Law Review* 1156, 1211–12 (2015).

35 The privilege of the Writ: U.S. Constitution Article I, § 9, cl. 2.

36 Just as Congress can: Ex parte *Bollman 4 Cranch* 75, 94 (1807).

36 Federal habeas law has: Other problems include procedural default, and mandatory exhaustion of claims in state court before going to federal court.

36 AEDPA creates the following: Under AEDPA, a litigant must obtain leave from the federal court of appeals before filing a second habeas petition in federal district court, thus restricting the availability of relief to habeas petitioners. That said, what qualifies as a "successive petition" is extensively litigated and challenged.

38 Indeed, the Supreme Court: *Cavazos v. Smith*, 565 U.S. 1, 4 (2011). Available at: www.supremecourt.gov/opinions/11pdf/10-1115.pdf.

38 And yet, when President: clintonwhitehouse6.archives. gov/1996/04/1996-04-24-president-statement-on-antiterrorism-bill-signing.html.

38 Courts have habeas jurisdiction: *Dobbs v. Zant*, 506 U.S. 357 (1993). (No longer good law, but historically *McCleskey v. Zant*, 499 U.S. 467 (1991)).

38 But courts, if they choose: *Coleman v. Thompson*, 501 U.S. 722 (1991) ("federal habeas review of the claims is barred unless the prisoner can demonstrate [among other things] that failure to consider the claims will result in a fundamental miscarriage of justice").

39 Traditionally, if a defendant's: *Moore v. Dempsey*, 261 US 86 (1923).

39 Furthermore, procedural barriers: *Engle v. Isaac*, 456 U.S. 107, 135 (1982).

39 A conviction lacks the due: *Brown v. Allen*, 344 US 443 (1953).

39 However, in 2013, the U.S.: *McQuiggin v. Perkins*, 569 U.S. 383, 387 (2013).

39 This new approach to post-conviction: Stephanie Hartung, "The Confluence of Factors Doctrine: A Holistic Approach to Wrongful Convictions," 51 *Suffolk University Law Review* 369 (2018).

40 The approach accounts for: Stephanie Hartung, "The Confluence of Factors Doctrine: A Holistic Approach to Wrongful Convictions," 51 *Suffolk University Law Review* 369 (2018).

40 The Supreme Court and: Jordan Steiker, "Innocence and Federal

Habeas," 41 *University of California Los Angeles Law Review* 303, 339–41 (1993).

40 As a potential corollary: Stephanie Roberts Hartung, "Missing the Forest for the Trees: Federal Habeas Corpus and the Piecemeal Problem in Actual Innocence Cases,"10 *Stanford Journal of Civil Rights & Civil Liberties* 108 (2014).

40 AEDPA added the: "The § 2244(b)(2)(B)(ii) and § 2255(h)(1) standards—including their 'evidence as a whole' provisions—were added to § 2244 and § 2255 with the enactment of AEDPA in 1996." *See* Antiterrorism and Effective Death Penalty Act of 1996.

40 This provision, and standard: *McCleskey v. Zant*, 499 U.S. 467 (1991).

40 Simply put, the evidence: *United States v. MacDonald*, 641 F.3d 596, 598 (4th Cir. 2011).

40 Quoting the Supreme Court: *Schlup v. Delo*, 513 U.S. 298, 327–28 (1995). This standard of "evidence as a whole" is applicable in federal court to both litigants in federal prisons and litigants in state prisons, under very similar statutes, 2255(h) and 2244(b)(2).

40 Finally, courts have the: *United States v. Williams*, 790 F.3d 1059, 1075–76 (10th Cir. 2015) (referencing common law and pre-AEDPA miscarriage of justice exception to procedural bars).

41 It must exist: this authority: *McQuiggin v. Perkins*, 133 S.Ct. 1924, 1931 (2013).

43 Dr. Moak gave Deputy Simmons: In the medical notes, Dr. Moak wrote "the appropriate authorities have been alerted."

46 Research indicates that over: Shima Baradaran Baughman, "How Effective Are Police? The Problem of Clearance Rates and Criminal Accountability," 72 *Alabama Law Review* 47 (2020), www.law.ua.edu/lawreview/files/2020/12/2-BaughmanArticle-47-112.pdf.

48 In his eyes, the video: (Trial Transcript, p. 89).

51 Within that caste system: Isabel Wilkerson, *Caste: The Origins of Our Discontents* (2020).

51 Sharon Beckman, director: Interview with Sharon Beckman, Director of the Boston College Innocence Program (2020).

51 It's clear that an essential: Interview with Sharon Beckman, Director of the Boston College Innocence Program (2020).

51 Massachusetts courts implement: *Commonwealth v. Rosario*, 74 N.E.3d 599, 607 (Mass. 2017).

52 In September 2020: Mem. of Decision and Order on Def. Frances Choy's Mot. for Postconviction Relief.

52 Soon after, the prosecutor's: The National Registration of Exonerations: Frances Choy, Oct.11, 2020. Available at: www.law.umich.edu/special/exoneration/Pages/casedetail.aspx?caseid=5815

52 Massachusetts is leading: Other states include Illinois, Kentucky.

52 The confluence of factors: Stephanie Hartung, "The Confluence of Factors Doctrine: A Holistic Approach to Wrongful Convictions," 51 *Suffolk University Law Review* 369 (2018).

53 The California Racial Justice Act: "California Legislature Confronts Racial Discrimination in New Criminal Justice Reform Package," *American Bar Association*, Oct. 28, 2020. www.americanbar. org/groups/committees/death_penalty_representation/project_press/ 2020/fall-2020/california-criminal-justice-reform-package.

53 For defendants with old: leginfo.legislature.ca.gov/faces/ billNavClient.xhtml?bill_id=201920200AB2542.

53 The Centers for Disease Control: *Disability and Health Overview*, CDC (last updated Sept. 16, 2020), www.cdc.gov/ncbddd/ disabilityandhealth/disability.html.

54 The institutionalized ableism: Sherina Poyyail, "Black and Disabled: How Racial Discrimination Is Amplified by Ableism," *Reset* (June 8, 2020), resetfest.com/black-and-disabled-how-racial-discrimination-is-amplified-by-ableism.

54 More than 50 percent: Natasha A. Baloch & Wesley J. Jennings, "A Preliminary Investigation of the Intersection of Race and Disabilities among Inmates in the U.S. State Prison System," 46 *Journal of Youth & Adolescence* 1424, 1451 (2017).

54 The disability rate: Jennifer Bronson et al., "Disabilities Among Prison and Jail Inmates," 2011–12, *Bureau of Justice Statistics* 2, 12 (2015).

54 Their desire to please authority: *Death Row Exonerations for People with Intellectual Disabilities,* ACLU), www.aclu.org/other/ death-row-exonerations-people-intellectual-disabilities; Samson J. Schatz, "Interrogated with Intellectual Disabilities: The Risks of False Confession," 60 *Stanford Law Review* 643, 690 (2018).

55 In a more widely followed: Interview with Amy Knight (March 2020).

55 This map helps guide: humaneborders.org/migrant-death-mapping. The Pima County Medical Examiner's Office also collaborates with Humane Borders to create these maps and documents the deaths in their yearly reports.

55 They're looking at tracks: Interview with Amy Knight (March 2020).

55 He calls his ongoing project: bitterrootmag.com/2019/07/12/in-the-sonoran-desert-an-artist-commemorates-where-dreams-die/; www.democracynow.org/2019/8/21/alvaro_enciso_unique_crosses_sonoran_desert.

56 In contrast, similar charged: Interview with Amy Knight, March 2020, noting that similar violations of environmental regulations to protect the refuge were waived.

56 In defense attorney Amy: Interview with Amy Knight (March 2020).

57 After this decision: Paul Ingram, "Judge reverses convictions of 4 No More Deaths volunteers," *Tucson Sentinel* (Feb. 3, 2020). Available at: www.tucsonsentinel.com/local/report/020320_no_more_deaths/judge-reverses-convictions-4-no-more-deaths-volunteers.

58 He took photos of: (Stubbs Clerks File p. 88).

59 He found a "match": (Trial Transcript, p.12).

59 All of which is consistent: (p. 89 Stubbs Clerk File. 4.21.2000 Letter from Mike West to Det. Nolan Jones).

69 West and Hayne are perhaps: My former boss, Tucker Carrington, and *Washington Post* reporter Radley Balko wrote a book on Hayne and West and their roles in multiple wrongful convictions, *The Cadaver King and the Country Dentist: A True Story of Injustice in the American South* (2019).

70 Many people have died: Alon Steinberg, "Prone Restraint Cardiac Arrest: A Comprehensive Review of the Scientific Literature and an Explanation of the Physiology," *Medicine, Science and the Law* 2021 Jul;61(3):215–26. Studies have additionally been conducted in San Diego and King County, Seattle. *See also* Shaila Dewan, "Subduing Suspects Face Down Isn't Fatal, Research Has Said. Now the Research Is on Trial," *New York Times* (Oct. 2, 2021).

70 Hayne labeled the: ebwiki.org/cases/debbie-denise-loggins.

70 Including Debbie's own son: Jerry Mitchell, Mississippi Center for Investigative Reporting, "'Y'all Going to Kill Me?' Years Apart, Mother and Son Die in Police Restraints," *The Marshall Project* (November 30, 2021). Available at: www.themarshallproject.org/2021/11/30/y-all-going-to-kill-me-years-apart-mother-and-son-die-in-police-restraints.

70 The police who sat: *Alice Loggins Hill v. Carroll County, Mississippi*, 587 F.3d 230 (5th Cir. 2009).

72 Hayne: That's correct. Transcript, January 23–24, 2007. *State of Mississippi v. Linda Griffin*, Cause No. 497-06. Even the prosecutor got confused about cause of death at trial:

PROSECUTOR: Are you saying that the ethylene glycol caused a
    heart attack or are you saying that he had a heart attack but that
    was not the reason that he died, he died from ethylene glycol
    poisoning?
HAYNE: He died from ethylene glycol poisoning, Counselor: I
    ruled it homicide.

72 He would also start: Frankie would also start showing symptoms of poisoning within half an hour. Frankie was working the night shift after having dinner with his wife, so he was around his coworkers. His coworker picked him up and dropped him off again at home after the shift ended at 3:00 A.M. To all appearances, Frankie seemed fine. When his wife Linda woke in the morning, Frankie was dead, in bed.

72 That's what I feel: Transcript, January 24, 2007. *State of Mississippi v. Linda Griffin*, Cause No. 497-06.

73 In its 2009 Report: *Nat'l Research Council of the Nat'l Acads., Strengthening Forensic Science in the United States: A Path Forward* 175–76 (2009); www.ncjrs.gov/pdffiles1/nij/grants/228091.pdf [perma.cc/Z9VR-ADYV].

73 The NAS Report reserved: Jennifer D. Oliva and Valena E. Beety, "Regulating Bite Mark Evidence: Lesbian Vampires and Other Myths of Forensic Odontology," 94 *Washington Law Review* 1769 (2019).

73 Reverend Burroughs was: Radley Balko, "It Literally Started with a Witch Hunt: A History of Bite Mark Evidence," *Washington Post* (Feb. 17, 2015, 7:57 A.M.), www.washingtonpost.com/news/the-watch/wp/2015/02/17/it-literally-started-with-a-witch-hunt-a-history-of-bite-mark-evidence [perma.cc/2KTD-F3PH].

73 Neither of these beliefs: The NAS Report concluded that the discipline had failed to scientifically establish "[t]he uniqueness of human dentition," and "[t]he ability of the dentition, if unique, to transfer a unique pattern to human skin and the ability of the skin to maintain that uniqueness." NAS Report at 175.

73 Instead, the NAS Report: NAS Report at 174.

73 Bite mark analysts also: NAS Report at 175–76, finding no "standard for the type, quality, and number of individual characteristics required to indicate that a bite mark has reached a threshold of evidentiary value."

73 Analysts cannot accurately: *Construct Validity Bitemark Assessments Using the ABFO Bitemark Decision Tree,* Adam Freeman & Iain Pretty, Presentation at the 2016 Annual Meeting of the American Academy of Forensic Scientists: *Construct Validation of Bitemark Assessments Using the ABFO Decision Tree* (2016), online.wsj.com/public/resources/documents/ConstructValidBMdecision treePRETTYFREEMAN.pdf [perma.cc/WX9E-79MX].

74 Instead, bite mark evidence: Augenstein, "Bite-Mark Evidence Should Be 'Deceased,' Dentist Says," *Forensic Magazine* (Nov. 5, 2018, 12:22 P.M.), www.forensicmag.com/news/2018/11/bite-mark-evidence-skin-should-be-deceased-dentist-says [perma.cc/KL3E-RF3Z].

74 In a habeas petition: *Brewer v. State,* 819 So. 2d 1169, 1172 (Miss. 2002).

75 Nearly a year before: Radley Balko, "A Forensic Charlatan Gets Caught in the Act," *REASON* (May 15, 2009, 1:30 P.M.), reason.com/archives/2009/05/15/a-forensics-charlatan-gets-cau [perma.cc/WG5Y-T8VN]. The entire sting is captured on video that is available online on the Reason website. *Id.*

75 West confidently concluded: Jennifer D. Oliva and Valena E. Beety, "Regulating Bite Mark Evidence: Lesbian Vampires and Other Myths of Forensic Odontology," 94 *Washington Law Review* 1769 (2019).

75 According to the treatise on: David L. Faigman et al., "The Judicial Response to Expert Testimony on Bitemark Identification," 4 *Modern Science Evidence* § 35:4 (2016–2017).

75 Courts simply rely on: *See PCAST Report* at 22 ("[R]eviews by competent bodies of the scientific underpinnings of forensic disciplines and the use in courtrooms of evidence based on those disciplines have revealed a dismaying frequency of instances of use of forensic evidence that do not pass an objective test of scientific validity.").

76 Forensic testimony can: *See* Jennifer L. Groscup et al., "The Effects of Daubert on the Admissibility of Expert Testimony in State and Federal Criminal Cases," 8 *Psychology, Public Policy & Law* 339 (2002).

76 Judges admit evidence: Jennifer D. Oliva and Valena E. Beety, "Regulating Bite Mark Evidence: Lesbian Vampires and Other Myths of Forensic Odontology," 94 *Washington Law Review* 1769, 1771 (2019).

76 In 2009, the publication: Committee on Identifying the Needs of the Forensic Science Community, National Research Council, No. 228091, *Strengthening Forensic Science in the United States: A Path Forward* (2009).

77 Even the U.S. Supreme Court: *Melendez-Diaz v. Massachusetts,* 557 U.S. 305, 319 (2009). The Supreme Court also mentioned how "[o]ne commentator asserts that '[t]he legal community now concedes, with varying degrees of urgency, that our system produces erroneous convictions based on discredited forensics.'" *Id.* at 319 (quoting Pamela R. Metzger, "Cheating the Constitution," 59 *Vanderbilt Law Review* 475, 491 (2006)).

78 The highest court in: Crucial to this investigation was the assistance and effort of George Castelle, public defender for Kanawha County, West Virginia.

78 Compelled by the widespread: *Zain I,* 438 S.E.2d 501, 506–07 (W. Va. 1993).

78 The state also has: Other states can do the same: we know faulty testimony with regards to hair microscopy, bite mark evidence, fire science, and roadside drug tests, has contributed to wrongful convictions. States can affirmatively fund reviews of cases, to identify wrongful convictions and free people. While a junk science writ allows individuals to petition courts for relief, a statewide review can free wrongfully convicted people en masse.

78 State crime lab directors: Notification from the ASCLD/LAB Board of Directors to Interested Parties Concerning Potential Issues with Hair Comparison Testimony.

79 [That case] is from 1954: As Garcia told me, "the first bite mark case . . ." Valena Beety interview with Lynn Garcia (2019).

79 The Texas Forensic Science Commission's: *Justice Through Science: Forensic Bitemark Comparison Complaint Filed by National Innocence Project on Behalf of Steven Mark Chaney—Final Report,* Texas Forensic Science Commission (April 12, 2016). Available at www.txcourts.gov/media/1440871/finalbitemarkreport.pdf.

79 And to fix it you really: Valena Beety interview with Judge Barbara Hervey (2019).

80 No way, no how. Valena Beety interview with Patricia Cummings (2020).

81 The flipside of that: Valena Beety interview with Cynthia Garza (2019).

81 The Texas legislature became: *Texas Code of Criminal Procedure Annual,* art. 11.073.

82 Bad news: as a recent Wyoming: *Parkhurst v. State,* 443 P.3d 834, 837 (Wyo. 2019) (citing *Wyo. Stat. Ann.* §7-12-403(b)) (stating that the law "requir[es] every petition filed pursuant to the Factual Innocence Act to 'contain an assertion of factual innocence' supported by 'newly discovered evidence'").

83 The Court ruled that the changed testimony: In re *Richards,* No. E049135, 2010 WL 4681260, at *1 (Cal. Ct. App. Nov. 19, 2010), aff'd, *Richards* I, 289 P.3d at 860–61.

83 The *California Lawyer* derided: Gerald F. Uelmen, "New Balance at the California Supreme Court," *California Lawyer* (Aug. 2013), www.callawyer.com/Clstory.cfm?eid=930177 [perma.cc/6XBG-Z9SP].

84 The Houston Forensic Science: Sandra Guerra Thompson, Nicole B. Casarez, "Building the Infrastructure for 'Justice Through Science': The Texas Model," 119 *West Virginia Law Review* 711 (2016).

84 According to former board: *Id.* at 1046.

84 Prosecutors are required under: Miriam H. Baer, "Timing Brady," 115 *Columbia Law Review* 1, 44 (2015) ("If ninety-five percent of the defendant pool pleads guilty, then resource-deprived prosecutors should rationally delay some of their preparation for trial until they know for sure whether a given defendant plans to plead not guilty.")

84 Nationally, state court criminal: Erica Goode, "Stronger Hand for Judges in the 'Bazaar' of Plea Deals," *New York Times* (Mar. 22, 2012), www.nytimes.com/2012/03/23/us/stronger-hand-for-judges-after-rulings-on-plea-deals.html [perma.cc/6SM8-YK4Z].

96 The San Antonio Four are: Their wrongful convictions are documented in the film *Southwest of Salem: The Story of the San Antonio Four*, www.southwestofsalem.com

96 Less than 5 percent of women: Jessica Henry, Smoke but No Fire: Convicting the Innocent of Crimes That Never Happened (2020).

96 Anna described herself: Interview with Anna Vasquez (2020).

97 Anna was so frustrated: Interview with Anna Vasquez (2020).

97 That is really hard for: Interview with Karen Thompson (2019).

98 Psychiatrists historically labeled: "Sexual Deviations— Homosexuality: This category is for individuals whose sexual interests are directed primarily toward sexual acts not usually associated with coitus. . . . Even though many find their practices distasteful, they remain unable to substitute normal sexual behavior for them." *American Psychiatric Association*, 1968.

98 They also labeled enslaved: Drapetomania, from Greek drapeteusis "an escape" and mania "madness": "A runaway slave is mania mad or crazy. Its diagnostic symptoms be absconding from service, is well known to our planters and overseers. . . . The cause in most cases that induces the Negro to run away from service is as much a disease of the mind as any other species of mental alienation, and much more curable as a general rule." Dr. Samuel Cartwright, "A Report on the Diseases and Physical Peculiarities of the Negro Race," (1851).

98 Scholars discuss these labels: Joey Mogul, Andrea Ritchie, Kay Whitlock, *Queer (In)Justice: The Criminalization of LGBT People in the United States*, 69–70, xi, xii (2012) (interrogating how our criminal legal system targets and abuses queer people, and particularly queer people of color).

98 Around World War II: Kathryn Ann Farr, "Defeminizing and Dehumanizing Female Murderers: Depictions of Lesbians on Death Row," *Women and Criminal Justice* Vol. 11(1) at 54 (2000).

98 They went to trial: Kathryn Ann Farr, "Depictions of Lesbians on Death Row," *Women and Criminal Justice* Vol. 11(1) (2000).

98 Even if they were not: *Id.*

98 Instead, the narrative: Ruthann Robson, *Lesbian (Out) Law: Survival Under the Rule of Law* (1992).

98 LGBTQ+ identities are criminalized: Joey Mogul et al., *Queer (In)Justice* (2011).

99 Years later, media still publicly: *See also* Knox's insightful podcast episode, Labyrinths: Getting Lost with Amanda Knox, The Pleasure of Pain (Aug. 29, 2021) podcasts.apple.com/us/podcast/the-pleasure-of-pain-mistress-cyan/id1494368441?i=1000533314281.

99 These stories overlap: *Queer (In)Justice* at 23–24.

99 The proliferation of sumptuary: Bennett Capers, "Cross Dressing and the Criminal," 20 *Yale Journal of Law & the Humanities* 1, 8–10, 18–19, 21 (2008).

99 As LGBTQ+ subcultures: Bennett Capers, "Cross Dressing and the Criminal," 20 *Yale Journal of Law & the Humanities* 1, 8–10, 18–19, 21 (2008).

100 Butch lesbians had to: Sexuality scholar Katherine Franke notes, "butch lesbians experienced the weight of these rules every day during the 1950s when police would arrest them if they could not prove that they were wearing at least three pieces of women's clothing." Katherine Franke, "The Central Mistake of Sex Discrimination Law: The Disaggregation of Sex From Gender," *U. Penn. L. Rev.* (1995).

100 In New York, individuals: *Queer (In)Justice* at 12.

100 Then in 1915, the state: 1915 California State Penal Code 288a. William N. Eskridge, Jr., *Gaylaw: Challenging the Apartheid of the Closet*, 3, 20 (1999).

100 In the *Making Gay History* podcast: makinggayhistory.com/podcast/episode-19-donaldson-smith.

101 Herbert: it would have: *Excerpt from Making Gay History* podcast, makinggayhistory.com/podcast/episode-19-donaldson-smith.

101 "Lewd conduct" laws: truthout.org/articles/the-ghosts-of-stonewall-policing-gender-policing-sex.

101 By the 1960s, famed: Imani Perry, *Looking for Lorraine: The Radiant and Radical Life of Lorraine Hansberry* (2018).

102 This marked a wave: Justin Woods, "LGBT Identity and Crime," 105 *California Law Review* 667 (2017).

103 The first satanic ritual: National Center for Reason and Justice; www.law.umich.edu/special/exoneration/Pages/casedetail.aspx?caseid=-3011.

103 Organizers led "die-ins": Original Working Document, ACT UP/New York (2003).

103 Their two-prong strategy: ACT UP's protests ultimately led the FDA to adopt parallel-track studies for AIDS medication and to move more quickly to approve promising treatments.

103 That year, 2003, the: *Lawrence v. Texas*, 539 U.S. 558 (2003).

104 They view this as: *Lawrence v. Texas*, Scalia dissent. www.law.cornell.edu/supct/html/02-102.ZD.html.

104 The Mississippi statute: *See* House Bill 761 (2020), "An Act to amend Section 97-29-59 Mississippi Code of 1972 to revise the unnatural intercourse law to remove the word 'mankind.'" The bill was referred to Judiciary B on 2/10/20 and died in committee on 3/3/20.

104 Fourteen states still have: FLORIDA: Fla. Stat. 800.02, outlawing "unnatural acts"; GEORGIA: O.C.G.A. Sec. 16-6-2; IDAHO: I.C. Sec. 18-6605, "infamous crime against nature" statute; KENTUCKY: KY. Rev. Stat. Sec. 510.100; LOUISIANA: LA Rev. Stat. 14:89; MASSACHUSETTS: MGL Ch. 272, Sec. 34; MGL Ch. 272, Sec. 35; MICHIGAN: MCL Secs. 750.158, 750.338, 750.338(a)-(b); MISSISSIPPI: Miss. Code Sec. 97-29-59; NORTH CAROLINA: G.S. Sec. 14-177; OKLAHOMA: Sec. 21-886; SOUTH CAROLINA: S.C. Code Sec. 16-15-60; and TEXAS: Tx. Penal Code Sec. 21.06, outlawing "homosexual conduct."

104 Whether the law is: www.huffpost.com/entry/louisiana-police-sting-gay-men-anti-sodomy-law_n_3668116.

105 Dr. Laura would claim: Michael Mello, "For Today, I'm Gay: The Unfinished Battle for Same-Sex Marriage in Vermont," 25 *Vermont Law Review* 149, 153–54 (2000).

105 A Newsweek poll for March: Michael Mello, "For Today, I'm Gay: The Unfinished Battle for Same-Sex Marriage in Vermont," 25 *Vermont Law Review* 149, 153–54 (2000).

106 Passing as straight may: Kenji Yoshino, *Covering: The Hidden Assault on Our Civil Rights* (2007).

106 My body was given back: Frantz Fanon, *Black Skin White Masks*, 113 (1967).

109 I'm always getting into: (Trial Transcript, p. 466).

109 Dr. West explained: (Trial Transcript, p. 510).

110 Focusing on Kim's nipples: (Trial Transcript, p. 511).

110 But you have Virginia Slims: (Trial Transcript, pp. 514–15).

110 Only this area: (Trial Transcript, p. 512).

111 A lot of the fine detail: (Trial Transcript, p. 529).

112 And it's more than just: (Trial Transcript, p. 531).

112 **And notice we have:** (Trial Transcript, p. 636).

112 **I'm just documenting them:** (Trial Transcript, p. 513).

112 **These injuries are – lead me:** (Trial Transcript, p. 513).

113 **After all the scientific:** (Trial Transcript, p. 601).

113 **Dr. West warned them:** (Trial Transcript, p. 533).

114 **It's mine and Detective Jones':** (Trial Transcript, p. 535).

115 **Checks the doors and then:** (Trial Transcript, p. 546).

116 **And I believe that that is:** (Trial Transcript, p. 547).

116 **When the teeth drag:** (Trial Transcript, p. 555).

117 **Well, of course, we go:** (Trial Transcript, p. 560).

117 **Almost:** (Trial Transcript, p. 559).

118 **There was plenty of:** (Trial Transcript, p. 562).

118 **We always tell them:** (Trial Transcript, p. 566).

119 **Curiously, he said:** (Trial Transcript, p. 568).

120 **"Dr. West, how do:** (Trial Transcript, p. 573).

120 **"The only way I think:** (Trial Transcript, p. 575).

121 **"That's the big problem:** (Trial Transcript, pp. 577–78).

122 **"I believe with no reservations:** (Trial Transcript, p. 583).

122 **But his evidentiary reports:** (Trial Transcript, p. 591).

122 **Dr. West bragged that:** (Trial Transcript, p. 598).

122 **"We got volunteers from:** (Trial Transcript, p. 604).

123 **He told Dr. West:** (Trial Transcript, p. 608).

123 **He ruled the complaint:** (Trial Transcript, p. 609).

123 **The judge urged Barnett:** (Trial Transcript, p. 610).

123 **"They caught me smoking:** (Trial Transcript, p. 611).

124 **"I can't give you someone:** (Trial Transcript, p. 619).

124 **They will come in and say:** (Trial Transcript, p. 617).

124 **It's two different things:** (Trial Transcript, p. 630).

124 **Dr. West dismissed the treatise:** (Trial Transcript, p. 632).

124 **And the judge again:** (Trial Transcript, p. 633).

125 **Barnett pointed out that:** (Trial Transcript, p. 641).

125 **Tracy was being paid:** (Trial Transcript, p. 668).

125 **The first, of course:** (Trial Transcript, p. 645).

125 **I asked them to spread her legs:** (Trial Transcript, p. 646).

126 **And if you had one of:** (Trial Transcript, p. 646).

126 **Now, if she was conscious:** (Trial Transcript, p. 647).

126 **There's basically not a:** (Trial Transcript, p. 650).

127 **It's not a rubber stamp:** (Trial Transcript, p. 655).

127 Can I completely duplicate: (Trial Transcript, p. 655–656).

128 Trying to force her in: (Trial Transcript, p. 668).

128 I believe the blows occurred: (Trial Transcript, p. 669).

128 So on an unconscious, injured: (Trial Transcript, p. 658).

128 That's all I was doing: (Trial Transcript, pp. 658–59).

128 I resent you saying: (Trial Transcript, p. 659).

129 Why don't you get your own: (Trial Transcript, p. 661).

129 But when someone tells: Gary L. Wells, *Eyewitness Testimony,* Iowa State University, lib.dr.iastate.edu/psychology_pubs/75.

130 Dr. West wasn't 100 percent: (Trial Transcript, p. 661).

130 He even conceded: (Trial Transcript, p. 662).

130 That came after the study: (Trial Transcript, p. 663).

130 Something black and long that: (Trial Transcript, p. 675).

130 I took the truck and put it: (Trial Transcript, p. 675).

131 I don't believe it's probable: (Trial Transcript, p. 677).

131 That's what I see: (Trial Transcript, p. 679).

132 Those are the photographs: (Trial Transcript, pp. 677–78).

132 No more questions: (Trial Transcript, pp. 686–87).

133 In 2008, Brooks and Brewer: Radley Balko & Tucker Carrington, *The Cadaver King and the Country Dentist: A True Story of Injustice in the American South* (2018).

133 She approached the stand: (Trial Transcript, p. 703).

134 "No," Kim responded: (Trial Transcript, pp. 703–4).

136 We consume visual images: Carol J. Adams, *The Sexual Politics of Meat* (1990).

136 There is something of a power trip: Carol J. Adams, *The Pornography of Meat* (2019).

136 I don't believe that it's beyond reason: (Trial Transcript, p. 650)

136 They are body parts to: In *The Sexual Politics of Meat,* Carol Adams explores how women become less than human, positioned as animals like bitch, pig, chick, old biddy—and ultimately inanimate pieces of meat. Carol J. Adams, *The Sexual Politics of Meat* (1990).

137 Women survivors of revenge: Cressida J. Heyes, "Dead to the World: Rape, Unconsciousness, and Social Media," 41 *Signs: Journal of Women in Culture and Society* 2 (2016).

138 Before the American Medical Association: Deirdre Cooper Owens, *Medical Bondage: Race, Gender, and the Origins of American Gynecology* (2017).

139 The unheralded Black women: Deirdre Cooper Owens, *Medical Bondage: Race, Gender, and the Origins of American Gynecology* (2017). *See also* The Mothers of Gynecology Park and Monument, Montgomery, Alabama, www.anarchalucybetsey.org.

139 Because of racism, Black: Last Week Tonight, *Bias in Medicine: Last Week Tonight with John Oliver (HBO)*, YouTube (Aug. 18, 2019), www.youtube.com/watch?v=TATSAHJKRd8 (12:02–12:32).

139 They concocted an: In medical journals Black women were reduced to their reproductive organs. As Dr. Cooper Owens describes, "this 'biologically rooted racism,' . . . further strengthened the anti-African racism of white Americans. Educated white people employed myriad methods to justify their belief in African inferiority and slavery . . . men of medicine and science wrote voluminous accounts of the biological failings of black people as a degenerate race." Deirdre Cooper Owens, *Medical Bondage: Race, Gender, and the Origins of American Gynecology*, 22–23 (2017).

142 So we checked her into: (Trial Transcript, p. 716).

143 I've never seen any: (Trial Transcript, p. 718).

143 There did appear to be saliva: (Trial Transcript, p. 726).

144 She compared those hairs to: (Trial Transcript, p. 740).

145 She was one of those that was willing: (Trial Transcript, pp. 757–58).

145 There was no trauma to: (Trial Transcript, pp. 764–65).

146 Dr. Galvez testified that: (Trial Transcript, p. 765).

146 You can leave so many teeth marks: (Trial Transcript, p. 771).

146 Problematically, fourteen years later when: Adam Freeman & Iain Pretty, Presentation at the 2016 Annual Meeting of the American Academy of Forensic Science: *Construct Validation of Bitemark Assessments Using the ABFO Decision Tree* (2016), online.wsj.com/public/resources/documents/ConstructValidBMdecisiontreePRETTYFREEMAN.pdf [perma.cc/WX9E-79MX]; Radley Balko, "A Bite Mark Matching Advocacy Group Just Conducted a Study that Discredits Bite Mark Evidence," *Washington Post* (Apr. 8, 2015), www.washingtonpost.com/news/the-watch/wp/2015/04/08/a-bite-mark-matching-advocacy-group-just-conducted-a-study-that-discredits-bite-mark-evidence/?noredirect=on [perma.cc/S2DL-ZREX].

148 That's the same word: (Trial Transcript, p. 810).

149 I did. Leigh didn't: (Trial Transcript, p. 816).

149 They have their own sources: (Trial Transcript, p. 818).

157 West: Almost: (Trial Transcript, p. 559).

158 It was a small town and I knew: Dara E. Purvis & Melissa Blanco, "Police Sexual Violence: Police Brutality, #MeToo, and Masculinities," 108 *California Law Review* 1487 (2020).

158 West: I don't believe that: (Trial Transcript, p. 650).

159 Mississippi first criminalized sodomy: *Doe v. Hood*, 345 F.Supp.3d 749, 752–53 (S.D. Miss. 2018).

159 making "unnatural intercourse" a felony: *State v. Davis*, 79 So.2d 452 (Miss. 1955).

159 A 1950s Mississippi Supreme Court: *State v. Davis*, 79 So.2d 452 (Miss. 1955).

159 When Dr. West testified about: (Trial Transcript, p. 646).

163 Tasha, Leigh, and Tami were: "2017 study, 86% of the women who had been detained in jail were survivors of sexual assault." Jamelia N. Morgan, "Reflections on Representing Incarcerated People with Disabilities: Ableism in Prison Reform Litigation," 96 *Denver Law Review* 973 (2019).

163 Transgender and gender nonconforming people: Jamelia N. Morgan, "Reflections on Representing Incarcerated People with Disabilities: Ableism in Prison Reform Litigation," 96 *Denver Law Review* 973 (2019).

163 The purpose of strip searches: Lisa Guenther, *Solitary Confinement: Social Death and Its Afterlives* (2013).

163 A prison in Illinois was: *Henry v. Hulett*, 930 F.3d 836, 837 (7th Cir. 2019).

166 That is undisputed: (Trial Transcript, p. 583).

208 Lisa Jo Chamberlin was sentenced: Michelle Liu, "Michelle Byrom, Who Narrowly Escaped Execution After 14 Years on Mississippi's Death Row, is Dead at 62," *Mississippi Today* (April 4, 2019), mississippi-today.org/2019/04/04/michelle-byrom-who-narrowly-escaped-execution-after-14-years-on-mississippis-death-row-is-dead-at-62.

168 Not many women are sentenced: Sandra Babcock, "Judged for More Than Her Crime," Cornell Law School, Cornell Center on the Death Penalty Worldwide (2018), www.deathpenaltyworldwide.org/wp-content/uploads/2019/12/Judged-More-Than-Her-Crime.pdf.

168 Why didn't she just leave: Ronni Mott, "An Innocent Woman? Michelle Byrom vs. Mississippi," *Jackson Free Press* (March 19, 2014), www.jacksonfreepress.com/news/2014/mar/19/innocent-woman-michelle-byrom-vs-mississippi.

169 Journalists uncovered four written confessions: Ronni Mott, "An Innocent Woman? Michelle Byrom vs. Mississippi," *Jackson Free Press* (March 19, 2014), www.jacksonfreepress.com/news/2014/mar/19/innocent-woman-michelle-byrom-vs-mississippi.

169 In a shocking move: Ronni Mott, "Michelle Byrom Gets Stunning Sentencing Reversal," *Jackson Free Press* (April 1, 2014), www.jacksonfreepress.com/news/2014/apr/01/michelle-byrom-gets-stunning-sentencing-reversal.

170 Her son, Eddie: Michelle Liu, "Michelle Byrom, Who Narrowly Escaped Execution After 14 Years on Mississippi's Death Row, is Dead at 62," *Mississippi Today* (April 4, 2019), mississippitoday.org/2019/04/04/michelle-byrom-who-narrowly-escaped-execution-after-14-years-on-mississippis-death-row-is-dead-at-62.

170 In her own powerful book: Sabrina Butler Smith, *Exonerated: The Sabrina Butler Story*, sabrinabutler.webs.com.

171 Solitary confinement has: *See generally* David Shapiro, "Solitary Confinement in the Young Republic," 133 *Harvard Law Review* 542 (2019).

173 Howard Patrick testified that: Ward Schaefer, "The Tragic Case of the Scott Sisters," *Jackson Free Press* (Nov. 3, 2010), www.jacksonfreepress.com/news/2010/nov/03/the-tragic-case-of-the-scott-sisters.

173 Gladys was pregnant: Ward Schaefer, "The Tragic Case of the Scott Sisters," *Jackson Free Press* (Nov. 3, 2010), www.jacksonfreepress.com/news/2010/nov/03/the-tragic-case-of-the-scott-sisters.

173 He ordered them released: Holbrook Mohr Associated Press, "Jamie, Gladys Scott Out of Prison in Kidney Deal," *SFGATE* (Jan. 8, 2011), www.sfgate.com/news/article/Jamie-Gladys-Scott-out-of-prison-in-kidney-deal-2462306.php.

176 Ninety-one percent of trafficking survivors: Jessica Emerson, *State Report Cards: Grading Criminal Record Relief Laws for Survivors of Human Trafficking* (2019). Available at scholarworks.law.ubalt.edu/all_fac/1079.

176 Black girls are more likely: Jasmine Sankofa, "From Margin to Center: Sex Work Decriminalization is a Racial Justice Issue," *Amnesty International* (Dec. 12, 2016).

177 Their adultification means that: Monique Morris, *Pushout: The Criminalization of Black Girls in Schools* (2016).

177 Traffickers interviewed by: Samantha Davey, "Snapshot on the State of Black Women and Girls: Sex Trafficking in the U.S.," *Congressional Black Caucus Foundation,* www.cbcfinc.org/publications/ health/snapshot-on-the-state-of-black-women-and-girls-sex-trafficking-in-the-u-s.

177 Black girls have been hypersexualized: Rebecca Epstein, Jamilia Blake, and Thalia González, *Girlhood Interrupted: The Erasure of Black Girls' Childhood* (June 27, 2017), papers.ssrn.com/sol3/papers.cfm?abstract_id=3000695.

177 They disproportionately profile: Melissa Gira Grant, *Playing the Whore* (2014).

177 Police, however, frequently: Int'l Women's Human Rights Clinic, CUNY Law & Trafficking Victims Advocacy Project, Legal Aid Society of N.Y., *Criminalization of Trafficking Victims* (April 2015).

178 Thirty-five states have enacted: Shared Hope Int'l, *National State Law Survey: Expungement and Vacatur Laws* (2017), sharedhope.org/wp-content/uploads/2016/03/NSL_Survey_ Expungement-and-Vacatur-Laws.pdf.

178 Crack babies became a symbol: Cortney E. Lollar, "Criminalizing Pregnancy," 92 *Indiana Law Journal* 947, 953 (2017).

178 Dubious charities like: D. A. Frank, M. Augustyn, W. G. Knight, T. Pell, & B. Zuckerman, "Growth, Development, and Behavior in Early Childhood Following Prenatal Cocaine Exposure," 285 *JAMA* 1613, 1626 (2001). Nearly thirty years ago, acclaimed legal scholar Dorothy Roberts wrote "Punishing Drug Addicts Who Have Babies: Women of Color, Equality, and the Right of Privacy," 104 *Harvard Law Review* 1419 (1991).

178 In fact, the use of crack: D. A. Frank, M. Augustyn, W. G. Knight, T. Pell, & B. Zuckerman, "Growth, Development, and Behavior in Early Childhood Following Prenatal Cocaine Exposure," 285 *JAMA* 1613, 1626 (2001).

178 In twenty-three states: Emma Milne, "Putting the Fetus First—

Legal Regulation, Motherhood, and Pregnancy," 27 *Michigan Journal of Gender & Law* 149, 153 (2020).

179 In 2014, Tennessee legislators: Wendy A. Bach, "Prosecuting Poverty, Criminalizing Care," 60 *William & Mary Law Review* 809 (2019).

179 One legislator described: Wendy A. Bach, "Prosecuting Poverty, Criminalizing Care," 60 *William & Mary Law Review* 809 (2019).

179 Another legislator supported: Wendy A. Bach, "Prosecuting Poverty, Criminalizing Care," 60 *William & Mary Law Review* 809 (2019).

179 The statute only stayed: Wendy A. Bach, "Prosecuting Poverty, Criminalizing Care," 60 *William & Mary Law Review* 809 (2019).

180 In 2011, 14 percent: Valena E. Beety, "Mississippi Initiative 26: Personhood and the Criminalization of Intentional and Unintentional Acts by Pregnant Women," 81 *Mississippi Law Journal Supra* 55 (2011).

180 As the Maryland Supreme Court: Valena E. Beety, "Mississippi Initiative 26: Personhood and the Criminalization of Intentional and Unintentional Acts by Pregnant Women," 81 *Mississippi Law Journal Supra* 55 (2011).

180 In Alabama, legislators passed: Ala. Code § 26-15-3.2 (2021).

180 Many state courts have ruled: New Mexico, Arizona, Nevada, Florida, and Maryland are among those states. Amicus Brief to *Kimbrough v. Alabama* 246 So.3d 1010, ACLU, footnote 1, www.aclu.org/legal-document/kimbrough-v-alabama-amicus-brief?redirect=reproductive-freedom/kimbrough-v-alabama-amicus-brief.

181 Having a prescription: A mother who uses a drug without a prescription—including drugs that treat substance abuse disorder—can be charged with endangering the child even if the child is born healthy. And a mother who was using the exact same drug with a prescription during pregnancy will—usually—not be charged with endangering the child, even if the child is born with health problems.

181 Prosecutors alleged that: Valena E. Beety, "Mississippi Initiative 26: Personhood and the Criminalization of Intentional and Unintentional Acts by Pregnant Women," 81 *Mississippi Law Journal Supra* 55 (2011).

181 The language of the statute: Miss. Code Ann. § 97-3-37 (2006).

181 They may also be factually innocent: Valena E. Beety, "Mississippi Initiative 26: Personhood and the Criminalization of Intentional and Unintentional Acts by Pregnant Women," 81 *Mississippi Law Journal Supra* 55 (2011).

181 With the resurgence of: Emma Milne, "Putting the Fetus First—Legal Regulation, Motherhood, and Pregnancy," 27 *Michigan Journal of Gender & Law* 149, 169 (2020).

182 A positive test means: Cortney Lollar, "Criminalizing Pregnancy," 92 *Indiana Law Journal* 947, 953 (2017). Available at papers.ssrn.com/sol3/papers.cfm?abstract_id=2806691.

182 The American Medical Association: ACLU, Position Statement of Medical Associations Opposing Criminal Sanctions for Pregnant Women With Substance Abuse Problems, www.aclu.org/files/assets/2010-7-6-Position_Statements_of_Medical_Associations_Opposing_Criminal_Sanctions_for_Pregnant_Women_With_Substance_Abuse_Problems.pdf.

182 According to the American Academy: American Academy of Pediatrics, Committee on Substance Abuse, 1994 to 1995, "Drug-Exposed Infants," 96 *Pediatrics* 365–66 (1995).

183 The Sylvia Rivera Law Project: *Sylvia Rivera Law Project,* srlp.org.

183 Police arrest and courts convict: Phoenix Municipal Code § 23-52(A)(3). Megan Cassidy, "Transgender Woman is Convicted of Prostitution-Related Charge," *AZ Central* (April 11, 2014).

183 When trans people are low income: *Sylvia Rivera Law Project,* "Systems of Inequality: Criminal Justice," srlp.org/files/disproportionate_incarceration_1.pdf.

183 Trans and queer people: Angie Martell, "Diversity in the Law: Legal Issues Facing Transgender and Gender-Expansive Youth," 96 *Michigan Bar Journal* 30 (Dec. 2017).

183 Prosecutors bring statutory: Angie Martell, "Diversity in the Law: Legal Issues Facing Transgender and Gender-Expansive Youth," 96 *Michigan Bar Journal* 30 (Dec. 2017).

184 In some states: Carrie Buist & Emily Lenning, *Queer Criminology: New Directions in Critical Criminology,* 76–77 (2015).

184 A straight teen in Texas: Caitlyn Silhan, "The Present Case Does Involve Minors: An Overview of the Discriminatory Effects of Romeo and Juliet Provisions and Sentencing Practices on Lesbian, Gay, Bisexual, and Transgender Youth," 20 *Law & Sexuality* 97, 111–12 (2011).

184 Approximately one fourth: Angie Martell, "Diversity in the Law: Legal Issues Facing Transgender and Gender-Expansive Youth," 96 *Michigan Bar Journal* 30 (Dec. 2017).

184 Furthermore, 20 percent of incarcerated: Daiana Griffith, "LGBTQ Youth are at Greater Risk of Homelessness and Incarceration," *Prison Policy Initiative* (Jan. 22, 2019), www. prisonpolicy.org/blog/2019/01/22/lgbtq_youth. Angela Irvine & Aisha Canfield, "The Overrepresentation of Lesbian, Gay, Bisexual, Questioning, Gender Nonconforming and Transgender Youth Within the Child Welfare to Juvenile Justice Crossover Population," 24 *American University Journal of Gender, Social Policy & Law* 243 (2015).

184 Prosecutors and police also: Amelia Roskin-Frazee, "The Danger of Statutory Rape Laws After Orlando," *Hu Post* (July 26, 2016), www.huffpost.com/entry/the-danger-of-statutory-rape-laws-after-orlando_b_5794fa0ae4b0e002a31393ef. *See also* Michael J. Higdon, "Queer Teens and Legislative Bullies: The Cruel and Invidious Discrimination Behind Heterosexist Statutory Rape Laws," 42 *University of California Davis Law Review* 195 (2008).

185 Darnell refused to plead: Although the prosecutor, defense attorney, and judge all referred to Wilson as "Darnell" and as "he," Wilson's appearance and presentation in court were feminine.

187 CeCe McDonald is an: *Free CeCe!* Documentary by Jacqueline Gares (2016).

187 In June 2011: Sabrina R. Erdely, "The Transgender Crucible," *Rolling Stone* (July 30, 2014), www.rollingstone.com/culture/culture-news/the-transgender-crucible-114095.

187 The insults escalated: "CeCe McDonald, Minnesota Transgender Woman, Pleads Guilty in Manslaughter Case Despite Supporters' Defense," *Hu Post* (Feb. 2, 2016), www.huffpost.com/entry/cece-mcdonald-minnesota-transgender-woman-manslaughter_n_1472078.

188 CeCe would wait two months: "CeCe McDonald, Minnesota Transgender Woman, Pleads Guilty in Manslaughter Case Despite Supporters' Defense," *Hu Post* (Feb. 2, 2016), www.huffpost.com/entry/cece-mcdonald-minnesota-transgender-woman-manslaughter_n_1472078.

188 The judge allowed the prosecutors: Michelangelo Signorile, "CeCe McDonald, Transgender Activist, Recalls Hate Attack, Manslaughter Case," *Hu Post* (Feb. 2, 2016), www.huffpost.com/entry/cece-mcdonald-manslaughter-case_n_4831677.

188 She told the court how: Guilty Plea Transcript, supportcece.files.wordpress.com/2012/08/mcdonald-chrishaun-11-16485-5-2-12-plea.pdf.

188 As Mara Keisling: Staff, "Chrishaun 'CeCe' McDonald Begins Jury Selection; Judge Rules to Exclude Contextual Evidence," *Fightback! News* (May 1, 2012), www.fightbacknews.org/2012/5/1/chrishaun-cece-mcdonald-begins-jury-selection-judge-rules-exclude-contextual-evidence.

189 Some prosecutor offices actively: As one example, the Fair Michigan Justice Project, a Michigan non-profit organization that advocates on behalf of the LGBTQ+ community and provides a special assistant prosecutor to the Wayne County (Detroit) Prosecuting Attorney's Office, and who vertically prosecutes felony cases involving LGBTQ+ victims of crimes. www.waynecounty.com/elected/prosecutor/fair-michigan-justice-project-lgbtq-unit.aspx.

190 The U.S. Supreme Court: *United States v. Morgan*, 346 U.S. 502, 512 (1954).

190 Constitutional law scholars identify: Akhil Reed Amar, *America's Unwritten Constitution: The Precedents and Principles We Live By* (2012).

190 In 1980, a Congressional Commission: The Commission on Wartime Relocation and Internment of Civilians. The Commission issued a report finding that the relocation and incarceration of Japanese Americans was not militarily necessary. Instead, "race prejudice, war hysteria and a failure of political leadership" led to the orders and to Congressional support. Indeed, the Commission's Report stated that "a grave injustice was done to American citizens and resident aliens of Japanese ancestry who, without individual review or any probative evidence against them, were excluded, removed and detained by the United States during World War II."

191 The general who ordered: "Final Report, Japanese Evacuation from the West Coast" (1942) prepared by General DeWitt. *See also Korematsu v. US*, 584 F.Supp. 1406 (NDCA 1984).

191 The court in Hirabayashi's case: *Hirabayashi v. United States*, 828 F.2d 591 (9th Cir. 1987) (granting writ of coram nobis).

191 Although Korematsu and Hirabayashi: *Hirabayashi v. United States*, 828 F.2d 591 (9th Cir. 1987).

191 As the Supreme Court said: *Davis v. United States*, 417 U.S. 333 (1974).

192 As recently as 2018: *Doe v. Hood*, 345 F.Supp.3d 749 (S.D. 2018).

194 Among Lampton's final words: (Trial Transcript, 856–57).

195 Talk show *The Dividing Line*: James White, "Recording of Gay Christianity Debate with Rick Schaeffer and Initial Review of Berry," *Alpha and Omega Ministries* (May 26, 2001), www.aomin.org/aoblog/the-dividing-line/recording-of-gay-christianity-debate-with-rick-schaeffer-and-initial-review-of-barry.

195 The report was based: Drury Sherrod & Peter M. Nardi, *Homophobia in the Courtroom: An Assessment of Biases Against Gay Men and Lesbians in a Multiethnic Sample of Potential Jurors.*

198 Based on the video: Letter from Dr. Souviron to Sheila Stubbs (May 10, 2005).

200 Old southern families: Becca Andrews, "The Racism of 'Ole Miss' is Hiding in Plain Sight," *Mother Jones* (July 1, 2020), www.motherjones.com/politics/2020/07/racism-university-mississippi-nickname-ole-miss-confederate-history-elma-meeks.

202 Every document was: Pete Stubbs affidavit (Dec. 8, 2010).

204 Mumma—now with a defense attorney: Anne Blythe, "NC Bar Admonishes Innocence Advocate Christie Mumma," *The Charlotte Observer* (Jan. 14, 2016), www.charlotteobserver.com/news/local/crime/article54743530.html#storylink=cpy.

205 The North Carolina bar admonished: Disciplinary Order, www.ncbar.gov/handlers/DisciplinaryOrderHandler.ashx?url=\Mumma, %20Christine%2015DHC20%20Admon.pdf&keyword=.

205 And I just think: Anne Blythe, "NC Lawyer Who Fights for the Wrongfully Convicted Goes Before Disciplinary Panel," *The Charlotte Observer* (Jan. 12, 2016), www.charlotteobserver.com/news/state/north-carolina/article54273370.html#storylink=cpy.

205 When victims ask for mercy: Danielle Sered, *Until We Reckon: Violence, Mass Incarceration, and a Road to Repair* (2019).

206 Henry's death would not: Roslyn Anderson, "Victims and Family of Death Row Inmate Want Execution Halted," *WLBT on Your Side* (June 4, 2012), www.wlbt.com/story/18700158/victims-and-family-of-death-row-inmate-want-execution-halted.

206 To affirmatively support defendants: Jocelyn Simonson, "Who are 'The People' in Criminal Procedure," *Law and Political Economy* (NOV. 26, 2018), lpeproject.org/blog/who-are-the-people-in-criminal-procedure. *See also* Raj Jayadev, "Participatory Defense—Transforming the Courts Through Family and Community Organizing," AC Justice Project (Oct. 17, 2014), acjusticeproject.org/2014/10/17/participatory-defense-transforming-the-courts-through-family-and-community-organizing-by-raj-jayadev.

207 Police have adopted alternative: The PEACE Method is one example (Preparation and Planning, Engage and Explain, Account, Closure, and Evaluate).

207 They reversed convictions: Interview with Kate Germond (Dec 9, 2020).

209 She also made a statement: Joyce Ann Brown, The National Registry of Exonerations, www.law.umich.edu/special/exoneration/Pages/casedetail.aspx?caseid=3061.

209 The pivotal coverage of: Center on Wrongful Convictions, *Northwestern Pritzker School of Law*, www.law.northwestern.edu/legal-clinic/wrongfulconvictions/exonerations/tx/joyce-ann-brown.html.

210 In their defense: *United States v. Yee*, 134 F.R.D. 161 (N.D. Ohio 1990).

211 The police officer who: LZ Granderson, "O.J. Trial Exposed Blatant Racism Inside U.S. Police Department," *The Undefeated* (June 17, 2016), theundefeated.com/features/o-j-trial-exposed-blatant-racism-inside-u-s-police-departments.

211 We all knew what: LZ Granderson, "O.J. Trial Exposed Blatant Racism Inside U.S. Police Department," *The Undefeated* (June 17, 2016), theundefeated.com/features/o-j-trial-exposed-blatant-racism-inside-u-s-police-departments.

212 The duo shared their policy: Robert J. Norris, *Exonerated: A History of the Innocence Movement* (2017).

212 As Justice Scalia stated: In Re *Troy Anthony Davis*, 557 U.S. 952 (2009) (cert. denied) (J. Scalia, dissenting). www.supremecourt.gov/opinions/08pdf/08-1443Scalia.pdf.

212 In the innocence community: Valena Beety, "Justice Antonin Scalia's Rebuke of Innocence," *Oxford Human Rights Hub* (Mar. 8, 2016), ohrh.law.ox.ac.uk/justice-antonin-scalias-rebuke-of-innocence.

214 If anything, after five years: George H. Ryan & Maurice Possley, *Until I Could Be Sure: How I Stopped the Death Penalty in Illinois* (2020).

216 In this follow-up letter: Appendix F—Disclosed letter to the FBI April 13, 2000.

216 Dr. West said he would continue: FBI's response to the FOIA request.

218 Years later, he still believed: John Ott Affidavit.

218 Neither McNees: Walter Wood Affidavit.

222 Thus, he recommended: OAG Public Integrity Division Memo Inv. Keith Milsap to Inv. Tony Green, May 22, 2008.

222 The date was over: OAG Public Integrity Division Memo Inv. Keith Milsap to Karl Pree September 15, 2009.

223 Together, their research findings: Peter and Dr. Mary Bush Affidavit.

224 1930s Southern prosecutors: For a thorough history of the rules of criminal procedure and their connection to Jim Crow, *see* Ion Meyn, "Constructing Separate and Unequal Courtrooms," 63 *Arizona Law Review* 1 (2021).

226 Helen: Helen Ervin passed away on April 20, 2020, at the age of eighty-four. This chapter is a fictional re-envisioning of her perspective, and recounts events that happened after the trial.

231 The key document: Vorder Bruegge Deposition.

232 It basically means: Vorder Bruegge Deposition p. 36.

233 I'm pretty sure: Vorder Bruegge Deposition p. 37.

233 That would be standard procedure: Vorder Bruegge Deposition p. 49.

233 Dr. Vorder Bruegge also: Vorder Bruegge Deposition p. 50.

233 That's a long-winded way: Vorder Bruegge Deposition pp. 51–52.

233 Dr. Vorder Bruegge had spent: Vorder Bruegge Deposition p. 52.

234 Nothing—no new evidence: Transcript Feb. 2, 2012 Hearing, West Deposition p. 7.

235 I don't have any independent: West Deposition p. 28.

235 I think you should use DNA: West Deposition pp. 36–37.

235 And if I was asked to testify: West Deposition p. 38.

236 And for that reason: West Deposition p. 39.

236 He gave me the VHS: West Deposition p. 48.

236 And they didn't have: West Deposition p. 51.

237 Oh yeah, I don't know: West Deposition pp. 62–63.

237 Not to Mike West: West Deposition p. 79.

238 You're going to need a big: West Deposition p. 95.

241 Jerry Rushing took the: (Trial Transcript, Habeas Hearing).

249 Prosecutors and police are often: Steve McCartney & Rick Parent, *Ethics in Law Enforcement* (2015).

251 In the early 2000s, prosecuting: Aya Gruber, *The Feminist War on Crime: The Unexpected Role of Women's Liberation in Mass Incarceration* (2020).

252 As the old saying goes: Jordan Flaherty, *No More Heroes: Grassroots Challenges to the Savior Mentality* (2016).

253 The governing rules: For a thorough history of the rules of criminal procedure and their connection to Jim Crow, *see* Ion Meyn, "Constructing Separate and Unequal Courtrooms," 63 *Arizona Law Review* 1 (2021).

253 Anyone can be susceptible: Sherry Nakhaeizadeh, Itiel E. Dror, & Ruth M. Morgan, "The Emergence of Cognitive Bias in Forensic Science and Criminal Investigations," 4 *British Journal of American Legal Studies* 527, 529 (2015). Alafair S. Burke, "Improving Prosecutorial Decision Making: Some Lessons of Cognitive Science," 47 *William & Mary Law Review* 1587, 1596 (2006).

253 Noble cause corruption leads: Michael A. Caldero & John P. Crank, *Police Ethics: The Corruption of Noble Cause* (2014).

253 Over half of exonerations involve: *Nat'l Registry Exonerations, Government Misconduct and Convicting the Innocent* (2020), www.law.umich.edu/special/exoneration/Documents/Government_Misc onduct_and_Convicting_the_Innocent.pdf (last visited Sept. 24, 2021).

254 A perverse incentive exists: As legal scholar Peter Joy has stated, "[prosecutors] do it to win. They do it because they won't get punished. They have done it to defendants who came within hours of being executed, only to be exonerated." Peter A. Joy, "The Relationship Between Prosecutorial Misconduct and Wrongful Convictions: Shaping Remedies for a Broken System," 2006 *Wisconsin Law Review* 399 (citing Ken Armstrong & Maurice Possley, "Trial & Error; How Prosecutors Sacrifice Justice to Win; The Verdict; Dishonor," *Chicago Tribune*, January 10, 1999, at 1.). Jessica Brand, "The Epidemic of Brady Violations: Explained," *The Appeal* (Apr. 25, 2018), theappeal.org/the-epidemic-of-brady-violations-explained-94a38ad3c800.

254 There's even less risk: *See About, Veritas Initiative,* veritasinitiative.scu.edu/?page_id=2 (last visited July 1, 2015). *See also* Maurice Possley & Jessica Seargeant, "First Annual Report: Preventable Error—Prosecutorial Misconduct in California 2010," *Northern California Innocence Project* (Mar. 2011), www.veritasinitiative.org/wp-content/uploads. 2011/03/ProsecutorialMisconduct_FirstAnnual_Final8.pdf.

254 Bernard would have: *Bernard v. United States,* No. 20A110, 141 U.S. 504 (2020). (Sotomayor, J., dissenting from denial of certiorari) www.supremecourt.gov/opinions/20pdf/20a110_1972.pdf.

261 Maybe they're experienced enough: Alexi Jones, "Reform without Results: Why States Should Stop Excluding Violent Offenses from Crim. Justice Reforms," *Prison Policy Initiative* (April 2020), www.prisonpolicy.org/reports/violence.html; David J. Harding, "Do Prisons Make Us Safer?" *Scientific American* (June 19, 2019), www.scientificamerican.com/article/do-prisons-make-us-safer.

262 Leigh and Tami didn't ever have: "The Court instructs the jury that to constitute possession, there must be sufficient facts to warrant a finding that the defendants, or either of them, were aware of the presence of the particular substance and were intentionally and conscientiously in possession of it. It need not be actual physical possession. Constructive possession may be shown by establishing that the substance involved was subject to the defendant's domain or control" (Trial Transcript, 794-95).

265 It is simply policy: Dwayne Betts, in his poetry collection *Felon,* repeatedly writes "it is the policy" representing bureaucratic justification. Reginald Dwayne Betts, *Felon: Poems* (2019).

265 It is the punishment that: Angela Davis, *Are Prisons Obsolete?* (2003).

266 At our current rate: U.S. Prison Decline Insufficient to Undo Mass Incarceration, *Sentencing Project*, www.sentencingproject.org/wp-content/uploads/2020/05/U.S.-Prison-Decline-Insufficient-to-Undo-Mass-Incarceration.pdf (last visited Sept. 24, 2021).

266 In 2085 we won't be back: Tara O'Neill Hayes & Margaret Barnhorst, "Incarceration and Poverty in the United States," *American Action Forum*, www.americanactionforum.org/research/incarceration-and-poverty-in-the-united-states (last visited Sept. 24, 2021).

266 People who most fear: *See, e.g.,* Rafael Prieto Curiel & Stephen Richard Bishop, "Fear of Crime: The Impact of Different Distributions of Victimization," 4 *Palgrave Commission* 46 (2018), doi.org/10.1057/s41599-018-0094-8.

266 We know that police arrest: Shima Baradaran Baughman, "How Effective Are Police? The Problem of Clearance Rates and Criminal Accountability," 72 *Alabama Law Review* 47 (2020), www.law.ua.edu/lawreview/files/2020/12/2-BaughmanArticle-47-112.pdf.

266 Common Justice is a restorative justice: Danielle Sered is also the author of *Until We Reckon: Violence, Mass Incarceration, and the Road to Repair* (2019).

267 Ninety percent of these survivors choose Common Justice: Brooklyn Law School, *Book Talk: Until We Reckon: Violence, Mass Incarceration, and a Road to Repair*, YouTube (Oct. 14, 2019), www.youtube.com/watch?v=PWkWRcqaUN4&ab_channel=BrooklynLawSchool.

267 And certain victims—namely middle: *See generally* Danielle Sered, *Until We Reckon: Violence, Mass Incarceration, and a Road to Repair* (2019).

267 Race and class cultivate: *See generally* Valena Beety, "Forensic Evidence in Arizona: Reforms for Victims and Defendants," 52 *Arizona State Law Review* 709 (2020).

267 Jennifer Henry, the Former Chief Prosecutor: *See* Legal-Ease Podcast, *COVID-19 Pandemic Impact on Tribal Communities*, SoundCloud, at 46:01 (June 26, 2020), soundcloud.com/legaleasepod/covid19tribalcommunities [perma.cc/5Z2V-JHP8].

267 So often a defendant today: Legal-Ease Podcast, *COVID-19 Pandemic Impact on Tribal Communities*, SoundCloud, at 45:50 (June

26, 2020), soundcloud.com/legaleasepod/covid19tribalcommunities [perma.cc/5Z2V-JHP8].

267 This is a similar message: "Analysis & Vision," *Survived and Punished,* survivedandpunished.org/analysis (last visited Sept. 24, 2021).

267 In some women's prisons: "Analysis & Vision," *Survived and Punished,* survivedandpunished.org/analysis (last visited Sept. 24, 2021).

268 For example, the Prosecuting Attorney's Office: Matt Markovich, "King County Council Oks plan to Let Community Groups Decide Some Punishment—Not Judges," *KomoNews,* komonews.com/news/operation-crime-justice/king-county-council-approves-program-to-let-community-groups-decide-punishment (Nov. 17, 2020).

268 Dehghani-Tafti believes in incorporating: Zoom interview with Parisa Dehghani-Tafti, Commonwealth Attorney for Arlington County and the City of Falls Church (June 2, 2020).

268 State legislatures can incorporate: Lara Bazelon, *Rectify: The Power of Restorative Justice After Wrongful Conviction* (2018).

269 The United Nations established: "The ICTR in Brief," *United Nations Int'l Residual Mechanism for Crim. Tribunals,* unictr.irmct.org/en/tribunal (last visited Sept. 24, 2021).

269 Ultimately, Gacaca decided: The Gacaca courts exhibited both successes and failures. They sometimes failed to provide reparations for genocide survivors, for example, but they also are seen as contributing to the successful post-genocide rebuilding of Rwanda as a stable country; *But see* "Rwanda: Justice After Genocide—20 Years On," *Human Rights Watch,* rightforeducation.org/2020/02/19/gacaca-courts (last visited Sept. 24, 2021).

269 In Gacaca, the focus: The broad goals were: enable the truth to be revealed about Genocide and crimes against Humanity in Rwanda; speed up the trials of those accused of Genocide, Crimes against Humanity and other crimes; put an end to the culture of impunity in Rwanda; reconcile the people of Rwanda and strengthen ties between them; revive traditional forms of dispensing justice based on Rwandese culture; demonstrate the ability of local communities to solve their own problems; solve some of the many problems caused by Genocide. "Gacaca Courts," *City of Kigali,* www.kigalicity.gov.rw/index.php?id=36 (last visited Sept. 24, 2021).

270 Their message is that: Lara Bazelon, *Rectify: The Power of Restorative Justice After Wrongful Conviction* (2018).

270 Director Katie Monroe told me: Zoom interview with Katie Monroe, Executive Director, Healing Justice (June 12, 2020).

270 Jennifer Thompson spoke with me: Zoom interview with Jennifer Thompson, Founder, Healing Justice (June 15, 2020).

PLAYLIST, 2012

Music was my best companion during my long rides through the Mississippi countryside, going from my home to prisons, to courthouses, and to the homes of witnesses. Carol and Will at the Mississippi Innocence Project often made "mixtapes" to accompany our trips. We had music for everything—hope, grief, celebration, and the fun of driving across the state and eating at rural gas stations (which had really great catfish). This was one mix that I made. You can find it on Spotify at: open.spotify.com/playlist/6PpKgTfqVcl7NYRwZVhusI?si=58cee59291be49a2.

Sam Cooke, "A Change Is Gonna Come"

Doobie Brothers, "Black Water"

Mattie Delaney, "Tallahatchie River Blues"

Son House, "Death Letter Blues"

Bobbie Gentry, "Mississippi Delta"

Dusty Brooks, "Chili Dogs"

Mash Up: Alison Krauss & Gillian Welch, "I'll Fly Away"; The Troggs, "Love Is All Around"; Taylor Swift, "Our Song" (thanks to Michael Coenen)

Howlin' Wolf, "Evil (Is Going On)"

Rufus Wainwright, "Oh What a World"

Stevie Wonder, "As"

George Michael, "Freedom"

ACKNOWLEDGMENTS

The success story of this book would not exist without the Mississippi Innocence Project, renamed the George C. Cochran Innocence Project in 2015, and Leigh Stubbs and Tami Vance who entrusted their case to us. Big thanks to Tucker Carrington, Will McIntosh, and Carol Mockbee, our MIP crew at the time. Thanks to all the students, interns, and visiting fellow, K.C. Meckfessel, who worked on Leigh and Tami's case and at MIP more broadly. The support from Ole Miss colleagues, the board, and the school made the broader innocence work possible, then and today.

Tucker and Radley Balko wrote an extraordinary book that dives into the many cases and lives impacted by Dr. West and Dr. Hayne titled *The Cadaver King and the Country Dentist: A True Story of Injustice in the American South.* I highly recommend it. Radley has also singlehandedly taken the conversation on repealing AEDPA to another level through his ongoing investigative journalism, alongside his commitment to exposing faulty forensics and challenging police brutality.

Many attorneys have guided my own legal path. In West Virginia, that's my colleagues at West Virginia University College of Law, retired Kanawha County public defender George Castelle, Lonnie Simmons, Al Karlin, Melissa Giggenbach, and all the attorneys, fellows, and students who worked in the West Virginia Innocence Project. The attorneys fighting for justice in West Virginia will always have my gratitude. Thank you for believing in change and refusing the status quo.

The women in the Innocence Network, and particularly the women who founded innocence organizations like Cookie Ridolfi, Linda Starr, Jackie McMurtrie, and Theresa Newman, and the women who were part of the creation of the Innocence Project like Nina Morrison, Vanessa Potkin, Aliza Kaplan, and soon thereafter Maddy Delone and Rebecca Brown, have transformed the legal landscape. I look forward to writing my next book about all of you. Thank you in particular to my friend and mentor Jackie McMurtrie. From the first time I walked into a room of innocence litigators and saw you knitting while calling the shots, you have been my hero. You have unabashedly known your truth and lifted up the truths of others, including me. Thank you for your friendship and support.

To the families of Leigh and Tami—you never gave up. You are the true reason they are free. Sheila and Pete, Sandy, Lori, Kristi and Steve, you exemplify the meaning of the words *family*, *commitment*, and *love*.

Judge Michael Taylor, you took a courageous step of truly reexamining Leigh and Tami's case, and then an even more courageous step of reversing their convictions. You transformed the destinies of Tami, Leigh, and myself. I know you have touched many lives during your time on the bench, but I'm particularly appreciative of these three.

For the women exonerees who have shared their stories with me, and for those who fight to free other people as well, thank you. To my clients, you have given me more than you may know; it is a privilege to represent you. To all the wrongly convicted people still incarcerated, I hope the tools in this book assist in your freedom.

When this was just a book proposal, some writers stepped up and vouched for me. Thank you to these inspiring writers and advocates: Alison Flowers, Liliana Segura, Jen Marlowe, Jessica Blank, Jennifer Thompson, Radley Balko, and Maurice Possley.

Pulitzer Prize–winning journalist and author Maurice Possley kindly helped edit this book and shared his expertise on wrongful convictions and criminal justice. Thank you to him, and his spouse Cathleen Falsani, for early advice on my book proposal and finding an agent. You were both there at the beginning!

Thank you to my friends in academia and in the innocence world who gave me important feedback for the many topics I tried to cover in this book. This includes Jessica Henry, Mary Thomas, Lisa Pruitt, Joshua Jones, Jordan Woods, India Thusi, Anthony Kreis, Aziza Ahmed, Larry Levine, Josh Sellers, Keith Findley, Dara Purvis, Richard Leo, Bruce Green, Ron Wright, Doug Starr, Ira Robbins, Lee Kovarsky, Eve Hanan, Stephanie Hartung, Aya Gruber, Sandra Guerra Thompson, and Nicole Casarez. Thank you also to my colleagues at the Decarceration Law Profs Works in Progress gathering each summer, and to Jamelia Morgan, India Thusi, and Ngozi Okidegbe for organizing this thoughtful and compassionate group of people. Finally, thank you to Deirdre Cooper Owens for your ground-breaking work on the Black and Irish mothers of Gynecology, and for your friendship in Mississippi and today. We made it.

Koa Beck has laid a blueprint for equality and social change in her thought-provoking book *White Feminism*, and generously wrote the forward. Koa, I aspire to be as discerning and discovering as you are, and for my writing to be as forthright and honest as your writing. You set a high bar.

Thank you to my nimble and ingenious agent Jill Marr at Sandra Dijkstra Literary Agency who saw my book proposal and could envision what it would become, even before I fully did. Thank you to my editor at Kensington Books, Michaela Hamilton, who then made that vision a reality with particular kindness and beneficence. I appreciate your patience working with a novice like myself.

At Arizona State University, thank you to my colleagues in the Academy for Justice, and particularly Commissioner Dawn Walton and Suzanne Stewart. Many research assistants helped me with interviews, footnotes, and the small but important things I couldn't do on my own: Zach Stern, Alejandra Molina Curiel, Tihanne Marshall, and Alyssa Padilla. Research assistants Jill Mceldowney and Priyal Thakkar are impressive poets and kindly gave me feedback and editing tips.

Thank you to my family, my parents, my aunt Martha and uncle Kent, my aunt Chris and uncle Tom, and my cousins Dean, Julie, and Stephan. I love you across any distance!

Thank you to my close friends who have been godsends for years—and who truly stepped up to help me with framing and creating this book. They contributed edits, insights, and encouragement when I was full of self-doubt. Nora Niedzielski-Eichner and Cara Kuball, you helped me with this book when it was just a jumble of ideas. Emily Bernstein, Jacqueline Speir, and Maya Ganguly, you helped me get out of my lawyer-head and out of my own way to make this book better.

I never had writing partners—until this book. Now, I don't know what I would do without either of these dear friends and our writing time together. Lara Bazelon, our friendship was one of the few good things to come of the COVID pandemic, and I appreciate how our friendship deepened through sharing our work. I'm glad we'll keep writing together long after our current projects. Holly Warren, you've been an impressive writer since we were in college. Thank you for sharing the struggle days and the victory days of writing.

Thank you most of all to my wife, Jennifer Oliva. You've seen my obsessive work tendencies, my writing insecurities, and my meltdowns. Through it all, you encouraged me and loved me. You let me know you were proud of me, and proud of me for writing this book. I hope you know how integral you are to it, and to all of my endeavors. I love you.

DISCUSSION QUESTIONS

1. The book shares the case and story of Leigh Stubbs and Tami Vance. Was it difficult to believe this wrongful conviction could happen? What was most surprising about their case?

2. Which other stories in the book were memorable to you? Were you angry? Saddened?

3. Beety quotes Patti Digh, "The shortest distance between two strangers is the story." How is *Manifesting Justice* about who gets to tell their own story, or who tells their story for them? Why does it matter? What about the role of the author's perspective in sharing these stories?

4. Did you see Kim as a victim? How does the author try to explain different ways that women are victimized by using Kim's experiences as examples? Are some victims more—or less—sympathetic? Why?

5. Beety proposes expanding and transforming post-conviction law—habeas law—as part of a legal Third Reconstruction. But she also proposes building restorative justice alternatives to incarceration. What is restorative justice, and could it lead us out of mass incarceration?

6. Beety discusses the historical criminalization of queer people, and how it still happens today. Did this resonate with you? What does "deviant" mean today? How do you think queer identity intersects with race and gender?

7. Prosecutors are very powerful in who they charge with crimes and how. In your opinion, is this a power for good or a power that needs to be restricted?

8. After reading this book, what do you think innocence work is?

9. Beety introduces the legal concept of manifest injustice to reverse criminal convictions. What is manifest injustice? Do you think convictions should be reversed because they are unjust? Why or why not?

10.   What is meant by the War on Drugs? How does the War on Drugs connect with wrongful convictions?

11.   What is forensic evidence? How has faulty forensic evidence caused wrongful convictions? How can we reduce this problem?

Index

Ableism, 53–54, 138, 279
Abolition movements, 266
Absolute certainty, 129–30
Accountability, 266–68, 281
ACT UP (AIDS Coalition to Unleash Power), 6, 103
Adams, Randall, 210
Alabama, "chemical endangerment" law, 180–81
Alcoholics Anonymous, 11, 19, 193
Alford pleas, 170, 260–62, 280
Allgood, Forrest, 133, 171
American Bar Association Resolution of 2017, 280
American Medical Association, 138, 182
American Society of Forensic Odontology, 122–23, 223
Amnesty International, 177
Angero, Dan, 71–72
Anti-Asian bias, 51–52
Antidepressants, 11, 13, 23
Anti-sodomy laws, 99, 102–4, 159, 192
Anti-Terrorism Effective Death Penalty Act (AEDPA), 28, 34, 35–41, 278

allowing federal courts to review state decisions de novo, 37–38, 278
eliminating one-year filing deadline, 38–39, 278
"evidence as a whole" review, 40–41, 278
Armbrust, Shawn, 213
Aung San Suu Kyi, 204
Autism, 53–54

Baldwin, James, 256
Banks v. State, 108–9
Baptist Memorial Hospital, 58, 88
Baran, Bernard, 103
Barbour, Haley, 173, 280
Barnett, Bill, 197, 201, 218
    closing arguments, 150–51
    Mills's testimony, 90–91
    plea offer, 64–65
    Sheila's testimony, 141–42
    West's testimony, 121–33
Bathory, Elisabeth, 240
Beck, Koa, ix–x
Beckman, Sharon, 51
Bernard, Brandon, 254

Bernstein, Elizabeth, 252
Bite mark analysis, 274–75
    as faulty scientific evidence, 73–74,
        77
    of West. *See* West, Michael, bite
        marks analysis of
    wrongful convictions and, 74–75,
        79
Black Belt, 19
Black Codes, 29, 31–32
Black Trans Lives Matter, 183
Blalock, Kim, 181
Bloodsworth, Kirk, 213, 214
Bodies. *See* Women's bodies as objects
Bondwomen, 138, 140
Boston College Innocence Program, 51
Bourn, Johnnie, 121–22
Bowers v. Hardwick, 102–3
Brady v. Maryland, 80, 84–85, 219,
        242, 246, 254
Brewer, Kennedy, 170, 171, 281
    deposition of West, 234–35
    false bite mark evidence, 74–75,
        132–33
    investigating West, 222, 224
    West and trial of Leigh and Tami,
        108, 124
    West's faulty testimony, 69–70,
        108, 124, 132–33
Brookhaven Comfort Inn, 24–26
Brookhaven Comfort Inn surveillance
        video, 24, 92, 152, 247–48
    FBI involvement and report, 132,
        197, 202–3, 216–19, 236–37
    toolbox theory, 48–49, 60–61
    Vorder Bruegge and, 216–17, 231–
        33, 234
    West's deposition, 236–37
    West's testimony, 113–16, 119–20,
        130–31, 245–46
Brookhaven *Daily Leader,* 116, 129,
    258

Brooks, Levon, 171, 222, 234–35
Brown, Jerry, 38
Brown, Joyce Ann, 207–9, 210
Brown, Larry, 200
Brown, Samantha "Sam," 13, 92–93
Brown v. Board of Education, 29
Bryant, Phil, 205–6
Bullard, Arch, 168–69
Buprenorphine, 19, 20, 277, 284*n*
Burger, Warren, 102
Bush, George W., 228, 249–50
Bush, Mary, 223
Bush, Peter, 223
Butch lesbians, 100, 297*n*
Butler, Sabrina, 170–71
Butler, Walter, 170–71
Byrom, Eddie, 168–70
Byrom, Michelle, 168–70, 280

Cady Hill Recovery Center, 9–13, 19–
    20, 62, 193–94
California, 30
    anti-sodomy laws, 100–101
    Junk Science Writ, 82–83
California Racial Justice Act, 52–53, 57,
    279
"Carceral feminism," 252
Carr, James G., 210–11
Carrington, Tucker, 68, 201–2, 233–38,
    245–46
Carter, Rubin "Hurricane," 29–30
Cásarez, Nicole Bremner, 84
Cavazos v. Smith, 37–38
Cellphone surveillance, 45
Centers for Disease Control and Pre-
    vention, 53–54, 167
Central Mississippi Correctional Facil-
    ity for Women, 161–72
    Leigh and Tami at, 1–2, 162–64,
        220–21
    organizing community activism to
        free women, 172–74

Shelby case, 164–67, 171–72
strip searches, 163–64
women on death row, 167–71
Central Park Five, 206
Centurion Ministries, 207–9, 210, 212
Chain of custody log, 203, 231–32
Chamberlin, Lisa Jo, 168, 171
Chaney, James, 250
Chaney, Steven, 78–82, 279
Chemical endangerment, 180–81
Child sex abuse and queers, 96–97
Choctaw Nation, 23–24
Choy, Frances, 51–52, 82, 279
Cifizzari, Gary, 198
"Citizen's arrests," 31–32, 287n
Civil Rights Act of 1964, 29
Civil rights movement, 24, 29, 32–33
Civil War, 29, 41, 255
Clemency, 8, 38, 173, 264, 280
Clinton, Bill, 38
CODIS (Combined DNA Index System), 44–45, 204–5
Colom, Scott, 171
Colonel Reb, 199–200
Comfort Inn. See Brookhaven Comfort Inn
Common Justice, 266–68
Compromise of 1850, 30
Compton's Cafeteria riot of 1966, 102
Confluence of factors review, 39–40, 51–52, 82, 278, 283n
Consent, 59, 137
Convicted by Juries, Exonerated by Science (report), 211–12
Coram nobis, 5–6, 39, 189–92, 278
Corey, Dorian, 105
COVID-19 pandemic, 254, 272
Coxwell, Merrida "Buddy," 231–38, 241–42, 247–48
"Crack babies," 178–79
Criminal legal system, 3, 27–28, 279

narrative of finality, 3, 33–35, 205, 275
"Cross-dressing," 99–101
Cummings, Patricia, 79–80

Dail, Dwayne, 205
Daughters of Bilitis, 101–2
David, Jon, 204–5
Davis v. United States, 191–92
DeAngelo, Joseph James (Golden State Killer), 45–46
Death Penalty Information Center, 213
Death row, 98, 167–71, 212–15, 255
Dee, Henry Hezekiah, 250–51
Defense Of Marriage Act (DOMA), 105, 159
Dehghani-Tafti, Parisa, 268
DeLone, Madeline, 214
De novo, 37–38, 278
Digh, Patti, 1
Disabled persons, 53–54
"Dixie" (anthem), 198–99
DNA evidence, 2–3, 7, 43–47, 204–15
history of DNA cases, 207–12
innocent people on death row, 212–15
Leigh and Tami's case, 43–44, 46–47
Maryland v. King, 45
DNA testing, 45, 210–11
Donaldson, Herbert, 100–101
"Drapetomania," 98, 296n
Dred Scott v. Sandford, 30–31, 32, 190
Drug Abuse Treatment Act (DATA Act), 284n
Drug laws, 20–22, 28, 244–45, 277
mass misdemeanor wrongful convictions, 176
War on Drugs, 2, 20–22, 29, 41, 252, 277
Drug testing, 47, 176, 181–82

Drug use, 19–22, 103, 277
  criminalizing to "help" pregnant
    mothers, 179
  during pregnancy, 175, 178–79,
    180–81, 277–78
Dry Prong, Louisiana, 11, 13, 23, 61–62
DuBoise, Robert, 197–98
Due process, 32, 35, 39, 82, 212, 283n
Dukes, Jim, 64
Duke Wrongful Convictions Clinic,
  213

Edmunds, Audrey, 167
Edwards, Charles, 250
Emerson, Irene, 31
Ervin, Emmit "Peanut," 13–15, 61, 112,
  230
Ervin, Helen, 13–14, 227–30
Ervin, James, Sr., 227–28, 229
Ervin, James "Dickie," 10, 12, 13–16,
  227–30
  police interview, 60
  trial of Leigh and Tami, 89, 93–94,
    112, 133–34, 138
"Evidence as a whole" review, 40–41,
  278, 289n
Expungement, 262–63, 280

Fair Michigan Justice Project, 308n
False confessions, 169–70
Fanon, Frantz, 106
Faulkner, William, 200
Faulty drug convictions, 176
Faulty forensic evidence, 4, 67–85, 279
  courts reversing convictions based
    on, 78, 279
  enacting statewide reviews, 76–77,
    279
  ending wrongful convictions based
    on, 75–85
  faulty scientific evidence, 73–74

  funding pre-trial forensic experts,
    76, 279
  junk science writs, 77, 78–82, 279
  recognizing post-conviction, 76–
    77, 279
  releasing lab findings directly to
    prosecutors and defense at-
    torneys, 83–85, 279
  testimony, 69–72
Faulty testimony, 69–72, 75–76
FBI, involvement and report, 132, 197,
    202–3, 216–22, 241–42, 246–
    48
  chain of custody log, 203, 231–32
  comparing West's findings, 238–39
  Dunn's deposition, 233, 236–37
  Judge Taylor's opinion, 259
  Vorder Bruegge's deposition, 231–
    33
Fifteenth Amendment, 29
Fifth Amendment, 211
Finality, 3, 33–35, 205, 275
Findley, Keith, 213
First Reconstruction, 29, 31–32
Food and Drug Administration
    (FDA), 103
Force Act of 1833, 30
Forensic evidence, faulty. See Faulty
    forensic evidence
Forensic Justice Project, 76, 279
Forensic witnesses, funding pre-trial,
    76, 279
Forrest, Nathan Bedford, 200
Fourth Step journal, 193–95
Fourteenth Amendment, 32
Freedmen, 32
Freedom of Information Act (FOIA),
    197, 232
Fugitive Slave Act of 1793, 30
Fuhrman, Mark, 211
"Fundamental miscarriage of justice
    exception," 6, 39–40

Galileo Galilei, 7

Galvez, Rodrigo, 145–48, 152, 240, 242–43

Garcia, Lynn, 79, 81

Gardner, Thomas, 169

Garza, Cynthia, 80–81

Gates, James Earl, 234

Gay and Lesbian Alliance Against Defamation (GLAAD), 240

"Gay panic" defense, 105–6, 189

Gender disparity in incarceration, ix–x, 175

Genocide, 251–52, 268–70

Germond, Kate, 207–9

Gibbs, Rennie, 181

Gideon v. Wainwright, 32–33

Giglio v. United States, 242

Gillis, Joey, 168–69

Ginsburg, Ruth Bader, 37–38

Glen, Karrie, 272

Goldman, Ronald, 211

Goodman, Andrew, 250

Good Samaritan laws, 22, 274–75, 277

Griffin, Linda and Frankie, 70–72

Gross, Sam, 215

Grove, The (Ole Miss), 198–99

Guede, Rudy, 99

Gynecology, 138–40

Habeas corpus, 29–36, 192, 278
   civil rights from Civil War to present, 31–33
   ideas for changing federal and state laws, 36–41
   principle of finality, 33–35
   slavery and, 29–31

Habeas Corpus Act of 1867, 32

Habeas corpus post-conviction laws, 35–41, 50–57, 246–48, 266, 278
   AEDPA and, 35–36. *See also* Anti-Terrorism Effective Death Penalty Act
   allowing federal courts to review state decisions de novo, 37–38, 278
   considering "confluence of factors" review, 39–40, 51–52, 82, 278
   dropping racially discriminatory charges, 54–57
   "evidence as a whole" review, 40–41, 278
   prohibiting charges, convictions, or sentencing based on race, ethnicity, or national origin, 52–53
   recognizing ableism as a cause of wrongful convictions, 53–54

"Hallmarks of wrongful conviction," 207, 209–10

Hannah, Barry, 200

Hansberry, Lorraine, 101

"Harmless error," 4, 52, 82, 278, 283n

Hartung, Stephanie Roberts, 52

Hayne, Steven, 69–72

Healing Justice, 270–71

Heckler v. Chaney, 78–82, 279

Hell's Angels, 210–11

Henderson, Arlustra, 15

Henry, Jennifer, 267

Herrera, Lionel, 212–13

Herrera v. Collins, 34, 212–13

Hervey, Barbara, 79

Hirabayashi, Gordon, 190–91

HIV/AIDS, 5–6, 102–3

Hoffman, Natalie, 55

Holcomb, Oona, 55

Homophobia, 106, 189, 260
   Leigh and Tami case, 137–38, 140, 158–59, 195–97, 239–43, 260

Homophobia in the Courtroom (report), 195–97

Hood, Jim, 169, 222

Hooker, Evelyn, 102
Hooks, bell, 283–84*n*
Houston Forensic Science Center, 84
Howard, Eddie Lee, 171, 219, 246
Howard v. State, 246
Humane Borders, 55
Huse, Madeline, 55

Incarceration rates, 5, 28
    gender disparity in, ix–x, 175
Indian Removal Act of 1830, 24
Innocence and the Death Penalty (re-
    port), 213
Innocence movement, 1–8, 35, 204–15,
    274–75
    checklist of tools, 277–81
    history of DNA cases and, 207–12
Innocence Network, 213–15
Innocence Project, 212, 213, 215
Innocence Project Northwest, 213
Innocence Project of New Orleans, 67
Innocence Protection Act of 2004, 214
International Criminal Tribunal for
    Rwanda, 251, 269–70, 315*n*
Intersectionality, 54

Jackson, Christina, 234
Jackson, Henry Curtis, 205–6
Jackson, Regina, 205–6
Jailhouse informants, 206–7, 208–9
Japanese American Internment
    Camps, 190–91, 278, 308*n*
Jayne, Samuel, 24
Jim Crow laws, 32, 200, 253
Johnson, Justin Albert, 69, 133
Jones, Kathy, 93
Jones, Nolan, 43–44, 201–2, 233, 246–
    47, 263
    interview of Leigh and Tami, 47–
        48
    toolbox theory, 48–49, 59–61, 119–
        20

trial testimony, 91–92, 158–59
West and bite marks evidence, 58–
    61
Junk science writs, 77, 78–82, 279,
    294*n*
Justice, Jay, 54

Kalra, Ash, 53
Kaplan, Aliza, 76, 212
Keisling, Mara, 188
Keko, Anthony, 234–35
Kennedy, John F., 199
Kennedy, Meredith, 214
Kercher, Meredith, 99
Key, Joe, 193–97, 201–2
Killebrew, Paul, 67
"Killer lesbian," 240–41
King, Martin Luther, Jr., 274
King's Daughters Medical Center, 26,
    42–45, 59–60
Kinsey, Alfred, 102
Klingfuss, Jeff, 246–47
Knight, Amy, 55
Knox, Amanda, 99
Korematsu, Fred, 190–91, 278
Korematsu v. United States, 190–91,
    278
Ku Klux Klan (KKK), 160, 199–200,
    250–51
Kyoto, Glendale, 205–6

Ladd, Donna, 250–51
Lambda Legal Defense and Education
    Fund, 189
Lampton, Dudley, 86–87
Lampton, Dunn, 222, 228–29
    closing arguments, 152–53, 194–95
    criminal indictment, 62
    FBI report, 197, 217, 236–37, 238–39
    Galvez's testimony, 147–48
    Jones's testimony, 91–92
    Kim's testimony, 133–35
    lack of DNA evidence, 46–47

Mills's testimony, 88–91
noble cause corruption, 249–51
plea offer, 64–65
Sheila's testimony, 142–43
West's testimony, 109–10, 111, 113,
116–19, 123–24, 132
Lawrence v. Texas, 103–4
LeFanu, Joseph Sheridan, 240–41
Lesbians. *See also* Queer people
arguing queer bias, 239–44
over-representation on death row,
98
passing as straight, 96, 97, 106–7
Lesbian vampire myth, 240–41
Lewd conduct, 100–101
LGBTQIA+. *See* Queer people;
Transgender people
Limbaugh, Rush, 105
Lincoln, Abraham, 255
Loggins, Debbie, 70
Louisiana State Penitentiary, 161–62
Loveall, Kathy, 258
Lumumba, Chokwe, 173

McCleskey v. Kemp, 52–53, 279
McCloskey, Jim, 207–9, 210
McDonald, CeCe, 184, 187–88, 192
McIntosh, Will, 201–2, 217–18, 233–38,
257, 258–59
McMurtrie, Jacqueline, 213
McNees, Ken, 66, 119–20, 135, 145,
149–50, 218
McQuiggin v. Perkins, 39, 40–41
McVeigh, Timothy, 36
Magna Carta, 35
Magnolia Grove Monastery, 161
Male gaze. *See* Women's bodies as ob-
jects
Mandatory minimum sentencing, 252
Mandela, Nelson, 171
Mandela Rules, 171–72
Manifesting justice, checklist of tools
for, 277–81

Manifest injustice, 3–8, 28, 76–77
Manifest injustice standard, 51–52, 78
Marcus, Eric, 100–101
Marley, Bob, 274
Marquez, Rosemary, 56–57
Maryland v. King, 45
Massachusetts Colony, 73
Mass misdemeanor wrongful convic-
tions, 176
Mattachine Society, 101–2
Maximum Security Unit (MSU), 7,
162–63, 171–72
Maxwell, Larry, 123, 234
Meckfessel, K.C., 257
Medical Bondage (Owens), 138–39
Melendez-Diaz v. Massachusetts, 294n
"Menacing social types," 98
Meredith, James, 199
Methadone, 19–20, 277, 284n
Mid-Atlantic Innocence Project, 213
Mills, Judy, 87–91
Milsap, Keith, 222
Mississippi Code 97-29-59 (unnatural
intercourse), 104–5, 159, 192
Mississippi Crime Laboratory, 44,
46–47, 143–44
Mississippi Innocence Project (MIP),
162, 171, 198–99, 255
arguing queer bias, 239–41
Brooks case, 67–69
investigating the case, 201–2
post-conviction depositions, 231–
38
post-conviction petition, 218–21
Mississippi Sex Offender Registry, 192
Mississippi State Insane Asylum, 161
Mississippi State Penitentiary. *See*
Parchman Farm Prison
Mississippi State University, 13
Mississippi Supreme Court, 75, 159,
237
post-conviction petition, 218–21
Mississippi Territory, 24

Mitchell, Jerry, 250–51
Moak, Joe, 43–44, 49, 63, 94–95, 148–52, 155, 194, 195
Mock, Janet, 105–6
Mockbee, Carol, 257
Model Penal Code, 102
Mogul, Joey, 239
Monroe, Katie, 270
Moore, Charles Eddie, 250–51
Morphine, 10, 14, 16, 62, 118, 135, 148, 149, 150
Morris, Errol, 210
Morrison, Nina, 212
"Motherblame," 181–82
Mumma, Chris, 44, 204–5
Music playlist, 317

Nanticoke Nation, 50
Napue v. Illinois, 254
Narcan (naloxone), 26, 118–19, 122, 274
National Academy of Sciences (NAS), 73, 76–77, 108, 223
National Center for Transgender Equality, 188
National Conference on Wrongful Convictions and the Death Penalty, 213–14
National Institute of Justice, 211–12
National Registry of Exonerations, 77, 97, 189, 215, 262–63
Navajo Nation, 267–68
Neufeld, Peter, 210–12, 213, 222
New England Innocence Project, 52
Newman, Theresa, 213–14
Nhat Hanh, Thich, 161
Nichols, Terry, 36
Noble cause corruption, 249–51, 253–54, 280
No-contact orders, 18, 172
No More Deaths/No Más Muertes, 54–57
North Carolina Center for Actual Innocence, 204–5

Northern California Innocence Project, 213
North Hill Square Apartment Complex, 258

Objectification. See Women's bodies as objects
Oklahoma City bombing, 35–36
Oliva, Jennifer, 50, 157–58
Opioid crisis, 19–20, 178–79, 179, 277
Opioid use disorder (OUD), 19–20, 277, 284n
Oppie, Mark, 234
Oregon Innocence Project, 76
Oregon Measure 110, 21
Origin stories, 17–19
Orozco-McCormick, Zaachila, 55
Oshinsky, David, 255
Ott, John, 63–64, 218
Owens, Deirdre Cooper, 138–39
Oxycontin, 10, 23, 25, 26, 62, 262

Parchman (Oshinsky), 255
Parchman Farm Prison, 65, 161–62, 173, 255, 274
Paris Is Burning (documentary), 105
Patrick, Howard, 173
People v. Ka Yang, 283n
Personhood amendments, 180
Pierre Part, Louisiana, 16
Pine Grove Behavioral Health Center, 9–11, 142
Plourd, Christopher, 75
Police abolition movement, 266
Police crime labs, 83–85, 279
Polygraph tests, 47–48, 63
Pose (TV series), 105
Possley, Maurice, 215
Post-conviction hearing of Leigh Stubbs and Tami Vance, 231–48
arguing queer bias, 239–41

comparing West and FBI findings, 238–39

the hearing, 241–48

Vorder Bruegge's deposition, 231–33

West's deposition, 233–38

Post-conviction petition of Leigh Stubbs and Tami Vance, 218–21

Potkin, Vanessa, 74, 212, 222

Pray, John, 213

Pree, Karl, 222

Pregnant women, 178–82

fallout from criminalizing, 181–82

interpreting laws to control behavior of, 179–81

myths and realities of drug use during pregnancy, 178–79

Shelby's case, 164–65

prison abolition movement, 266

Prosecutors

drug laws and, 20–22

principle of finality, 3, 33–35, 205, 275

as white saviors, 178, 252–53

Prosecutor misconduct, 3, 7, 249–54

noble cause corruption and, 249–51, 253–54, 280

Prosecutor reform, 280–81. *See also* Restorative justice

Alford pleas, 170, 260–62, 280

creating accountability with restorative justice, 267–68

dropping racially discriminatory charges, 54–57

releasing scientific findings directly to prosecutors, 83–85, 279

Prostitution, 175–78

legal innocence and, 176–78

mass misdemeanor wrongful convictions, 176

transgender people, 185–87

youth and Safe Harbor laws, 178, 182, 280

Punishing identity, 157–60

Queer (In)Justice (Mogul, Ritchie and Whitlock), 239

Queer people (queerness), 33, 96–107

assisting wrongfully on the sex offender registry, 191–92

criminalization at time of Leigh and Tami's trial, 104–6

fighting to change the narrative, 101–4

history of criminalizing, 99–101

labeling, 98

passing as straight, 97, 106–7

pathologizing, 97–99

punishing identity, 157–60

San Antonio Four, 96–97

suicides of, 195, 272–73

Race and racism, 3, 7, 50–53, 106, 209–10. *See also* Slavery

considering "confluence of factors" review, 51–52, 279

dropping racially discriminatory charges, 54–57

historical creation of gynecology and medicine, 138–40, 301*n*

at Ole Miss, 198–201

prohibiting charges, convictions, or sentencing based on, 52–53

prostitution and, 176–77

Rankin prison. *See* Central Mississippi Correctional Facility for Women

Rape kits, 44, 46–47

Rasco, Evelyn, 173

Reagan, Ronald, 103

Reconstructions, 28–29, 31–33

Rehnquist, William, 212–13

Reno, Janet, 211–12

Restorative justice, 264–71, 280–81
  healing from a genocide with, 268–70
  Healing Justice, 270–71
  prosecutors creating accountability with, 267–68
  seeking safety and accountability, 266–67
Richards, William, 82–83
Riddick, LeRoy, 166–67
Ridgen, David, 250–51
Ridolfi, Cookie, 213–14
Ritchie, Andrea, 239
Rivera, Sylvia, 183
Rix, James, 75
Robinson, Harriet, 31
Robson, Ruthann, 239–41, 243–44
Rocky Mountain Innocence Project, 270
Ross, John, 234
Rule 52(b) of the Federal Rules of Criminal Procedure, 40
Rushing, Jerry
  criminal indictment of Leigh and Tami, 62
  FBI report, 197, 203, 216, 217, 218, 231
  post-conviction hearing, 238–39, 241–42, 246
  trial of Leigh and Tami, 64, 143–44, 148–50
  West and bite marks evidence, 58, 59
Rwanda, 251, 269–70, 315n
Ryan, George, 214

Safe Harbor laws, 178, 182, 280
Safety and accountability, 266–67, 281
Same-sex marriage, 105, 159
San Antonio Four, 96–97
Sanders, Marvin, 233–38
Satanic panic, 96, 103
Savior mentality, 178, 252–53

Scalia, Antonin, 104, 212–13
Scheck, Barry, 210–12, 213
Schlessinger, Laura, 105
Schlup v. Delo, 40
Schmitz, Dean, 188
Schwerner, Michael, 250
Scott, Dred, 30–31, 32
Scott, Gladys, 172–72, 280
Scott, Jamie, 172–72, 280
Seale, James Ford, 250–51
"Second look" sentencings, 22, 277
Second Reconstruction, 29, 32–33
Section 1983 claims, 70
Sequential lineups, 129
Sered, Danielle, 266–68
Sex and pregnancy, criminalization of. *See* Pregnant women
Sex offender registries, 184, 191–92
Sex trafficking, 177–78
"Sexual deviants," 98–99, 105, 107, 196, 242, 296n
Sexual shame, 2, 194–95, 239
Sex work. *See* Prostitution
Shaken Baby Syndrome, 37–38, 165–67
Shelby, Tasha Mercedez, 162–67, 171–72, 174, 272
Silver Dollar Group, 250
Simmons, Janet, 42, 43–44, 46–47
Simmons, Lonnie, 78
Simmons, Truett, 14–15, 42, 43, 89
Simpson, Nicole Brown, 211
Simpson, O.J., 210, 211
Slavery, 29, 98, 138–39, 177, 255
  habeas corpus and, 29–31
  historical creation of gynecology and medicine, 138–40, 301n
Sledge, Joseph, 204–5
Smith, David, 168–70
Smith, Evander, 100–101
Smith, Lamar, 24
Smith, Mike, 64, 90, 154–56, 162, 196
Smith, Shirley Ree, 37–38

Sodomy laws, 99, 102–4, 159, 192
Solitary confinement, 162–63, 171–72,
        188
Sotomayor, Sonia, 254
South Mississippi Correctional Insti-
        tute, 224
Souviron, Richard, 197–98
Starr, Linda, 213
*State of Mississippi v. Vance and
        Stubbs*, 222
State-sanctioned sexual assault, 163–64
State v. Bourn, 121–22
State v. Tully, 283*n*
Statewide reviews, 76–77, 279
Statutory rape, 183–84
Staubus, Barry, 179
Stillbirths, 181
Stinney, George, 6
Stonewall Riot of 1969, 102
*Strengthening Forensic Science in the
        United States* (report), 73–
        74, 77–78
Strickland v. Washington, 259
Strip searches, 163–64, 279
Stubbs, Leigh
    Alford plea of, 260–62
    at Brookhaven Comfort Inn, 24–
        26
    at Cady Hill, 9–13
    criminal indictment of, 62
    discharge from Cady, 13–15
    drug use of, 9–10, 19, 23, 25, 149–
        50, 155, 194
    expungement of records, 262–63
    FBI report and, 132, 197, 202–3,
        216–18
    freedom for, 256–59
    homophobic bias and, 137–38, 140,
        158–59, 195–97, 242–43, 260
    investigating West, 221–22
    Jones interview of, 47–48
    Kim's overdose, 43–44
    passing as straight, 106–7

    post-conviction hearing of. *See*
        Post-conviction hearing of
        Leigh Stubbs and Tami
        Vance
    post-conviction petition, 218–21
    at Rankin prison, 1–2, 162–64,
        220–21
    threats against, 61–62
    trial of. *See* Trial of Leigh Stubbs
        and Tami Vance
Stubbs, Pete, 9–10, 63, 257–58
Stubbs, Sheila, 9–10, 12, 25, 26, 201
    FBI report, 197, 198, 216–18, 232
    freedom for Leigh, 257–58, 259
    police interview, 47–48, 90
    pre-trial problems, 63–64
    trial of Leigh, 131, 132
    trial testimony, 141–42
    undisclosed evidence, 193, 195, 197,
        198, 202, 203
Stubbs Mobile Home Park, 9–10
Sudden Infant Death Syndrome
        (SIDS), 37
Sullivan, Tina, 144–45
Sumptuary laws, 99–100, 102
Sykes, Wanda, 139
Sylvia Rivera Law Project, 183, 189

Taney, Roger, 31
Taylor, Michael, 221, 257, 259
    attempt to depose West, 224–25
    life after hearing, 263
    post-conviction hearing, 243–44,
        246–47, 248, 259, 263
Taylor, Renee, 208–9
Texas
    forensic science reform, 78–82
    Romeo and Juliet law, 184
Texas Court of Criminal Appeals, 80–
        81
Texas Forensic Science Commission,
        78–82
Thibodeau, Shelley, 85

Thin Blue Line, The (documentary), 210

Third Reconstruction, 28–29, 33, 41

Thompson, Bryan, 164–67

Thompson, Jennifer, 270–71

Thompson, Karen, 97, 275

Thompson, Sandra Guerra, 84

Toolbox theory, 48–49, 59–61, 109, 113–16, 130–31

Trafficking Victims Protection Act (TVPA), 177–78

Transgender people, 28, 33, 105, 162–63, 183–92
    coram nobis, 189–91
    McDonald case, 184, 187–88
    proposed solutions for victims of violence and of wrongful convictions, 189–92
    Wilson case, 184–87

"Trans panic" defense, 105–6, 189

Trial of Leigh Stubbs and Tami Vance, 86–95
    Cady Hill witness testimony, 92–93
    closing arguments, 148–53
    criminalization of queerness at time of, 104–6
    defense case, 141–53
    Ervin's testimony, 93–94
    exculpatory evidence, 216–25
    Galvez's testimony, 145–48
    Jones's testimony, 91–92
    jury selection, 86–87
    Kim's testimony, 133–35
    lack of DNA evidence, 43–44, 46–47
    Mills's testimony, 87–91
    Moak's testimony, 94–95
    pre-trial problems, 63–66
    punishing identity, 157–60
    Sullivan's testimony, 144–45
    trial date, 63–64

undisclosed evidence, 193–98
verdict and sentencing, 154–56
West's testimony. *See* West, Michael, trial testimony of
Winters's testimony, 143–44

"Trial penalty," 224

Trump, Donald, 254

Trump border wall, 54–55, 56

Tunnel vision, 84, 207, 253–54, 280

Underground Railroad, 30

United Nations Mandela Rules, 171–72

University of Mississippi ("Ole Miss"), 162, 198–201

University of Southern Mississippi, 87, 122

Valdez v. State, 283n

Vance, Sandi, 61–62, 193, 201, 224, 272
    FBI report, 197, 202, 203, 216, 217–18, 232
    freedom for Tami, 257–58

Vance, Tami
    Alford plea of, 260–62
    at Brookhaven Comfort Inn, 24–26
    at Cady Hill, 11–16
    criminal indictment of, 62
    discharge from Cady Hill, 13–15
    drug use of, 11, 19, 23, 25, 149–50, 155, 194
    expungement of records, 262–63
    FBI report and, 132, 197, 202–3, 216–18
    freedom for, 256–59
    homophobic bias and, 137–38, 140, 158–59, 195–97, 242–43, 260
    investigating West, 221–22
    Jones interview of, 47–48
    Kim's overdose, 43–44
    life after prison, 263, 272–73

passing as straight, 106–7
post-conviction hearing of. *See*
    Post-conviction hearing of
    Leigh Stubbs and Tami
    Vance
post-conviction petition, 218–21
pre-trial problems, 63–66
at Rankin prison, 162–64, 220–21,
    225–26
trial of. *See* Trial of Leigh Stubbs
    and Tami Vance
Vasquez, Anna, 96–97
Velasco, Bernardo, 56
Vice Squads, 20–21
Victim Restoration Fund, 268
Vorder Bruegge, Richard, 216–17, 231–
    33, 234, 239
Voting Rights Act of 1965, 29

Wade, Steve, 257
Ward, Jesmyn, 200
Warden, Rob, 215
War on Drugs, 2, 20–22, 29, 41, 252,
    277
Warren, Scott, 55
West, Michael
    attempt to depose, 223–25
    background of, 108
    deposition of, 233–38
    investigation of, 221–22
    post-conviction hearing, 242–48
    post-conviction petition, 218–21
    toolbox theory, 48–49, 59–61, 109,
        113–16, 130–31
    trial testimony of. *See* West,
        Michael, trial testimony of
West, Michael, bite marks analysis of,
    58–60, 235–39, 261
    absence of blood, 121–25
    alleging vagina bite marks, 125–26
    Barnett's challenge to testimony,
        65–66

in Brewer case, 69–70, 74–75, 108,
    124, 132–33, 170, 224, 234–35,
    281
comparing FBI's finding, 238–39
exculpatory evidence, 216–23, 259
faulty testimony, 69–70
Galvez's testimony, 145–48
homosexual assaults theory, 116–17,
    157–58, 242–43
"hospital footage" video, 58–59,
    109–13
initial examination of Kim's body,
    58–60, 89

Judge Taylor's opinion, 259
Souviron and, 197–98
testimony in trial cases, 108–9
West, Michael, trial testimony of,
    108–33, 201
    absence of blood, 121–25, 152
    absolute certainty, 129–33
    alleging vagina bite marks, 125–26
    Comfort Inn surveillance video,
        113–16, 119–20, 130–31, 245–
        46
    cross-examination, 119–33
    gaps in theory, 117–19
    homosexual assaults theory, 116–17,
        242–43
    "hospital footage" video, 58–59,
        109–13
    mis-matched bruises, 126–29
    objectifying Kim's body, 58–60, 61,
        136–38, 140, 242
"West Phenomenon," 122, 123
White, Bukka, 274
Whitfield Hospital, 161–62
Whitlock, Kay, 239
Wilkerson, Amy, 272
Williams, Kim
    at Brookhaven Comfort Inn, 24–
        26

Williams, Kim (*Cont.*)
  at Cady Hill, 10–13, 193–94
  discharge from Cady Hill, 13–15
  drug overdose of, 25–26, 42–45
  drug use of, 10, 19, 23, 25, 135, 149
  Fourth Step journal of, 193–95
  objectifying the body of, 58–60, 61,
     136–38, 140, 242
  stealing of Dickie's medications,
     14–16, 26, 62
  trial of Leigh and Tami. *See* Trial
     of Leigh Stubbs and Tami
     Vance
  trial testimony of, 133–35
  West and bite marks evidence, 58–
     61. *See also* West, Michael,
     bite marks analysis of
Williamson, Lester F., Jr., 72
Willingham, Cameron Todd, 79, 279

Wilson, Darnell, 184–87, 192
Winters, Amy, 143–44
Wisconsin Innocence Project, 213
Women's bodies as objects, 136–40
  historical creation of gynecology
     and medicine, 138–40
  objectifying Kim's body, 58–60, 61,
     89, 136–38, 140
  state-sanctioned sexual assault,
     163–64
Wood, Walter, 218
Woodall, Glen, 78
World War II, 98
  Japanese American Internment
     Camps, 190–91, 278, 308*n*

Zain, Fred, 78
Zimmerman, Bonnie, 240

ABOUT THE AUTHOR

VALENA BEETY is a former federal prosecutor and innocence litigator. She has successfully exonerated wrongfully convicted clients, obtained presidential grants of clemency for drug offenders, served as an elected board member of the national Innocence Network, and was appointed commissioner on the West Virginia Governor's Indigent Defense Commission. She is currently a professor of law at Arizona State University's Sandra Day O'Connor College of Law and the deputy director of the Academy for Justice, a criminal justice center at the law school, which connects research with policy reform. Previously, she founded and directed the West Virginia Innocence Project at the West Virginia University College of Law and practiced as a senior staff attorney at the Mississippi Innocence Project, representing clients on death row. She and her wife live in Phoenix, Arizona. Please visit her at www.valenabeety.com.